Solaris™ Implementation

A Guide for System Administrators

George Becker
Mary E. S. Morris
Kathy Slattery

SunSoft
A Sun Microsystems, Inc. Business

The publisher offers discounts on this book when ordered in bulk quantities. For more information, contact: Corporate Sales Department, Prentice Hall PTR, 113 Sylvan Avenue, Englewood Cliffs, NJ 07632. Phone: 800-382-3419 or 201-592-2498, Fax: 201-592-2249, email: dan_rush@prenhall.com

Cover designer: *Anthony Gemmellaro*
Manufacturing manager: *Alexis R. Heydt*
Acquisitions editors: *Gregory G. Doench and Phyllis Eve Bregman*
Copyeditor: *Mary Lou Nohr*

10 9 8 7 6 5 4

ISBN 0-13-353350-6

SunSoft Press
A Prentice Hall Title

Contents

≡

Solaris Implementation: A Guide for System Administrators

Acknowledgments

This book is dedicated to the system administrators that have transitioned or will transition to Solaris 2.x. We understand how hard it is to adapt to a new environment. We are all in this together.

There are many people who provided insight and encouragement for this project throughout its long life. I hope to remember them all. First of all, I must graciously thank my mother and father, Bud and Kaye Becker, who taught me how to learn, not what to learn. I must thank my wife, Laurie, and children for their patience and understanding during all of the long hours and weekends. Special thanks go to Joe Baker, Bernard Bove, Pat Cashman, Brendan Doyle, Karl Gaffney, Bikram Gill, Dolores Hannick, Bill Leach, Joe Marceau, Long Nguyen, Roger Pease, Robert Rebiejo, Larry Rolla, Eric Smith, and anyone whom I've overlooked.

— George Becker

Special thanks to Lori Reid and Alvin Cura who shared their scripts and configuration files for AutoInstall with us and the reader. Thanks to Casper Dik who has allowed us to print parts of his FAQ (comp.unix.solaris). Appreciation to my significant other, Terry Haynes, for seeing me through this with a smile.

— Mary E. S. Morris

Many thanks are due to Chris Drake, Ron Ledesma, and Robert Robiejo who reviewed early versions of this book. I would also like thank my husband, Tim, for his continual support and patience.

— Kathy Slattery

Last, but definitely not least, we would all like to thank Karin Ellison of SunSoft Press for her endless enthusiam and support. Also, we would like to thank Phyllis Eve Bregman and the rest of the team at Prentice Hall for helping us over the long haul.

Preface

≡

As with all documentation, there is a large hole between the steps necessary to install and support a generic Solaris® environment and the real world of day-to-day systems administration. This book attempts to bridge the gap. It is not intended as a basic guide nor should it be used in place of the standard documentation, but it should be consulted by System Administrators who need more information.

How This Book Is Organized

Chapter 1, "An Introduction to Solaris," describes the most notable differences between the Solaris 1.x and 2.x environments.

Chapter 2, "Planning and Preparing for Installation," details the planning involved in setting up a Solaris 2.x installation and automating the installation process.

Chapter 3, "Installing Solaris," provides the reader with a few sample installations.

Chapter 4, "Admintool," details the ways in which to use the new admintool GUI and shows the longer manual processes to accomplish some of the same tasks.

Chapter 5, "Boot and Shutdown Files," describes some of the files consulted during the booting of a system and reviews changes that can be made to them.

Chapter 6, "Using the Network," discusses network topology and the different ways to use the Solaris environment on server systems.

Chapter 7, "Security," describes the theory of maintaining security and how to implement it in the Solaris 2.x environment.

Chapter 8, "Software Management," describes both the GUI and the command line-based tools for managing SVR4-standard software packages and patches for the operating system.

Chapter 9, "Disk Utilities," presents the standard Solaris 2.x utilities that are available for managing your disks and related common archiving procedures.

Chapter 10, "Solaris 2.x Products," describes the Wabi™ and Online: Backup™ products that are currently available for the Solaris 2.x environment.

Appendix A, "AutoInstall Samples," contains samples of actual AutoInstall scripts used at Sun.

Appendix B, "Sample Disk Configurations," contains examples of disk partitioning schemes and suggested sizes for the partitions.

Appendix C, "Sources of Information," contains excerpts from the comp.unix.solaris FAQ.

Related Books

- *All About Administering NIS+, Second Edition*, Rick Ramsey
- *Solaris System Administrator's Guide*, Janice Winsor
- *The UNIX C Shell Field Guide*, Gail Anderson and Paul Anderson
- *The KornShell Command and Programming Language, Second Edition*, Morris I. Bolsky and David G. Korn

What Typographical Changes and Symbols Mean

The following table describes the type changes and symbols used in this book.

Table PR-1 Typographic Conventions

Typeface or Symbol	Description	Example
AaBbCc123	The names of commands, files, and directories; on-screen computer output	Edit your `.login` file. Use `ls -a` to list all files. `system%` You have mail.

AaBbCc123	What you type, contrasted with on-screen computer output	<pre>system% **su**
		password:</pre>

AaBbCc123	Command-line placeholder: replace with a real name or value	To delete a file, type `rm` *filename*.
AaBbCc123	Book titles, new words or terms, or words to be emphasized	Read Chapter 6 in *User's Guide*. These are called *class* options. You *must* be root to do this.

Code samples are included in boxes and may display the following:

%	UNIX C shell prompt	system%
$	UNIX Bourne shell prompt	system$
#	Superuser prompt, either shell	system#

Solaris Implementation: A Guide for System Administrators

An Introduction to Solaris   1 ≡

The Solaris distributed computing environment runs on a variety of computer systems, from desktop workstations to large departmental file servers. The Solaris environment is inherently based on the UNIX® operating system and was originally developed for the Scalable Processor ARChitecture (SPARC®) platform. Currently, the Solaris product is branching out to other platforms, including the Intel® x86 machines. The Solaris product as a whole is not only an operating system designed on published standards, but it also includes a powerful user environment capable of running thousands of application programs, a networking subsystem, support for local and remote printing, electronic mail, and other productivity tools. Many of the features included in the Solaris environment are not available in the base environment of other popular operating systems, but must instead be purchased separately, often with unexpected results.

The power of the Solaris environment is most apparent in large networked environments where large amounts of data are exchanged. Although fully functional in a standalone or nonnetworked environment, the Solaris environment is network oriented. Many of the Solaris benefits cannot be utilized unless two or more systems are connected to a network, thus allowing file, printing, and other resource sharing.

Major Solaris Components

The Solaris product can be divided into three major parts: the SunOS™ operating system, the ONC™ networking technology, and the OpenWindows™ development environment. There are two Solaris releases, and although they include the same functional parts, the operating software is very different so it is important to be aware of the differences.

The operating system is tasked with making sure that it can communicate with other systems on the network, keeping track of files on one or many disks, and allowing a windowing system to run on top of itself. These duties are not trivial.

1

The networking packages can be used to connect various hosts together so that data and other resources can be shared. The software is intended to be independent of the operating system, hardware architecture, and the transport protocol. This software allows for many different types of hosts running different software to co-exist on one network.

The windowing system is the tool that can increase human productivity when used correctly. It certainly makes the system much more manageable. Solaris ships with OpenWindows but different GUIs are available, starting with generic X and ending with Motif®.

Some of the features that are in both the Solaris 1.x and the Solaris 2.x environments are:

- ONC, Sun's open systems distributed computing environment, which includes:
  - NFS®, a distributed computing filesystem
  - NIS (Network Information Service)
  - RPC (Remote Procedure Calls)
- Remote File Sharing (Solaris release 1.x, 2.0, and 2.1 only)
- OpenWindows Version 3 (OWv3) development environment, which includes:
  - DeskSet™ utilities
  - Drag-and-drop file management
  - The ToolTalk® service
  - Local and remote display capabilities

Solaris 1.x

The Solaris 1.x operating environment contains SunOS release 4.1.2 or 4.1.3, the SunView™ graphical user interface, and OpenWindows Version 2.0 or 3.0. The Solaris 1.x environment runs on all SPARC systems except the sun4d architecture.

Solaris 2.x

The Solaris 2.x environment is Sun's current standard software environment for a variety of computer systems. The Solaris 2.x environment is predominantly based on UNIX System V, release 4 (SVR4) and is fully compliant with the System V Interface Definition III (SVID III) and other industry standards, including POSIX 2.3 and XPG 3.2.1. This compliance ensures easy portability of applications between unlike hardware types.

As with Solaris 1.x, the pieces of the Solaris 2.x environment have similar names, but the version numbers are different: SunOS 5.0 (Solaris 2.0) marked the first time that a release was based on SVR4. All releases prior to SunOS 5.x were based on Berkeley's Standard Distribution (BSD) UNIX system.

The Solaris 2.3 environment is available for all single and multiprocessor SPARC machines, including the entire family of systems from Sun Microsystems Computer Corporation and the SPARC clones, which include Axil (i.e., Hyundai) and Solbourne®.

The Solaris 2.x product is now available for Intel 80x86 machines. The primary difference between x86 systems and SPARC systems is the hardware. The physical device names and some device access methods are different, but the differences end there. Because the x86 world has such a diverse range of hardware devices, exploring Solaris 2.x on specific x86 platforms is beyond the scope of this book, but readers will find discussions on the distributed file system and general system administration to be of value, because a common command set is used on all architectures.

New Solaris 2.x features which are not in the Solaris 1.x product include:

- Standard device naming

- Automatic device configuration

- `admintool`, an administration tool

- Standard software packaging

- New installation environment and method

- ASET, an automated security enhancement tool

- JumpStart™, an autoinstall tool

- Kerberos and DES authentication

- The ONC+™ suite of products, which includes:
  - TI-RPC (Transport-Independent Remote Procedure Calls)
  - NIS+ (Network Information Service Plus)
  - NFS Version 3, Sun's distributed computing file system
  - TLI (Transport Layer Interface)

- Volume Management

SunOS

The SunOS operating system has evolved on many different hardware platforms, beginning with the Motorola 68000 Multibus-based systems, on through to SPARC systems of today. SunOS 1.0 was first released in 1982, nearly a direct port of the Berkeley Standard Distribution (BSD) UNIX version 4.2, and was not very robust compared to today's standards. Over the years, the ongoing development and refinement of SunOS has pioneered many popular standards of today, such as Remote Procedure Calls (RPC), the NFS system, and the Network Information Service (NIS).

The SunOS operating system is the base on which everything else sits. It is the SunOS system that transparently provides the interface between the user and the hardware, including all networking functions, print services, electronic mail activity, disk and tape services, and audio capabilities.

SunOS 4.x

The SunOS system began to change dramatically beginning with release 4.1. The need for a standard interface between applications and operating system motivated this change. While still based on BSD, the SunOS operating system included System V utilities, attempting to bridge the gap between the two camps. Application developers that were predominantly Berkeley-based now had an environment in which to port their products. The SunOS system was moving toward SVR4, and the framework was in place.

As new SPARC systems were developed, the SunOS 4.x system was revised but was still BSD-based, as are all SunOS 4.x releases.

The SunOS 4.1.3_U1 system contains asymmetrical multiprocessing capabilities for systems with more than one SPARC CPU. SunOS 4.x extensions make it compliant with the System V Interface Definition (SVID 3.2), POSIX and X/OPEN™ standards while still based on BSD 4.3.

SunOS 5.x

The multitasking, multithreaded SunOS 5.x operating system combines popular features from many UNIX versions, such as BSD, SunOS, XENIX®, and System V, into a single environment known as SVR4. The SunOS 5.x system also includes symmetric multiprocessing, a feature that provides effective load balancing between CPUs on machines with more than one installed SPARC processor. Each version of the SunOS 5.x system improves security, automates more system administration tasks, and adds to the networking sophistication of the overall Solaris product.

ONC Networking

The networking software is one of the most important parts of the software release. The networking is what makes this software so attractive to many users. It can allow for easy access to data and computing resources.

Remote Procedure Call (RPC) is a set of operations that execute procedures on a remote host. TCP or UDP are most often used as the transport protocol.

Another important piece of the ONC networking package is External Data Representation (XDR). It provides a way of encoding data that is architecture independent. This software would be used for copying files from a workstation to a PC.

OpenWindows

Another major part of the Solaris environment is the OpenWindows development environment, which includes productivity tools and utilities that manage system resources in addition to providing an environment in which to run application programs. The components of the OpenWindows environment include the OPEN LOOK® graphical user interface (GUI) from Novell, X11/NeWS®, Sun's network extensible windowing system which includes X11, Releases 3, 4, and 5 from the Massachusetts Institute of Technology, the ToolTalk service (an interapplication communication package), and the DeskSet (desktop) utilities.

The OpenWindows environment has evolved into an ideal distributed computing environment. First introduced in the SunOS 4.1 system, version 2.0 was an alternative windowing system to SunView. The SunOS 4.1 system allowed both environments to coexist and provided libraries to run SunView applications within the OpenWindows environment.

Although many applications were written for the SunView environment, its limits were pressed, especially in the area of distributed computing. Application developers needed a new framework for programs that used the network more efficiently within the client-server model. A more natural networked-based user environment was created under OpenWindows Version 3 by combining X11/NeWS, Sun's Network extensible Windowing System, and the OPEN LOOK GUI.

As the OpenWindows development environment became more powerful, window-based tools took the place of UNIX command-line programs. Drag-and-drop capabilities allowed file manipulation, creation, and removal by use of iconic representation. The Solaris 1.x product was born when both the SunOS 4.x system and the OpenWindows version 3 environment were included on the same install media.

OpenWindows 3.0

The OpenWindows Version 3.0 (OWv3) environment incorporates the X11/NeWS window server program that allows execution of both local and remote windowing programs, including drag-and-drop capabilities. OWv3 runs only on systems installed with the SunOS 4.1.1 and later BSD-based releases.

OpenWindows 3.1+

The OpenWindows Version 3.1 (and above) environment for the Solaris 2.x product is a near-direct port of OWv3 and is available in the SunOS 4.x system; it includes the X11/NeWS server and the OPEN LOOK Intrinsics Toolkit (OLIT).

The OpenWindows Version 3.x product has added more functionality and features with each new SunOS 5.x release. In the OpenWindows 3.3 release, included in the Solaris 2.3 product, the X11 server has remained, but the NeWS system has been dismantled, offering a faster, cleaner X-based windowing environment. OpenWindows 3.3 now includes Display PostScript™ instead of NeWS.

The OpenWindows Version 3.x development environment is but one of many graphical user environments available with the Solaris 2.x product, which also supports the OSF/Motif X11-based windowing system from Open Software Foundation. The OpenWindows environment is bundled with the Solaris 2.x product, whereas the OSF/Motif system must be purchased separately.

Systems installed with the Solaris 2.x product can also run Microsoft® Windows™ applications through the use of the Wabi product, Sun's MS-Windows application binary interface.

Device Name Changes

Disk-naming conventions in past releases of the SunOS system led to much confusion. Consistency was lacking, especially in the target-to-name translation of SCSI disks. On some systems, a disk configured as SCSI target three is translated to /dev/sd6, whereas other systems translated a SCSI target three to /dev/sd0. The confusion over naming disk devices is resolved with the implementation of the SVR4 standard naming convention. A SCSI target three is always a SCSI target three (i.e., c?t3d?s?). Controllers are also named as they appear in the probing routine—usually in ascending order of Sbus or VME slots.

There are no longer any "real" device nodes in /dev. All of the "real" nodes are located in /devices, and /dev is a directory tree filled with symbolic links that point to the special files in /devices. The device links are created when the system is booted with the -r option. A probing routine adds any new devices found and creates the necessary device nodes and symbolic links. It is no longer necessary to run MAKEDEV or to build a new kernel when new devices are attached to the system.

The /devices directory contains the actual device nodes for all physical and pseudo-devices that are used by the system. An example of a physical device is a disk or tape unit; an example of a pseudo-device is a shelltool window, a remote shell, or telnet session, or some other kind of window-based application. The device paths contained under /devices conform to those listed in the OpenBoot™ PROM specification. The device names in this directory can get quite deep, using long path names to even longer directory names until the real node is finally found.

The paths to particular devices are system specific, meaning that the /devices directory for any two SPARC systems may be different, depending on the kernel architecture of the machine. The multiprocessor systems, such as the SPARCstation™ 10 and SPARCserver™ 600, map some of the devices through an iommu device. The uniprocessor systems do not have an iommu and thus omit the iommu path in the /devices directory.

For example, on a SPARCstation IPX, the device node for SCSI target three, partition six uses the path:

```
/devices/sbus@1,f8000000/esp@0,800000/sd@3,0:g
```

Because this path is long and hard to remember, the node is symbolically linked to a more reasonable entry under /dev/dsk. This slice can now be easily referenced using the following path:

```
/dev/dsk/c0t3d0s6
```

Both of the above paths or device names access the same device. Notice that disk devices referenced in the /etc/vfstab file use the /dev/dsk and /dev/rdsk entries.

Disk Devices

For disks, the only path names of concern are for the /dev/dsk and /dev/rdsk directories. These directories equate to /dev/sdXX and /dev/rsdXX in Solaris 1.x and previous SunOS releases, where the former device is the "cooked" or block device and the latter is the "raw" or character device.

Realistically, the Solaris 2.x /dev directory is much better organized than previous versions of SunOS. As shown above, disk devices under /dev are now grouped under either /dev/dsk directory for the block devices, or the /dev/rdsk directory for the character devices. Both the /dev/dsk and the /dev/rdsk directories contain exactly the same file names. The differences lie in where the file names point. Arrangement of the disk devices is much more intuitive than in Solaris 1.x, where physical SCSI target three might be known as /dev/sd0 or /dev/sd1, depending on the system type.

Links are created when booting with the reconfigure option. For compatibility, symbolic links are also made to the appropriate /dev/sd* and /dev/rsd* device names.

SCSI and IPI disks use the following fields when naming disk devices:

controller#:target#:disk#:slice#

Thus, the device named `/dev/dsk/c0t3d0s0` indicates controller zero, target three, disk zero, slice zero. Most systems with built-in SCSI host-adapters identify the on-board controller as c0. When a disk controller is attached to a different bus, such as the VME or Sbus in addition to an on-board disk controller, the controller number is increased by one.

The controller field is necessary on all disks, but the target field is only relevant to SCSI and IPI disks.

The Sun® SCSI target and disk identification numbers have a little history. In the early days of Sun SCSI use, each target or controller could have more than one disk or tape attached. An emulator board between the SCSI bus and the peripheral device converted SCSI language into ST506 or QIC24. Although this type of arrangement is still valid, it is becoming less used as disk capacities have increased. Many SCSI devices now attach directly to the SCSI bus. The target number is *embedded* into the peripheral. Because of this, the additional disk connection per each SCSI target is lost. You may never see an embedded SCSI peripheral with a disk field greater than zero. Some of the older Sun peripherals may have nonembedded SCSI controllers that allow multiple disks per a single target.

Other disk devices such as the VME based Xylogics® SMD and ESMD disk controllers omit the target field but use the following convention:

controller#disk#slice#

The controller is numbered according to the order in which it is placed on the SBus or VME Bus. SBus options have a higher priority than VME devices since the SBus is built into the CPU board. The on-board SCSI controller on 4/600 models is always c0, unless no devices are attached to it. If an additional SCSI controller is placed in the first SBus slot, the prefix for devices attached to this controller is c1. If an IPI controller is installed on the VME bus in addition to the other two SCSI controllers, it will be known as c2, controller two.

Helpful Hint – Take care when you add new devices to an already installed Solaris 2.x system. If you add a controller and disk on a higher-priority bus than one that is already installed, you can effectively change the device name, resulting in mount problems for disk slices listed in the `/etc/vfstab` file.

Example: A deskside system 4/670 has two internal 1.3 Gbyte SCSI disks and an expansion IPI pedestal with four 1.3 Gbyte IPI disks. The device names for the internal SCSI disks are `/dev/dsk/c0t0d0` and `/dev/dsk/c0t1d0`. Both of these disks are connected to the on-board SCSI controller esp0. The four IPI disks are currently using the device names `/dev/dsk/c1t0d0`, `/dev/dsk/c1t1d0`, `/dev/dsk/c1t2d0`, and `/dev/dsk/c1t3d0`. Controller number one in this case is the VME-based IPI device called ipi3sc.

You purchase an additional Sbus-based SCSI controller and disks for this machine. You install the Sbus card and the disks and reboot the system with `boot -r` . Now, controller number one is the new Sbus card. The IPI controller is now called controller number two. References to the old `/dev/dsk/c1txdxsx` in the `/etc/vfstab` file will fail. They must be changed to `/dev/dsk/c2txdxsx`.

Helpful Hint – Consider this example fair warning. Always check the validity of the old device names after booting with the reconfigure option, especially when adding new hardware.

Tape Devices

Device names for magnetic tape devices are grouped under the `/dev/rmt` directory, complete with extensions that denote tape densities where applicable. Selecting the density of tape devices under the Solaris 1.x environment was not consistent. The device numbering scheme, under Solaris 1.x, was somewhat awkward, as it used a device name seemingly unrelated to low, medium, or high density encoding. The mechanism for tape drive densities is much clearer in the Solaris 2.x product.

Each device has several names, depending on features or options of the device that you want to use. A device name itself can be from one to five characters long.

- The first character is the device number. This value is always specified. Device numbers are relative to one another, not fixed to a specific SCSI ID, as SunOS used to be.

- The second character indicates the density of the device. This field is optional, and the device itself will be polled to determine the default if none is specified. Density is noted by an l, m, h, or u after the drive number to determine low, medium, high, and ultrahigh density. Not all tape devices have the ability to change write density.

- The third character indicates whether the data will be written out in normal or compress mode. A compressed output is indicated by a c. If this field is left blank, then normal output is assumed.

- The fourth character indicates whether the device is used with BSD style I/O. A BSD device is indicated by a b. If this field is left blank, then an SVR4 device is assumed.

- The fifth and last field is the rewind status of a device. If this field is blank, then the device can and usually will be rewound at the end of an operation. The n qualifier still indicates no rewind, but it is now placed at the end of the name instead of at the beginning.

Putting all of the pieces together, the first 8 mm tape drive will be

/dev/rmt/0, or

/dev/rmt/0n for the no-rewind device, or

/dev/rmt/0m for the 5.0G device name, or

/dev/rmt/0mb for the 5.0G BSD device name, or

/dev/rmt/0mcbn for the 5.0G compressed BSD no-rewind device name.

Tape devices are no longer limited to specific SCSI targets under Solaris 2.x as they are in 1.x. The SCSI target numbers four and five were reserved for /dev/st0 and /dev/st1 on the first controller and different targets for tape devices on other controllers. Determining the tape device on second and third controllers required reading the kernel configuration file.

Under Solaris 2.x, the only requirement for multiple targets on the same bus is that none of the targets share the same identification number. In other words, you cannot have a disk addressed as target four and a tape addressed as target four. If this is the case, usually neither device is seen, even though both are attached. Many systems provide a SCSI probing mechanism in the Boot PROM to diagnose this type of addressing conflict.

Frame Buffer Devices

The links to node names for frame buffer display devices are under /dev/fbs. Solaris 1.x placed the frame buffer devices in the topmost /dev directory. Some implementations of Solaris 2.x place a link from /dev/fb to /dev/fbs/<console_framebuffer> for the default OpenWindows frame buffer. If more than one frame buffer is installed on a system, the /dev/fb link points to the device that is probed first.

File Descriptors

A new directory called /dev/fd contains device nodes to keep track of file descriptors.

Directory Structure Changes

The directory structure is similar on all UNIX systems. Subdirectories under a single root directory in turn branch out into other directories containing the files to perform their specific function. Solaris 2.x remains bound to these constraints. There are some new directories in addition to the familiar directories found in /, such as /devices, /kernel, /opt, and /proc. In addition, the /etc directory has changed its appearance. Each new directory's purpose is explained next.

/devices and /dev

As explained above, the /devices directory holds the long, cumbersome physical device name. The /dev directory holds both the new SVR4 naming convention devices and the compatibility device names found in SunOS 4.x.

/kernel

"Where did /vmunix go?" The Solaris 2.x kernel is called /kernel/unix. The /kernel directory is a grand scheme. Under its branches are most of the device drivers and kernel modules needed for the system to run. These drivers and modules used to be built and linked into the kernel during a lengthy regeneration procedure. In Solaris 2.x they are objects automatically brought into the kernel memory by means of the modload command, see modload(1). It is no longer necessary to rebuild the kernel when new devices are added.

/net

The /net directory, while not new, is used by the NFS automounter. Shared NFS resources can be accessed through this directory by normal users, depending on how the directory is exported. The automounter is started by default on all Solaris 2.x systems because of entries in the /etc/auto_master file. In Solaris 1.x, the master automounter file is called /etc/auto.master.

/opt

The /opt directory is the home of SVR4 optional software packages. Many unbundled packages place their executables under /opt.

Helpful Hint – The size of /opt should be monitored at installation time on systems that will store unbundled software locally, as the install program does not allocate much disk space to this directory.

Often, the /opt directory is used as a mount point for NFS-shared unbundled products such as the SunPro™ Compilers or the AnswerBook® on-line documentation. Some OpenWindows optional packages are placed here as well.

/proc

The /proc directory is a special filesystem type that contains images of all processes that are running on the system. Each active process has an entry under /proc using the process ID as its file name. From an administrator's view, the /proc directory is a necessary system resource and should be left alone. However, see the proc(4) man page if you need more information about how to access these files.

/sbin

The /sbin directory is also known as single-user bin. Residing here are programs and startup scripts used during boot-up. Other files that reside in /sbin are such favorites as the Bourne shell, sh, init, and shutdown. The Solaris 1.x /bin directory that used to reside in the root partition has been completely moved to /usr/bin.

/tmp

Prior to Solaris 2.x, the /tmp directory was part of the root file system. This arrangement caused space problems, especially when mailtool was used to read large mail files or when a large compilation was executed. When /tmp got full, so did the root filesystem. The solution to this problem was to create a separate partition for /tmp.

In Solaris 2.x, /tmp is a temporary file system or *tmpfs*, allocated in virtual memory. It can still fill up, but all of the system's RAM and swap would first have to be exhausted. The tmpfs-mounted /tmp is actually a performance boost, not only because it runs in RAM but also because it caches write operations more effectively, saving the time it takes for normal I/O when writing to disk files.

/etc

The /etc directory has always held the configuration files for the system. As these files grew in number, the /etc directory became cumbersome. In Solaris 2.x, the /etc directory has been reorganized and subdirectories for specific functionality have been created.

- /etc/mail, /etc/lp, /etc/inetd, /etc/dfs, and /etc/cron have been created to hold the configuration files related to each service. In some cases, there is still a link to the Solaris 1.x location for the configuration file; restoring old files will break the link, and the configuration changes will not take effect. Such is the case with the old /etc/aliases, which now resides in /etc/mail/aliases.

- `/etc/default` holds configuration files that manage general administration defaults. `su`, `login`, and `passwd` control security restrictions that can be placed on user IDs and the login process. `cron` sets up the logging of the cron facility. `fs` and `tar` define default values.

- The `/etc/rc*.d` and `/etc/init.d` directories contain the system startup scripts.

Command Changes

With the change to SVR4, the System V version of commands is now the default. Many commands still retain their BSD counterparts in `/usr/ucb`. However, some of the system functions have not been carried forward. One notable example is the absence of `pstat`. To obtain the information supplied by this command, use the `swap` command for swap information. All other information must be obtained by setting up and using the `sar`, the system accounting utility.

Automatic Configuration

The automatic kernel configuration feature on Solaris 2.x may be one of its biggest assets. The kernel is now separated from the device and system drivers, which are loaded as needed at boot time. The system is probed, and, unless the device driver is specified to be loaded in the `/etc/system` file, device drivers are loaded only if a device is found.

Automatic configuration can be forced to run at boot time by means of the `-r` option to the boot command. Another way to reconfigure is to touch or create a file named `/reconfigure` before you reboot. The existence of this file name causes the probing and reconfiguration of the `/dev` and `/devices` directories.

For instance, to add a new SCSI disk to a Solaris 1.x system, first check to see if the device is configured in the kernel. This is accomplished by looking at the kernel configuration file for the running kernel. If the device is not present or is commented out, then build a new kernel and move it into the root directory. Then create the device nodes for that disk in `/dev` and reboot the system. If all goes well, everything should work. Last you partition the disk, create the filesystems, and add entries to `/etc/fstab`.

With the Solaris 2.x software, you can shut down the system, connect the new device, and reboot with the `-r` option. You can then partition the disk, create filesystems, and add the appropriate entries to the `/etc/vfstab` file for automatic mounting upon subsequent reboots. Much less of a burden than building a new kernel!

Use the same procedure when adding other devices, such as an additional frame buffer or system option card. First, shut down the system, install the board, and reboot with `-r` to automatically configure the necessary driver onto the kernel stream. Some system options require their own drivers; the installation software for a particular device usually places the driver in the proper directory so that it is available at boot time or at first reference.

Helpful Hint – Take care when adding, moving, or removing devices or controllers in the interim between reconfiguration boots.

If a new device, especially a SCSI controller, is placed between two other controllers on the bus, reconfiguring may cause the devices to renumber themselves, possibly causing existing mount points in the `/etc/vfstab` file to fail.

admintool

Solaris 2.1 introduced a GUI-based administration tool, `admintool`, which performs many of the routine administrative functions on local files and network-wide databases. `admintool` is the preferred method of administrating NIS+ because it has facilities to update data files directly, and it can be used to obtain information from NIS, although it cannot update data files. `admintool` can also update local files, often referred to as the `/etc` files.

Note – Don't confuse `admintool` with the System V utility, `sysadm`, which was based on single-system administrative tasks instead of on tasks that affected the network as a whole. The `sysadm` utility was removed from the Solaris 2.x implementation of SVR4.

Under `admintool`, adding and removing standalone, diskless, and dataless systems on the network is simple. `admintool` provides utilities for the creation and modification of user accounts, the installation of both local and remote printers, and serial port manipulation. `admintool` can also configure systems as remote installation or diskless clients.

When to Use admintool

If you are making the plunge into NIS+, then use `admintool`. The framework surrounding `admintool` is specifically targeted at the NIS+ environment. All the tasks that introduce a system on the network can be achieved with great ease under the `admintool`/NIS+ combination. This in turn affects how all other systems are configured. Diskless and dataless clients can be easily configured by touching a few buttons and entering necessary system data.

The biggest asset of `admintool` is in configuring local and remote print resources, because the commands to install printers under SVR4 tend to be long and cumbersome. Starting with Solaris 2.3, `admintool` can also be used to set up serial ports, including modem connections.

When Not to Use admintool

You cannot use `admintool` to administer a NIS domain. For instance, in Solaris 1.x, to add diskless client support on a server, you first enter its Ethernet address and hostname into the NIS databases, `ethers`, `hosts`, `bootparams`, and so on. You then build the NIS maps and make sure they are propagated throughout the domain. After the client is known on the network, you can execute the `/usr/etc/install/add_client` script on its server. The server then performs the remaining steps to enable that system to boot over the network.

Using `admintool`, you cannot add any host that already exists. To create diskless clients in a functional NIS domain, you literally have to cut off access to the domain before the clients will configure under `admintool`. Instead of making administrative tasks easier, using `admintool` with NIS can cause you to perform additional steps.

`admintool` also requires a special administrative group account to be known network-wide. Certain files are created with special permissions, allowing privileges only to this predefined group.

NFS

The functionality of NFS, Sun's distributed computing filesystem, remains intact across Solaris releases. However, the manner in which files and directories are made available as NFS resources has changed. The NFS system is now included under the Distributed File Systems (DFS) framework. Commands have been developed to control both NFS and RFS resource management. RFS has since been dropped from the Solaris release, beginning with Solaris 2.3.

The Solaris 1.x command to share NFS directories is `exportfs`, while the Solaris 2.x equivalent sharing for both NFS and RFS resources is `share`. For compatibility, Solaris 2.x software still supports the `exportfs` command, but the command itself is a shell script that maps the different options to the `share` command.

The file in which NFS shared directories are listed has also changed. Solaris 1.x uses a file called `/etc/exports` to define directories that are automatically exported at boot time. The Solaris 2.x equivalent is the file named `/etc/dfs/dfstab`, in which both NFS and RFS resources are automatically shared at boot time. The syntax of the entries between `/etc/exports` and `/etc/dfs/dfstab` is also different, mostly to accommodate RFS.

Name Services

The name service is a distributed database that contains the information about all the hosts and the users on the network. This information is often viewable and usable by all users, but only a selected few can alter the data. Without this service, it would be necessary to synchronize information about hosts and passwords on each individual host. Once a network has more than about ten hosts, the practice of manually sharing the data is not a good choice.

/etc/nsswitch.conf

A new file, found only in Solaris 2.x, is responsible for the order and location from which system and network data is retrieved. The /etc/nsswitch.conf file contains entries for specific system functions that are available both to the local files and the naming service databases. You can select what is to be looked at first, or last, and what can be omitted entirely. A file such as this is necessary when more than one name service is in use.

NIS and NIS+

NIS+ (Network Information Service Plus) is an entirely new naming service for Solaris 2.x. NIS+ provides much of the same functionality as NIS (Network Information Service) in previous SunOS releases. NIS+ is targeted at a distributed administrative framework, in which a group of system administrators are responsible for maintaining a single database in parallel instead of serially, whereas NIS is targeted more at a single master server, on which all database datafiles are modified and built.

The NIS+ root server is similar to the NIS master server in that it holds the master data files for its domain, but modifications to those files can be done with the GUI-based admintool or from the command-line interface of designated administrative accounts.

Some of the things to keep in mind concerning NIS and NIS+ are the following:

- Solaris 2.x systems can join existing NIS domains as clients using the same procedures that were used for SunOS 4.x clients.

- NIS+ domains can be set up to support both NIS and NIS+ clients. This is a good choice for sites that are transitioning to NIS+ or sites that need to keep SunOS 4.x installed on some systems. This is a good intermediate choice for sites that plan to convert entirely to NIS+.

- Solaris 2.x systems cannot become NIS master or slave servers with the bundled release. No NIS server processes are available in the bundled Solaris 2.x release. The NIS slave server package can be obtained through the normal system support channel.

Password Management

The password file is somewhat different in Solaris 2.x than in Solaris 1.x. The encrypted password is stored in a separate file, called /etc/shadow, where functions such as password aging and other user account management are defined. The command /usr/sbin/pwconv converts single password file accounts into the dual password scheme. The Solaris 2.x /etc/passwd file no longer needs special entries for the naming service as were necessary in Solaris 1.x. The management of name service lookups and priority is accomplished in the /etc/nsswitch.conf file.

User account creation and maintenance can be achieved through the useradd command on local systems or through the GUI-based admintool for both local and NIS+ wide administration.

The Printer Subsystem

The printer subsystem is completely different in Solaris 2.x as compared with the Solaris 1.x print spooler. A /etc/printcap file no longer defines printer attributes; instead, printers are defined through System V commands, such as lpadmin, lpsched, and pmadm. In addition, a function within the GUI-based admintool performs local and remote printer setup and maintenance.

Solaris 2.x systems can use network printers that are connected to Solaris 1.x systems, and vice versa. The administration of cross-OS architecture print services can be difficult to maintain, but is possible.

Serial Device Management

Serial devices are managed through the System V commands pmadm and sacadm. In Solaris 1.x, you only had to edit the /etc/ttytab file and send a signal to init. The management of serial ports is more difficult in Solaris 2.x, but is also more tunable. Serial device management can also be accomplished via the Solaris 2.3 admintool, a feature not provided in previous releases.

In conclusion, there are many changes to administering systems in the Solaris 2.x environment. The remaining chapters of this book will help make the transition as painless as possible, providing a single reference for most of the daily administrative tasks.

≡ *1*

Solaris Implementation: A Guide for System Administrators

Planning and Preparing for Installation

2 ≡

The manner in which a system is installed dictates the manner in which it can be used. You should consider many things before you begin to install the Solaris 2.x environment. In particular, you must understand how the machine being installed fits into the network as a whole. The most common system on the network is a general purpose workstation, able to run many user applications. Another common system type is one that performs a single purpose, for example, a network file server or a system that supplies naming service information to all or a selected number of systems. The gateway or router system connects two different network segments and allows systems on both networks to communicate with each other. Each of these functions can be created from a standalone Solaris installation.

Planning Installation

Helpful Hint – Be sure you know what function the system will perform before you begin installation.

The decisions made during the installation process can enable or disable certain functionality of a system. Of course, you can convert a system to perform almost any function after installation, but the steps become more complex when a machine is defined and installed for one purpose and ends up performing something entirely different.

Hardware Requirements

Before Solaris is installed on a system, some hardware requirements must be satisfied, beginning with the machine itself. Solaris 2.x can be installed on all SPARC systems, starting with the desktop systems, such as an SLC, continuing with the deskside and server systems, such as 4/200 and 4/600 series, and ending with the SPARCserver 1000 and SPARCcenter 2000 series systems. Each system requires a minimum amount of 16 megabytes of RAM. Twelve megabytes may actually suffice, but the response time is much better with 16 or more megabytes of RAM. Table 2-1 matches machine types that can run Solaris 2.x with their kernel architecture.

Table 2-1   Solaris 2.x System Types

Machine Type	Kernel Architecture
Sun 4100/200/300/400	Sun
SPARCstation SLC/ELC/IPC/IPX	Sun4c
SPARCstation 1/1+/2	Sun4c
SPARCclassic	Sun4m
SPARCstation LX/10	Sun4m
SPARCserver 600MP	Sun4m
SPARCserver 1000	Sun4d
SPARCcenter 2000	Sun4d

Each platform supports most, if not all, of the SCSI disk and tape devices that were released as options for those systems. The 4/200 series systems also support disks and tape devices attached to VME-based option cards, such as the Xylogics 451 and 7053 disk controllers and the Xylogics 472 tape drive controller. The 4/300 and 4/400 series systems can use the Xylogics 7053 disks, IPI and SCSI devices; the 4/600 series systems support only IPI or SCSI devices. The newer SPARCcenter 1000 and 2000 support both standard single-ended and differential fast SCSI devices.

Most SBus and VME frame buffer devices are also supported in Solaris 2.x, including many P4-Bus display cards, resident only on the 4100, 4300, and 4400 series systems.

Software Planning

The entire Solaris 2.x release is quite large, over 250 megabytes in size just for the binary files themselves. The amount of Solaris to be installed on a machine depends on the size of the local disk or disks, the function that machine will perform, and the type of network resources available. It is not wise or cost effective to install the entire release on every machine. Learn to use the network and NFS to obtain other resources on systems with smaller disks. This process, defined as workgroup computing, requires a fair amount of planning.

A common idea involves separating the Solaris environment into sections: the SunOS base operating system, the OpenWindows windowing system, optional bundled software packages, and home directories. These equate to files and subdirectories in the root or /, /usr, /usr/openwin, /opt, and /home directories. When major parts of the environment are distributed in this manner, system upgrades are much easier to manage. A windowing system upgrade is as simple as changing the NFS mount path. Operating system upgrades can be done without affecting other parts of the environment. Optional bundled and unbundled packages can be changed once in a central location instead of many times on a number of different systems. The home directory files are safe from accidental removal.

There is also a fine line between simply using NFS resources and making a workgroup too network bound. If too many clients rely on a single NFS server for operating system or other services, they will all be adversely affected if the server is overloaded. Tuning NFS servers is a balancing act that can only be done after collecting performance statistics on the live environment.

The Base Operating System

The UNIX operating system is a series of files and directories that are attached at the topmost directory, commonly called root or slash, /. Every system needs a dedicated root area, whether that area is on a local disk or over a network mount. Files contained in the root filesystem dictate specifics about the machine, including its hostname or nodename, the Internet Protocol address, and name service designation. For this reason, the root filesystem cannot be shared by more than one network node.

Also included under the root filesystem are kernel-specific files, based on the architecture of the installed SPARC processor. Systems from different architecture families cannot share kernel-specific executable files. For instance, a SPARCstation 10 cannot boot from a disk that was installed on a SPARCstation 2, because they are from different kernel architecture families, Sun4m and Sun4c, respectively.

In Solaris 2.x, there are three distinct systems configurations to select from during the installation process: dataless, standalone, and server. A dataless machine is one that relies in part on another system for necessary operating system resources, namely the /usr partition. A standalone machine is the most common system type, booting from its local disk and using both local and network resources. The term "standalone" means that the system needs only itself to run SunOS. In the context of installation, a server provides one or more client systems with operating system files or other resources.

Most of the files residing under /usr may be shared by all architectures but, for performance, are generally stored on the local disk. It is this area that is shared by both diskless and dataless systems on the Solaris server. These files are said to belong to the SPARC application architecture, as opposed to the kernel architecture. Also under the /usr directory are many of the shared object libraries and system utilities that are common in most UNIX implementations.

All files under the root and /usr filesystems are wiped clean and remade during system installations. Custom files and other nonoperating system files should not be kept in these two partitions or they will be lost. During system upgrades, as opposed to installations, the root and /usr filesystems are not destroyed. Instead, new files replace the older files, and many system-specific files, such as /etc/passwd and /etc/hosts, are saved.

The Windowing System

The OpenWindows development environment occupies the /usr/openwin directory. The complete windowing system can use up to 110 megabytes of disk space, which is quite a bit of space for most standalone systems. However, the entire 110 megabytes are not required by most systems, because a few large packages containing demonstration image files, development tools, and sample source code are generally not needed.

One way of conserving space on small disk systems is to NFS-mount the windowing system. The executable files under /usr/openwin also conform to the SPARC application architecture specifications, so systems from all SPARC architecture types can share the same copy simultaneously. Select a machine with enough disk space to be the OpenWindows server and install the entire windowing system files on that machine. Share the /usr/openwin directory as an NFS resource. When installing systems with smaller capacity disks, do not install OpenWindows. Instead, NFS-mount the /usr/openwin from server on the empty directory created during the install.

When you employ this strategy of an NFS-shared OpenWindows, you enable systems with small disks to have access to the entire windowing system instead of limiting them to what fits on their disk. (This strategy can also be used with windowing systems other than OpenWindows.)

Some window system drivers reside outside the /usr/openwin directory and must be installed before you can run OpenWindows, but the disk space used by these drivers is trivial compared to the entire 110 megabytes. The window system drivers are contained in one required package (or logical group of related files), SUNWowdrv, and are installed under the /kernel or /usr/kernel directories along with other system and device drivers during normal installation.

Optional Software

The /opt directory is designed for optional software packages. Several of the bundled operating system packages, such as the X-Imaging runtime libraries, SUNWxilrt, the SPARC compilers, and the SUNWsprot packages, are placed in /opt. Software that resides in /opt must be executable by all SPARC architectures. The /opt directory can easily become an NFS-shared resource, similar to /usr/openwin, saving space on small-disk systems.

Home Directories

User home directories can also be removed from the local disk when possible and placed on a common NFS server. This type of arrangement allows a central point for backup procedures and saves local disk space on all home directory clients. Another advantage to a home directory server is a simpler implementation of the NFS automounter, which is discussed in Chapter 6, in the section titled "The Automounter."

Disk Partitioning

Solaris 2.x systems can use a partition arrangement similar to that in Solaris 1.x, except for the size of the root or / partition. In BSD-based systems, a smaller root partition suffices, whereas in Solaris 2.x, more space is needed in root, specifically for the kernel modules and device drivers that reside in the /kernel directory. The amount of disk space needed by the /kernel subdirectory alone is nearly 12 megabytes, in addition to the files used by the /etc and /sbin directories, which are also resident in the root slice.

Helpful Hint – You will need to change the partition sizes on most systems that are upgrading from a Solaris 1.x base to Solaris 2.x; refer to Appendix B to determine the partition sizes that you need. You can change partition sizes either by using the manual format program or during the installation itself.

Minimum Disk Requirements

The minimum space requirement for a system depends on the available NFS resources. You can fit the base Solaris 2.2 and earlier releases on a 105-megabyte disk if you use a remotely mounted version of OpenWindows and omit other, less common packages. A few other modifications are necessary to successfully run Solaris 2.2 on a system with a single 105-megabyte disk, but it can be done. Consider making systems with smaller disks into dataless clients rather than standalone machines. This arrangement allows more local space for the root and swap partitions where it is needed most. Samples of common types of installation (end-user, developer, NFS server) are found in Appendix B. Rather than stating the minimum requirements as law, some general rules, discussed below, apply.

▼   The Root Partition

Configure the root partition with at least 20 megabytes of space for most systems. Fourteen of the 20 are used by the necessary root files, and, unless specifically configured otherwise, all email, print spooling, and calendar manager files are stored in the root partition. If you make the root partition too small, any one of these areas could quickly occupy all the free space.

Don't overlook the print spooler when setting the size of the root slice. Free space is used while attempting to spool up a large file for printing. When the print job is complete, the file is removed. Sending just one PostScript file to the printer could use up all the free space in the root filesystem.

Another problem that can result from insufficient root filesystem space has to do with receiving large email files, especially those with audio or other types of attachments. Both of these issues can be resolved by making a separate /var partition during installation. The minimum size of a dedicated /var partition can vary greatly, depending on the amount and type of email that is exchanged at a particular site. Other options are discussed in Chapter 3.

▼ Swap Space

The size of system swap space is another consideration often overlooked. The Solaris install program automatically configures the size of the swap partition by doubling the amount of installed RAM. For example, if the system has 16 megabytes of RAM and you accept the default disk parameters when you boot into the install program, then the swap partition will be given approximately 32 megabytes. If more memory is installed, then more swap is allotted.

Helpful Hint – It is a good idea to install any additional RAM on a system before you begin the Solaris Install process. If this is not possible, you can manually increase the swap size while in the install program's disk forms. You can also add swap space on a system on-the-fly while Solaris is running if necessary. For instructions on how to do this, refer to the section titled "Adding Swap Space" in Chapter 9. Again, the disk space must be available.

A full doubling of the amount of installed RAM is not always necessary because Solaris 2.x uses virtual memory space before touching the actual disk swap space. Swap activity is also specific to the amount of system load and the applications that are being executed. You may have to monitor the system once it is running its desired task to determine if more swap space is necessary.

▼ The /usr Partition

The complete Solaris 2.x release requires a minimum of 185 megabytes for the /usr filesystem, which includes the entire OpenWindows executable files and fonts. However, not every system needs the full complement of bundled packages; when everything is installed, many packages that are never used occupy precious disk space. The amount of needed /usr space depends on the function of the system being installed; general purpose workstations need a fair amount of /usr space because of the many different jobs they perform.

You may choose to split the 185-megabyte partition into two separate slices, designating one partition for the /usr filesystem and another for /usr/openwin, if OpenWindows is to be installed locally. With this arrangement, the /usr partition needs only 85 megabytes, and /usr/openwin needs 100. If you install the /usr partition with less than 85 megabytes, there may be a potential space problem if you ever decide to install additional bundled packages.

▼ Application Space

An area often overlooked on standalone systems is application space. Before starting installation, determine the size of the application programs that will be used on your machine. In most networked environments, application programs are stored on an NFS-shared directory, available to many systems simultaneously. In this case, you do not need to reserve local disk space. However, if you are installing a standalone system, you must reserve an area for user applications. If you are installing the NFS server of these applications, be sure you understand the size requirements for the total number of applications that will be installed. Strategies for such an arrangement are discussed in Chapter 6, "Using the Network."

▼ New Home Directory Designation

The Solaris 1.x standard, /home/<system-name> should be migrated to a different path in Solaris 2.x because the default automounter files specify /home as a mount point. Upon initial boot, the NFS automounter covers any directory or file that might be attached locally under /home. The newly designated path to local home directories is now /export/home, even if you do not plan to NFS-share your home directory.

You can implement user home directories in many different ways. To obtain maximum user mobility and ease of administration, arrange home directories together by workgroup on a remote home directory server. Use the automounter by way of an NIS-wide auto.home or auto_home map to automatically mount user home directories from any system in the NIS domain.

From Where Should You Boot?

One of the most puzzling parts of the installation process may be in deciding how to boot into the install system. You cannot install Solaris 2.x while the system is running Solaris 1.x, nor can you install Solaris 2.x while running a previous version of Solaris 2.x. You must use an alternate way of booting to gain access to the install program. In Solaris 2.x you have three choices: booting from a local CD-ROM device, booting from the preinstalled stub image, or booting from the network. Each of these boot processes is a means to the same end, the Solaris Install system.

There are three distinct parts of the installation process: booting the environment, a system identification query session, and the install query session. Each can be done manually or automatically. Boot commands can be entered at the monitor prompt, or a preinstalled image can automatically locate an install environment. You can choose to answer screen prompts each time they appear during this boot process or register the system to the naming service prior to booting, allowing the query session to be completely answered by the NIS or NIS+ name service entries. You can also choose to manually install each system or enable the install process to be fully automated with AutoInstall. Each of these processes is discussed below.

Manual Booting

Booting from a local CD-ROM is a matter of telling the system boot PROM where to start reading. You must have a CD-ROM device connected directly to the system that you wish to install. Depending on how many Solaris CDs and installable CD drives are in your possession, this method is how you probably will start. The local CD boot process is discussed in "Booting into the Install System from Local CD" in Chapter 3.

Not every machine has a local CD device, and some of the older systems do not even allow CD drives to be attached. In these instances, you can use the network to boot from a remote CD device as though it were local. This process of remote booting from a shared CD-ROM is effortless once you understand how it is set up. Remote installations may even become the preferred method. The setup for remote booting is discussed in "Preparing the Network for Automatic Booting" found later in this chapter.

Automatic Booting

Automatic booting can be defined as letting the system determine the location of the installation environment by looking for either a locally attached CD device or certain network shared resources. This automatic booting is accomplished with the preinstalled jumpstart boot image, installed at the factory.

New systems and new disk peripherals boot from the preinstalled image when they are first turned on. This preinstalled boot image, or "stub," has caused some confusion since its introduction in Solaris 2.1. Its sole purpose is to initiate a *hands-off* installation for end-users. The stub cannot be used as a standalone environment as in Solaris 1.x and previous SunOS releases. It can only be used to locate and boot the local or remote installation environment.

Using the Preinstalled Boot Image

When a new system is unpacked and a CD-ROM drive included, all the proper cables are plugged in; the Solaris Install CD can be inserted into its caddy and placed into the CD device. You then turn on the system and wait for some activity. Soon after the initial self-test, the system begins booting from the preinstalled image and looks first to see if the Solaris CD is installed. If it is found, the stub boot process is halted, and the locally attached CD is used as the boot device.

If there is no locally attached CD-ROM device, then the stub attempts to locate a network install server by probing the bootparams servers on the local network segment. If a server was configured and the match is found, the stub halts and initiates a remote boot from the install server just located.

If neither a local nor a remote Solaris Install device is located, the stub halts itself, reporting that it could not find a local or remote device. The options at this point are to find a CD device for this system or to configure it as an install client on a server system in the local network segment.

Boot Query Session—Manual Input

After either the manual or the automatic boot process is initiated, the next phase of reaching the install system is the boot query session, which involves such things as setting the hostname, Internet Protocol address, name service designation, local time zone, and time. A screen-based menu prompts the user for each required item before the install program can be entered. Systems that are not attached to a network must always go through this session when booting from the Solaris Install CD.

Systems that will be installed on an existing network can have all of their required data entered into the local name service prior to booting from the CD, thereby omitting this query session entirely. Systems that use a remote install server have some of this data entered by virtue of booting over the network. However, some manual intervention may still be necessary to completely boot into the install program.

Boot Query Session—Automatic Input

You can automate the manual boot query session for all systems booting from either the local CD or remote resource by entering data into the proper NIS or NIS+ name service. The required setup is discussed in "Preparing the Network for Automatic Booting" on page 39. You may find this part of the install process to be one of the most gratifying because the chance of improper hostname, IP address, and name service input by users is removed.

Manual Installations

Once you have completely booted from either a local or remote install medium, the Solaris Install program is started, offering a number of choices. Three types of installation configurations are offered, standalone quick, standalone custom, or server. The manual install is performed by working though a series of menu-driven screens that select the system type, software selection, and disk partitioning. The manual installations are covered in Chapter 4.

Automatic Installations

Automatic installations are performed by using network resources and name service databases to supply configuration information. By addition of the host, ether, and timezone information into the appropriate name service data, the Boot Query section of the installation can be bypassed.

Additionally, a configuration information directory can be specified, and the autoinstall process will complete the installation without any more manual intervention. System configurations are defined in files that select system type, explicit or automatic disk partitioning, and automatic or explicit software selection. This very powerful tool can make future installations and upgrades effortless.

For AutoInstall to be most effective, all the prior automatic procedures should be implemented. It would seem strange to automate only this part of the installation process, allowing the possibility of user error in the Boot Query session. AutoInstall information can be found in the AutoInstall section later in this chapter. Samples of AutoInstall scripts can be found in Appendix A.

Preparing to Install

You have many things to consider before attempting to install Solaris 2.x on a system currently running Solaris 1.x. First and foremost, save any user-modified files on a medium other than the system about to undergo installation. The Solaris Install system allows you to preserve existing partitions, but you can easily wipe clean a disk before you know what has happened.

The easiest and fastest method for saving files is to use the network, especially if a local tape device is not available. Choose an NFS server, ideally a machine that runs a nightly backup script. Mount the shared directory on your local machine and create a directory under the mount path with proper permissions. Copy the files you want to save using any of the many mechanisms available such as tar, cpio, or just plain cp. It is also a good idea to make a tape, just in case.

Special Files to Save

It is difficult to identify all of the files to save on each and every system. An experienced administrator knows which files need to be saved and probably already has backups of these files. Some of the more popular files to save are listed below.

From Solaris 1.x System

- `/.*` files (for your favorite root environment files: `.cshrc`, `.login`, `.profile`, `.rhosts`)
- `/etc/aliases` (mail aliases)
- `/etc/auto.*` (any other automounter files)
- `/etc/dumpdates` (for systems that use `dump` and `rdump` for backups)
- `/etc/hosts` (IP information)
- `/etc/fstab`
- `/etc/licenses` (software licensing)
- `/etc/passwd` (if local file is maintained)
- `/etc/printcap`
- `/var/spool/mail/*` (the email spooler)
- `/var/spool/calendar/*` (OpenWindows Calendar Manager files)
- `/var/spool/cron/*` (don't forget your cron jobs)

From Solaris 2.x System

- `/.*` files (for your favorite root environment files: `.cshrc`, `.login`, `.profile`, `.rhosts`)
- `/etc/mail/aliases` (mail aliases)
- `/etc/auto_*` (any other automounter files)
- `/etc/dumpdates` (for systems that use `ufsdump` for backups)
- `/etc/inet/hosts` (IP information)
- `/etc/vfstab`
- `/etc/licenses` (software licensing)
- `/etc/passwd` (if local file is maintained)
- `/var/mail/*` (the email spooler)
- `/var/spool/calendar/*` (OpenWindows Calendar Manager files)
- `/var/spool/cron/*` (don't forget your cron jobs)

Networking Requirements

The Solaris 2.x installation uses the network for several activities. If it cannot find the information that it needs, then it prompts you for this information. NIS+ is the default name service. If both NIS and NIS+ are found on the local subnet, NIS+ will be used, even if it does not supply the needed information.

Hostname and Internet Information

If you are upgrading a system from a Solaris 1.x or previous release, then you should already know the system's hostname and IP information. If not, you can obtain it by using the existing naming service databases or by looking in the /etc/hosts file before the system is shut down for installation. To extract the information from the NIS naming service, use the command:

```
% ypmatch `uname -n` hosts
192.9.200.1    harlie
```

If installing a new machine or moving a system from a different subnet, you will take different steps, depending on how the system will boot. In most cases, assign the system a hostname and Internet Protocol number prior to booting. This procedure is done differently depending on (a) whether a naming service is being used and (b) the naming services that are currently running.

If the system will boot from a local CD-ROM device and there is no naming service, then prior setup is unnecessary because the network information will be gathered during the boot query session. Once the system is installed, its hostname and IP address can be added to the /etc/hosts file of all other systems that will communicate with it. Those systems must also be added to its /etc/hosts file.

If the system will use a remote install server, then introduction to the network is necessary. Both Ethernet and Internet addresses must be registered with the install server before the system begins booting. Again, the procedures for this type of install differ according to the way the install client is created. If the GUI-based admintool sets up the client on the install server, then no prior introduction is necessary because the system's Ethernet and Internet addresses are used as input to the tool itself.

If the command-line-based add_install_client script is used to create the install client, then the system hostname must be known either in the local /etc/hosts file on the install server or in the naming service databases.

Naming Service

In addition to the hostname and Internet information, the naming service type and domain name must also be supplied. Solaris 2.x systems may join an existing NIS domain easily. To determine the NIS domain name, you can view the contents of the /etc/defaultdomain file or execute the domainname command from any other machine on the local network segment.

Helpful Hint – You will need this information when booting from the installation CD, so write it down.

A new naming service, NIS+, is available in Solaris 2.x. The NIS+ naming service also uses the /etc/defaultdomain file. However, there may not be any NIS+ servers running on your network. If you join a nonexistent domain, the system will have problems during the initial boot. It is far better to first install the machine without a naming service and then join the NIS+ domain as a client or create the NIS+ server after installation. A bogus name service designation also negatively affects the outcome of the installation.

Install Servers

Some systems cannot or do not have local CD-ROM devices attached. These machines can only be installed via remote CD. Systems that share their CD device to other machines are called install servers. Systems that use the install server are called install clients.

The Solaris CD-ROM can convert any machine with a local CD-ROM device to an install server of all SPARC architectures. However, not all machines can be used as install servers, because boot support is not included in their current kernel or because certain daemons are not running. The following section explains how to configure an install server.

Choosing an Install Server

Install clients must be attached to the same local network as their install server because they are essentially diskless clients while the installation is taking place. Because network booting cannot occur through a router, the install server should be connected to as many networks as possible. Figure 2-1 illustrates one option (not always possible): making the router system the install server to allow the most number of installation clients per install server.

In the figure, clients on networks B and C can boot and install from the install server "blue." Note that if "blue" had only one network attached, only clients from that network could use blue's boot services.

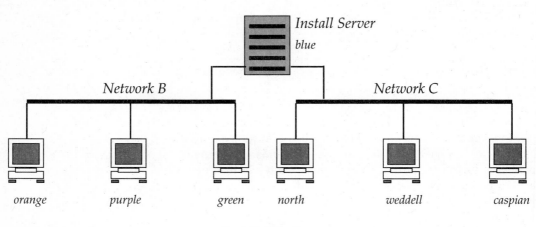

Figure 2-1   *Install Server and Clients*

To dedicate a system as an install server, choose one of the following procedures; both methods enable the network booting of clients for installation.

1. Mount the Solaris CD-ROM itself

   Advantages

   • Use this method if the system is installing only a few clients. By using a local CD, you can install a few clients in the same amount of time it takes to copy the UFS image.
   • Safe; that is, little risk of corruption.
   • You can use `admintool` to add remote install clients from a Solaris 2.x-based install server because the CD-ROM is assumed to be mounted or attached under a certain path name, as `admintool` expects.

   Disadvantages

   • Much slower than a disk drive (UFS image).
   • Installing many simultaneous installations greatly extends the installation time.

2. Copy the image of the Solaris 2.x CD-ROM, also known as the UFS image, to an exported disk.

   Advantages

   • The USF image; can handle many simultaneous installations much faster than can a mounted CD.
   • Reduces boot-up and installation time for remote clients.

   Disadvantages

   • You cannot use `admintool` to add remote install clients from a Solaris 2.x-based install server. However, you can use the command-line interface to add install clients.
   • Because the file is both readable and writeable, the image can be inadvertently corrupted.

Select an install server that gives you the most reward for your effort.

Install Server Base Operating Systems Requirements

You can use either a Solaris 1.x- or 2.x-based install server; network booting is enabled in both environments. If you decide to use a Solaris 1.x-based system as an install server, be sure to check the following system parameters:

• Server OS should be at least Solaris 1.0.1, SunOS 4.1.2

• GENERIC kernel or the following pseudo-devices enabled in the current kernel:

```
pseudo-device      snit          # streams NIT
pseudo-device      pf            # packet filter
pseudo-device      nbuf          # NIT buffering module
```

These devices enable operations necessary for the booting of diskless clients. If you are converting a normal Solaris 1.x-based standalone machine into a network install server, these devices may not be built into the current kernel. Before you boot clients, modify the kernel and reboot the system.

Install servers running Solaris 2.x should check the file `/etc/nsswitch.conf` to determine the order in which the ethers and bootparams data is located. If your install server is an NIS client, this file is set to look first in the NIS domain.

You should also try to select a somewhat powerful machine to be an install server. While any machine can do the job, the best results can be found when the install server has more memory and a somewhat faster CPU than its clients have. When in doubt, select later-model machines, such as the SPARCstation 10 or SPARCserver 1000 with its built-in CD-ROM device, as install servers.

Copying the Image

Use the `setup_install_server` script to install the contents of the CD-ROM on a system. This utility is located in the topmost directory of the Solaris installation CD. There must be no less than 300 megabytes of free disk space, preferably in a filesystem that serves no other purpose and is not already an NFS-shared resource. The process takes a couple of hours to complete.

Mounting the CD-ROM Volume

On Solaris 1.x-based systems, you must first mount the CD-ROM under an existing directory, then initiate the setup_install_server script, using the destination path as the first argument.

```
harlie# mount -rt hsfs /dev/sr0 /cdrom
harlie# /cdrom/setup_install_server /export/cdrom
```

The commands above copy the contents of the Solaris CD that is attached under /cdrom into the /export/cdrom directory.

On Solaris 2.x-based systems, a few conditions apply. A new utility in Solaris 2.2, called Volume Management, automatically mounts labeled CD-ROMs and diskettes to locations specified in the /etc/vold.conf file. When the Solaris CD-ROM is inserted into a system that is running the vold process, it is automatically mounted to the /vol/cdrom0/s0 directory. The command line for this arrangement is as follows:

```
harlie# /vol/cdrom0/s0/setup_install_server /export/cdrom
```

Releases prior to Solaris 2.2 do not contain the Volume Manager, so the CD-ROM must be mounted manually. The command line to mount the CD-ROM is shown below.

```
harlie# mount -F hsfs -o ro /dev/dsk/c0t6d0s0 /cdrom
harlie# /cdrom/setup_install_server /export/cdrom
```

As before, these commands copy the contents of the Solaris CD-ROM into the /export/cdrom directory, provided there is enough space.

Helpful Hint – Since you are copying nearly 300 megabytes from a relatively slow device, this procedure should be left running overnight or started several hours before it is actually needed.

Adding Install Clients

Install clients may be configured in one of two ways: by using the
add_install_client script in the topmost CD-ROM directory or by using the GUI-
based admintool. You must have already installed Solaris 2.x on the install server before
you can run admintool. Additionally, the install CD should be inserted into the CD
device.

Note – Add_install_client can be executed on systems running either Solaris 1.x or
Solaris 2.x. Do not execute add_install_client on Solaris 1.x-based servers while
another installation is occurring. Doing so may temporarily interrupt NFS services,
possibly causing an incomplete package install and a failed overall installation. The
temporary interruption of NFS services does not occur on systems running Solaris 2.x.

To use the command-line interface, enter the complete path to the mount point of the CD-
ROM or to the location of the CD-ROM image. If the CD is mounted to the /cdrom
directory, then add install boot support by running /cdrom/add_install_client,
supplying two arguments: the hostname of the system you are about to install and its
kernel architecture, which may be one of sun4, sun4c, sun4e, sun4m, or sun4d. See Table
2-1 for system kernel architectures with model numbers.

Assuming that the Solaris installation CD is mounted to /cdrom, the command in
Figure 2-2 shows how to add the installation client named "green."

```
blue# /cdrom/add_install_client green sun4c
saving original exports in /etc/exports.orig
Adding "/cdrom -ro,root=green" to /etc/exports.
enabling tftp in /etc/inetd.conf
"green" has an entry in the NIS bootparams map.
Please update it with the following entry:
green root=blue:/cdrom/export/exec/kvm/sparc.sun4c.Solaris_2.2
install=blue:/cdrom

updating /etc/bootparams
copying inetboot to /tftpboot
```

Figure 2-2   Running add_install_client

If the system is not properly configured into the naming service database, the command
will not complete and will list the missing data. Also seen in Figure 2-2 is a message that
states the client already has an entry in the NIS bootparams map and that the map should
be updated with new information. If the entries are different, the client could obtain the

wrong information and boot from an entirely different server, or not boot at all. Your choices to remedy this situation are to update the NIS database with the entry displayed or to remove the entry from the NIS bootparams map entirely.

After `add_install_client` returns to the shell prompt, boot the client system over the network.

Using admintool to Set Up Remote Installations

The GUI-based Administration Tool provides an effective way to enable remote installations on install servers that use the Solaris CD only. A more complete discussion of `admintool` is included in the "admintool" section of Chapter 4. You cannot use `admintool` to set up remote installations on systems with an image of the CD-ROM unless that image is mounted under `/vol/cdrom0/s0`.

To begin:

1. **Become root on the Solaris 2.x install server and enter admintool.**
   The window shown in Figure 2-3 is displayed.

2. **From the admintool window, Figure 2-3, position the mouse cursor over the Host Manager icon and use the SELECT mouse button to select the Host Manager screens.**

Figure 2-3   admintool

3. Select the naming service for the current session, as shown on the left side of Figure 2-4.

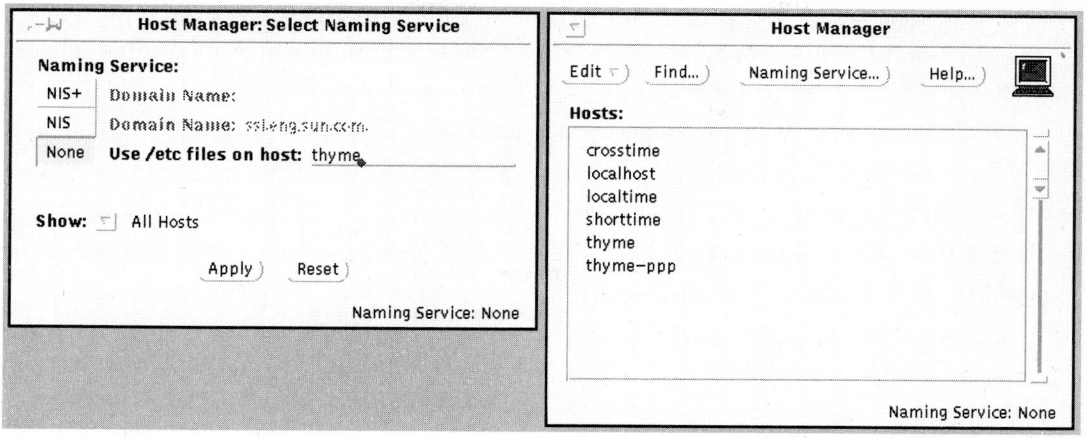

Figure 2-4   Host Manager Name Service and Host Selection Screens

The naming service selection depends on what already exists on the local subnet. If NIS+ is in use, then, of course, select NIS+. If the current network uses the Solaris 1.x-based NIS, then select None. The Host Manager cannot update NIS databases, so the local files must be updated first, then manually placed in the NIS databases. For networks with no naming service, select None. Make sure to check the Domain Name before hitting the Apply button.

When the name service screen is applied, all the known hosts in the local /etc/hosts file are displayed, as shown in the right side of Figure 2-4. If the system you wish to add is already known in the Host Manager, then continue below. If you are adding a new host to be installed, skip to Step 4-2, Adding New Remote Install Clients.

Enabling Remote Installs for Existing Systems

When you enable new or existing hosts for remote installation, the /etc/ethers file on the install server is updated with the client's Ethernet address, and the /etc/bootparams file is updated with the client's root, swap, and install partition mounting information for diskless install booting.

4-1. To enable a remote installation for an existing machine:

a. Click on the specified host in the center Host Manager window, then move the cursor over the Edit button in the top-left corner. Pull down the menu with the MENU mouse button, and highlight the "Enable Remote Install" menu item at the bottom of the popup menu.

The Remote Install screen is displayed, as shown in Figure 2-5.

Figure 2-5   Enabling Remote Install on an Existing Host

b. From the Remote Install screen, enter the Ethernet address and the kernel architecture of the existing client.

If the information can be obtained from the name service, this window is skipped.

c. Check the OS Release field in the center of the window. Place the cursor over the arrow next to OS Release, use the right mouse button to pull down the list of available client architectures, highlight the appropriate selection, then release the button. Then, click on Apply with the SELECT mouse button to begin the install client setup.

Adding New Remote Install Clients

4-2. To enable a remote installation for systems that are not in the local hosts file:

a. Use the Add Host option instead of the Enable Remote Install from the Edit pull-down menus. The Host Manager: Add Host menu is displayed, as shown in Figure 2-6.

b. From the Host Manager: Add Host menu, enter all the system data, such as the hostname, IP address, and Ethernet address. Use the pull-down method discussed above to select the timezone and OS Release architecture of the client. When the proper selections have been made, click the Add button at the bottom of the screen.

After a few minutes, the Add Host screen will return with the hostname, IP address, and Ethernet address fields empty. The main Host Manager screen should now have an entry for the new host.

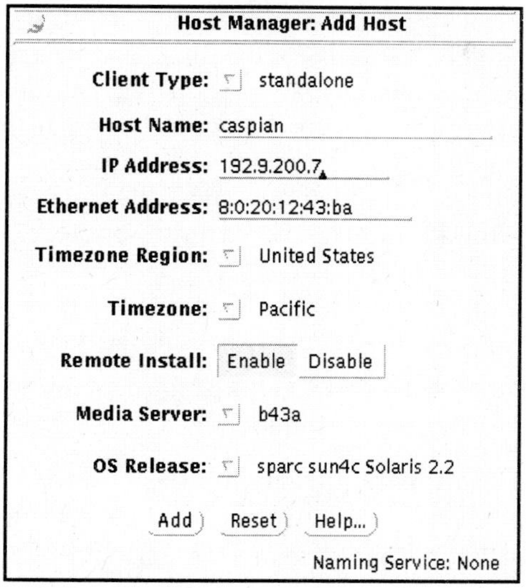

Figure 2-6   Enabling Remote Install on an Unidentified Host

When you enable new or existing hosts for remote installation, the /etc/bootparams file on the install server is updated with information about the client just configured. Notice that the client hostname appears first, followed by the path to root mount. Also notice that the directory to which the CD is attached has become a NFS-shared resource.

```
blue# cat /etc/bootparams
green root=blue:/cdrom/cdrom0/s0/export/exec/kvm/sparc.sun4c.Solaris_2.2
blue# share
- /cdrom/cdrom0/s0 ro,anon=0 ""
```

Preparing the Network for Automatic Booting

Preparing the name service to supply information to systems that boot from a local CD can greatly shorten the time to install even one system. When a few NIS maps and entries are properly updated, the entire query session explained previously can be automated. Before you can achieve total automation, you must verify the existence of certain network daemons. You may be required to rebuild or reboot the GENERIC kernel on install servers running Solaris 1.x. You may also have to reboot systems running versions of Solaris 2.x depending on the systems currently running on the network and their purpose.

2

The following procedure assumes that the NIS naming service is in use. The procedures for setting up maps in an NIS+ domain for booting installation clients can be applied, using similar NIS+ map names.

Reverse Address Resolution Protocol (RARP)

RARP is the service that answers *"whoami"* requests. There must be a system running rarpd on the local network segment to answer the RARP requests of booting systems. Usually this is handled by the install server, but not always. If the ethers map is NIS wide, any system running rarpd may answer RARP requests. As noted previously, all Solaris 1.x and earlier systems that are acting as install servers must have the following pseudo-devices included in the kernel that is currently booted:

```
pseudo-device    snit      # streams NIT
pseudo-device    pf        # packet filter
pseudo-device    nbuf      # NIT buffering module
```

These pseudo-devices are included in all GENERIC kernels and are already enabled if a server of diskless systems is running on the local net.

Solaris 2.x systems do not have this requirement. Files and directories that are created during the client setup procedure are themselves keys to starting the appropriate boot daemons after a subsequent reboot.

Existing NIS Domain Setup

In order for the proper information to be found, you must update or create the following NIS maps before booting the system to be installed.

Hosts

Update the hosts maps to include the hostname and IP address of the machine to be booted from the local CD. You must also specify a *timehost* for the domain so that the system time can automatically be found. Use the command

```
% ypmatch timehost hosts
```

to check for a timehost. If no matches are found, select a system as the timehost and add the nickname "timehost" to its entry in the NIS hosts datafile. The timehost must have the tcp and udp time service entries enabled in the /etc/services file before rdate requests are honored. Both time service routines are enabled in the default /etc/services file.

```
# # NIS hosts file for domain blegvad #
192.9.200.1      harlie nismaster timehost    # NIS master and timehost
192.9.200.5      hal
```

On the timehost, harlie, check for the time services in the /etc/services file, as follows:

```
harlie% grep ^time /etc/services
time 37/tcp timeserver
time 37/udp timeserver
```

If the above lines are present and are not preceded by a "#" sign, then the time services are enabled on the NIS timehost. The time services are enabled by default.

Ethers

You must update the NIS domain with the Ethernet address of every system that will use this method of booting. The probing sequence uses a protocol that broadcasts its Ethernet address on the local subnet and waits for a reply. The reply is returned only if the correct entry is found and translated to an IP address.

```
# NIS ethers file for domain blegvad
8:0:20:8:25:8b     hal
```

If a system's Ethernet address is missing or entered incorrectly, the message

```
no RARP replies received
```

is returned while attempting to boot from the network. If booting from a local CD-ROM without the Ethernet information, you will be asked to enter the host name and IP address before you can continue.

Bootparams

You must update or create a bootparams map on the NIS master and push the updated map out to, at the very least, the subnet on which the client will boot. If you prefer not to maintain an NIS-wide bootparams map, edit the /etc/bootparams file on the local bootparams server and add the hostname of the booting machine.

The actual bootparams entries can differ, depending on many factors. If you just want to allow a system to obtain the minimal amount of information from the network, then only a hostname is required. If you have set up a Solaris install server, then the bootparams information for clients of that server will again be different. Additional arguments are required in the bootparams file for systems using the AutoInstall automatic installation method.

The server's bootparams file is changed automatically each time you execute the add_install_client script or add an installation client via admintool. But just because the install server's entries are up to date does not ensure that those entries are globally available to the booting client. There may be an old entry in the NIS bootparams map for the booting client, left over from another OS install, or it may have once been a diskless client. Stale bootparams entries can really confuse matters.

Helpful Hint – Make sure not only the NIS or NIS+ bootparams map is correct, but also update any other bootparams servers that might respond to bootparams requests.

Systems that are boot servers start a process called `rpc.bootparamd` and `in.tftpd`, which provides for remote booting.

To enable hands-off booting from local CD-ROM, enter the hostname of the machine on a single line in the NIS bootparams map or designated bootparams server as follows:

```
# cat >> /etc/bootparams <RETURN>
hal <RETURN>
^D <CNTL-D>
#
```

Timezone

Timezone.byname is an NIS map that originated in the SunOS 4.1.1 revB release, as did much of this procedure. Its sole purpose is to supply new systems with the proper timezone information. If this map is not present, you must enter the timezone information during the boot phase. The timezone map is the only nonstandard map needed to enable a hands-off CD or network boot. To find out if the timezone map is present in your NIS domain, enter

```
$ ypwhich -m | grep timezone
```

If nothing is returned, set up the timezone map, as follows:

1. **Log in to the NIS master server as root or become the user that has permission to edit and create NIS maps.**

2. **Check the version of the NIS Makefile, as follows:**

   ```
   nis_master$ what /var/yp/Makefile
   /var/yp/Makefile: make.script 1.36 90/12/20 SMI
   ```

If the `make.script` version is older than 1.26, then a more current version is needed. You can obtain the necessary Makefile from any Sun-4 or 4c architecture machine running SunOS 4.1.1 revB or later by looking in the `/usr/lib` directory for a file called, `NIS.Makefile`. Simply copy the file over to your NIS master, replacing the current Makefile in the `/var/yp` directory. If you have custom NIS maps, then you may find it easier to cut and paste the necessary parts of the more current Makefile to your existing one, remembering that much of the preceding white space in the subroutines of the Makefile are *tabs*, not spaces.

If the command above indicates that the NIS Makefile is above version 1.26, then you can build and propagate the timezone map without trouble. You need only create or edit the /etc/timezone file to reflect the local timezone information and build the map. The syntax of the /etc/timezone file is

```
timezone     domainname
US/Pacific   blegvad.COM
```

If you attempt to build and push the new NIS maps at this point, you may have problems because the ypxfer program will not push a map to an NIS slave server unless a file of the same name already exists in its /var/yp/<*domainname*> directory. You can work around this minor hurdle by building any new NIS maps the first time with the NOPUSH option, forcing the NIS master to omit the yppush to slave servers. Then, from the slave server, you can execute the ypxfer program to pull the new map over. The complete procedure follows:

```
NISmaster# cd /var/yp;make timezone NOPUSH=1
updated timezone
```

On each NIS slave server, log in remotely as root and use the command below to manually transfer any new maps to the local slave server:

```
NISslave# /usr/etc/yp/ypxfer -h <your NIS master`s hostname> timezone
```

It is often better to include the IP address of the NIS master instead of its hostname in this command.

Netmasks

The netmasks map should be present if you are using network masks. If not, the same procedure explained above can be used to obtain a new NIS Makefile. You need a netmasks map if you are using IP standard subnetting.

After the hosts, ethers, bootparams, timezone, and netmasks maps have been updated and pushed, you can boot from the Solaris 2.x CD-ROM. No questions will be asked while booting, and the system will come up directly into the Solaris Install system's main menu, ready for installation.

AutoInstall

AutoInstall is the automated portion of the Solaris install process, available only in networked environments. Automatic booting and automatic system configuration are important parts of the process, but are not necessarily components of AutoInstall, which takes over the manual install process of determining the system type, choosing system software, and disk partition arrangement. AutoInstall is enabled by the system or network administrator by creating an NFS-shared directory with files that contain information about a system or group of systems ready to undergo installation.

AutoInstall is designed for persons who never want to peer at a format screen or select a prescribed set of software packages. Implementation of the AutoInstall process ensures reproducible system installations and upgrades. Workgroups of similar system types that run common applications can be set up to install the same bundled and unbundled packages completely hands-off, making life much easier for both the end-user and the administrator.

Using AutoInstall provides many advantages. You can easily place systems with similar requirements into installation workgroups. Disk partitioning can be automatic or explicit, based on disk type and size. You can implement pre- and postinstall scripts to do such things as add network printer support, install unbundled software packages, or place NFS mounts in the system's /etc/vfstab file. Customized postinstallation scripts can also perform procedures that cannot be done during a manual installation.

Another advantage is saving the system administrator's time. Most end-users do not know how to find a way to boot, decide how to partition their disk, or select the "proper" software to make their systems run. A knowledgeable person must be forever on-call to get most installations started correctly and then perform the postinstallation procedures necessary for the environment.

The AutoInstall setup process is mildly complicated. All pieces must be in place for total automation. The initial time spent setting things up is well worth it, because once the environment is there, both installations and upgrades to the latest Solaris 2.x release are possible without manual intervention. Automated upgrades alone are a good reason to initiate AutoInstall into your network environment, because new versions of Solaris 2.x are being released often, each one better than the previous one.

For example, suppose that a software engineer just received a new SPARCstation 10, which needed Solaris 2.2 installed right away. You could sit down and boot the machine from a local CD-ROM, answering all the pertinent information during the boot query session. You could also go through each of the installation screens, selecting the appropriate software and disk configuration for that software, as previously explained. Then you begin the install, go away for about an hour, come back and perform all of the manual postinstallation procedures, such as mounting remote applications, adding remote print services, enabling a root or administrative password entry on the new machine.

Suppose then that a second engineer also needs to be running Solaris 2.2 right away. Are you going to sit down and repeat the exact same steps as before? Probably at first, but this process can grow tiresome, especially if many other systems are waiting to be upgraded or installed with Solaris 2.x.

The solution to this scenario is to make these systems members of an *install class*, thereby enabling exactly the same partition arrangement, bundled software packages, and postinstallation procedures. As more similar systems are needed, they, too, can become members of the *install class*, ensuring proper installation of selected software packages and customization.

Requirement for AutoInstall

The three requirements to begin using AutoInstall are:

- Solaris 2.x medium; local, remote, or UFS Image

- An exported or shared *install_config* directory containing the appropriate files

- A functional NIS or NIS+ domain

The Solaris 2.2 medium contains all the "hooks" to enable AutoInstall, in addition to providing a sample *install_config* directory. The preinstalled boot image is not a requirement for AutoInstall. Any system can invoke the probing mechanism that searches for the *install_config* directory by adding arguments while booting the install environment.

The NIS or NIS+ setup is detailed in "Preparing the Network for Automatic Booting." Much of the required data for AutoInstall is obtained through the name service databases, most during the boot query stage.

How AutoInstall works

The AutoInstall process begins after the local or remote installation environment has been booted. AutoInstall probes the network bootparams servers for the location of an *install_config* directory, which it then mounts and searches. The first file it looks for is the `rules` file, in which comparisons to the booting system are made, based on a number of things, including hostname, kernel or application architecture, disk size, and the release currently installed.

The rules File

Complete comparison matching requirements are illustrated in the sample `rules` file, but generally, comparison rules follow the syntax below:

`<match_key> <match_value> <begin> <class> <finish>`

The fields are described below.

<match_key>, <match_value>
> Comparison matching occupies the first two fields of each `rules` entry. A match key can be almost anything, depending on how explicit you want to be. Table 2-2 lists the comparison matching that occupies the first two fields of each `rules` entry.

Table 2-2   JumpStart Comparison Rules

Comparison	Match	Data
any	ignores	- (always matches true)
arch	exact	application arch text string
domainname	exact	domainname as text string
disksize	disk range	disk device name, disk size as range of MB
hostname	exact	hostname as text string
installed	disk release	disk device name, OS release
karch	exact	disk device name, OS release
memsize	range	memory size as range of MB
model	exact	machine model, e.g., 4_75
network	exact	network as dotted decimal address
totaldisk	range	total amount of disk space as range of MB

> An AutoInstall client uses the first match found in any of the comparison fields of the `rules` file. Then, the remaining arguments of that line are executed from left to right.

Helpful Hint – This is important to remember if a system can satisfy more than one comparison.

> The third field, labeled **, is the file name of a begin script in the *install_config* directory. Begin scripts are executed before the actual installation takes place. They can be used to make backups of certain files and to obtain system specific information, such as current NFS mounts, disk partition sizes, or automounter file entries. Begin scripts are not a requirement and can be skipped.

Begin scripts can also be used to gather information about a machine to determine which *<class>* file is used. This process is called profiling. A common type of profiling is to check disk availability and sizes, or unbundled software that is currently installed on a system about to undergo installation.

<class>
The fourth field in the `rules` file syntax determines the class file to use. Class files are the input to the Solaris Install system and include the system type, partition arrangement, and list of packages or clusters to install. Class files may also include NFS mounts.

<finish>
The last field of the `rules` file syntax is the finish script, used to perform routine procedures after an installation has taken place. The finish script can be written to handle many of the manual postinstallation adjustments, such as setting kernel variables in the `/etc/system` file or adding a root password to each machine. Many administrators of large networks have longed for this kind of open functionality to customize their environment.

Writing Scripts

Example begin, class, and finish files are detailed in Appendix A. There are a few things to know about the workings of AutoInstall before you begin to write the scripts for the beginning and end.

What Mounts Where?

When AutoInstall finds an entry for either a begin or end script, it boots the system from the install server. Therefore, / is not the root of the system that it is working on. / is actually the root that is defined in the bootparams entry. Specific mountpoints are listed in Table 2-3.

Table 2-3   Mountpoints During AutoInstall

Mountpoint During AutoInstall	Filesystem in Real Life	Mounted For You?
/	export/exec/kvm/sparc.{arch}.{OS} under the location of the CD or UFS image	Yes
/tmp/install_config	AutoInstall files directory	Yes
/a (This mountpoint is provided for mounting the / directory. You can create and use other mountpoints if you prefer)	/	No

How to Mount an NFS Volume without a Name Service

If you are using a name service that is not on the local subnet, you may not have access to the hosts information. In cases like this, you can use the IP number of the system in place of the name. For example, to mount *snoopy*, which is IP 129.144.68.23, your mount line would look like the following:

```
mount -F nfs 129.144.68.23:/export/patches /tmp/patches
```

How to Debug a Script

There are a few methods of debugging scripts that you write. You can use echo statements to track the progress of the script. You can set the debug flag on your script with #!/bin/sh -x. Or lastly, you can start a shell at different places in the script.

Helpful Hint – One thing to watch for in starting these shells is that there is no prompt.

You should place an echo statement just before the /bin/sh line so that you know that you have stopped and are ready for interactive checking. When you are done with the shell, use Ctrl-D to return control to AutoInstall.

What Is Root and Where Does chroot Come In?

Since / is not the root partition of the system under construction, use chroot in cases where tools such as installpatch or pkgadd expect / to be the root partition. A sample chroot command would look like the following:

```
chroot /a /usr/sbin/pkgadd -a /tmp/admin -d /Unb -n -r /Unb/resp SUNWsteNP .
```

Customizing AutoInstall

AutoInstall can easily be set up on an existing network of systems running either Solaris 1.x or Solaris 2.x. To customize AutoInstall in your environment, select a system to become the *install_config* server, on which the rules and system class files will reside. The *install_config* directory is set up by mounting the Solaris installation CD and copying the contents of the CD's `auto_install_sample` directory to a directory, such as `/export/install`, created by you.

After the copy is made, create your own `rules` file or use the one that is provided. If you use the one that is provided, first comment out or delete the *any* system entry. If this is not done, every system will configure itself the same way, as dictated by the `any_system` class.

The next step is to define the key to be matched. Matching a single hostname is a good way to start before going on to groups of systems. Use the hostname key, followed by the hostname of the system to be installed.

You may define a *begin_script* if desired, but trying to do too much on the first pass may result in confusion.

The first example skips the *begin_script*, uses an install *class* file which has not yet been defined, and uses a *finish_script* that places a root password on the system. The `rules` file entry for a machine named *henry* would look like this:

```
hostname henry - henry_profile set_root_pw
```

After defining the system in the `rules` file, create or edit the class file. The system in this example is a SPARCstation IPC, with a single 207 megabyte disk. The software to be installed is the core system cluster, plus the man pages. The disk partitioning defined by the install program is not desired. Instead, an explicit partition arrangement is created. The root partition size is increased to 20 megabytes, and the `/usr` partition is decreased from the default 100 to 70 megabytes, because the windowing system is NFS mounted. To accomplish these feats, the custom profile for this particular machine would be similar to the output shown below.

```
# cat henry_profile
install_type initial_install
system_type standalone
partitioning explicit
filesys c0t3d0s0 20 / rw
filesys c0t3d0s1 40 swap
filesys c0t3d0s6 70 /usr rw
filesys c0t3d0s5 10 /opt rw
filesys c0t3d0s7 40 /export/home rw
cluster SUNWCreq
```

```
package SUNWman
package SUNWdoc
filesys harlie:/usr/openwin - /usr/openwin ro,intr
```

The first two lines of the custom profile are identical to the default, indicating that this is an *initial_install* instead of an *upgrade* and the system type is *standalone*. The third line specifies explicit partitioning, as defined by the next few lines using the *filesys* keyword. In the above example, the first disk slice, c0t3d0s0, is 20 megabytes in size, mounted to /, is readable and writeable. Subsequent disk slices are defined in the same manner.

The software information follows the slice definitions. In the example above, the cluster named SUNWCreq is installed first, followed by the software packages SUNWman and SUNWdoc. You can install SUNWman by itself, but in order to read the man pages, you need the SUNWdoc packages, which include `nroff` and `troff`.

The last line in the custom class file contains the NFS mount for the windowing system. This particular system mounts the /usr/openwin directory from the server `harlie`. The mount options `ro` and `intr` mount the resource read-only and allow keyboard interrupts on hard mounts, respectively.

The check Script

After you have defined the `rules` and custom *class* files, verify your work by using the `check` script, also located in the *install_config* directory. The `check` script validates the entries in both the rules and class files referenced by the `rules` file. This script can detect problems in your setup long before you boot any AutoInstall clients. Since both local and remote CD boot procedures take a long time to complete, it is worth your time to run the `check` script.

The output of a successful check run may be similar to the following:

```
# ./check
Checking validity of rules...
Checking validity of host_class file...
Checking validity of net924_sun4c file...
Checking validity of henry_profile file...
The auto-install configuration is ok.
```

After the `check` script is executed, a new rules file, called `rules.ok`, is created and is placed in the current directory. The `rules.ok` file is the actual file used during AutoInstall. This file needs to be regenerated after each change.

Preparing the install_config directory

There are two steps in setting up AutoInstall in the local environment: ensuring that the system about to undergo installation is properly configured in the name service databases, as described in "Preparing the Network for Automatic Booting"; and exporting the `install_config` directory as an NFS-shared resource.

▼ Sharing the install_config directory

On a Solaris 1.x `install_config` server, NFS sharing is accomplished by creating or appending to the `/etc/exports` file, inserting the following information:

```
<install_config_directory> <export arguments>
```

Then, use the `exportfs` command to make the directory available.

```
# exportfs -a
```

Note – If no other exported directories are on this system, then additional steps may be required, such as starting two required NFS daemons, `nfsd` and `in.mountd`.

In the current example, the `install_config` directory is located on the system `hal`, under the path, `/export/install_config`. The subsequent entry in the `/etc/exports` file on `hal` would be:

```
/export/install_config -ro
```

On a Solaris 2.x `install_config` server, NFS sharing is accomplished by adding the following information to the `/etc/dfs/dfstab` file in the format below:

```
share -F nfs -o <share arguments> <install_config_directory>
```

Again, using the current example, the contents of the `/etc/dfs/dfstab` file on the Solaris 2.x server would be the following:

```
share -F nfs -o ro /export/install_config
```

Once the `/etc/dfs/dfstab` file has been updated, make the NFS resource available by using the command below.

```
# /etc/init.d/nfs.server start
```

This command starts necessary NFS daemons in addition to sharing all of the NFS resources in the `/etc/dfs/dfstab` file.

▼ Updating bootparams

Systems using AutoInstall must have an entry in the bootparams map or in the local /etc/bootparams file of a server running bootparamd. How the bootparams entry appears depends on the type of install client you are booting. If the AutoInstall client will use a local CD-ROM device instead of a network install server, the bootparams entry must be manually entered, following the syntax shown below:

```
<hostname> install_config=<server>:<install_config_directory>
```

As directed, the local CD-ROM will boot, use the network to obtain the AutoInstall information from the install_config server, then return to the local CD for the actual install.

On systems that use an install server instead of a local CD device, a bootparams entry is automatically set up during the execution of the add_install_client script or admintool. The default entry does not contain any information about *install_config* unless a command-line argument is used.

Specify the name of the *install_config* directory by using the -c argument. In the current example, the install_config server is named hal while the machine being automatically installed is named harlie. Using these variables, the command that enables harlie to be an AutoInstall client of hal is shown below:

```
{hal}# /cdrom/add_install_client -c hal:/export/install_config harlie sun4c
```

The resulting bootparams entry for the command above is the following:

```
{hal}# grep harlie /etc/bootparams
harlie root=hal:/cdrom/export/exec/kvm/sparc.sun4c.Solaris_2.1 \
install=hal:/cdrom install_config=hal:/export/install_config
```

The install server named hal, provides to harlie both an installation environment and the install_config files necessary for AutoInstall.

Once the bootparams entry is in place, you are ready to boot the AutoInstall client.

Booting AutoInstall Clients

Newly purchased systems and disk peripherals are set to automatically boot the preinstalled stub image when turned on. After the kernel and device drivers are loaded, programs on the stub attempt to locate an installation environment by first checking if a Solaris 2.x CD is in the local CD drive. If so, the system reboots from the local CD and into the Solaris Install environment.

If the local CD-ROM condition is not met, a network probe for exported installation environments is begun. If the system has been added as a client on an installation server within the same subnet, as described earlier, then the system reboots from the just-found installation server.

If there is neither a local CD device with the Solaris CD installed nor a network install server with the proper information, the stub halts itself, as shown below.

```
Booting from: sd(0,0,0)
AutoInstall 1.0
Copyright (c) 1983-1993, Sun Microsystems, Inc.
Configuring the /devices directory
Configuring the /dev directory
no local boot CD, checking net...

No network boot server. Unable to install the system.
See installation instructions.

Halted
```

Any system can take advantage of AutoInstall capabilities by using the following boot arguments:

```
ok> boot [cdrom, net] - install
```

Or, from older systems without the Open Boot PROM:

```
> b ie() - install
```

The operative argument here is "- **install**," the keyword that begins the network probe for the *install_config* bootparams entries. Once the name service databases are correctly configured for a particular system, that system can be reinstalled or upgraded with AutoInstall by simply using the above argument to boot from the network.

The following output is from a system booting from the Preinstalled Boot Image. Notice that no user input was required for it to locate its *install_config* directory.

```
SPARCstation IPC, Type 4 keyboard.
ROM Rev. 1.6, 24 MB memory installed, Serial #1179.
Ethernet address 8:0:20:9:97:35, Host ID: 5200049b.
Testing
Booting from: sd(0,0,0)
AutoInstall 1.0
Copyright (c) 1983-1993, Sun Microsystems, Inc.
WARNING: clock gained 5 days -- CHECK AND RESET THE DATE!
Configuring the /devices directory
Installing from local cdrom
rebooting...
Booting from: sd(0,6,2) - FD=/sbus@1,f8000000/esp@0,800000/sd@3,0:a=32=24=X
SunOS Release 5.2 Version Generic [UNIX(R) System V Release 4.0]
Copyright (c) 1983-1993, Sun Microsystems, Inc.
WARNING: clock gained 29 days -- CHECK AND RESET THE DATE!
Configuring the /devices directory
Configuring the /dev directory
Searching for auto-install directory...using defaults.
The system is coming up. Please wait.
```

Summary

In summary, you should know the following items before initiating a local installation:

- Hostname and Internet Protocol address

- NIS or NIS+ Domain name and server on the local subnet

- Time zone information

- Installation system type

- Disk partition arrangement

- Local or remote windowing system files

- Local or remote home directory

- Local or remote user applications

After you have considered and planned for the above items, you are ready to boot into the Solaris Install system and start the installation.

Installing Solaris 3 ≣

The previous chapter detailed the process of planning for an installation and outlined how to automate the installation process. This chapter takes you through the installation of Solaris 2.x software on workstations and servers.

Booting into the Install System from Local CD

To perform a local CD boot, you need a CD-ROM device connected to the system, a Solaris 2.x CD, and a CD caddy. The procedure is begun by booting from the Solaris 2.x CD, which then prompts you to enter some essential information, such as a host name, an Internet Protocol address if attached to a network, and name service selection. After the boot process has completed, the install program is automatically invoked. You then select a type of install to perform, depending on your needs and experience level. The examples here show you every possible screen so that you can get through the CD boot process without being stalled by a particular screen that has no bearing on the final result.

To boot from a local CD-ROM, insert the Solaris 2.x CD-ROM into its caddy and then into the drive. Begin by issuing a command from the OpenBoot PROM monitor. Study Table 3-1 to determine which command to use to boot from a particular system.

Table 3-1   Local CD Boot Commands

Machine Type	Kernel Architecture	CD boot command
Sun 4300/400	Sun4	>b sd(0,30,1)
SPARCstation SLC/IPC	Sun4c	ok boot sd(0,6,2)
SPARCstation 1, 1+/2	Sun4c	ok boot sd(0,6,2)
SPARCstation ELC/IPX	Sun4c	ok boot cdrom
SPARC Classic	Sun4m	ok boot cdrom
SPARCstation LX/10	Sun4m	ok boot cdrom

Table 3-1   *Local CD Boot Commands (Continued)*

Machine Type	Kernel Architecture	CD boot command
SPARCserver 600MP	Sun4m	ok boot cdrom
SPARCserver 1000	Sun4d	ok boot cdrom
SPARCcenter 2000	Sun4d	ok boot cdrom

When the proper command is entered, the CD device activity light starts flashing, indicating that the medium is being read. After a few minutes, you are prompted to start entering information. Booting from CD is slower than booting from a normal disk because data access times are long on this type of medium. It may seem at times that the system is not doing anything, especially in the time between the clock warning message and Configuring devices message.

1. Enter a terminal type.

The first input screen may ask you to enter a terminal type as shown in Figure 3-1. If you are installing a system with a serial terminal as a console rather than a bit-mapped display, this screen is required. Otherwise, you will not see it. A probing mechanism in the CD boot process can determine the console type when using a standard Sun monitor and frame buffer and automatically starts the OpenWindows environment.

If using a terminal as the console, enter the terminal type and press RETURN. If a bit-mapped display is used as the console, as on most desktop machines, then OpenWindows is started, and the remaining query session is done from the Solaris 2.x Install window in the center of the screen.

```
ok boot sd(,6,2)
```
Booting from: sd(0,6,2)
SunOS Release 5.2 Version Generic [UNIX(R) System V Release 4.0]
Copyright (c) 1983-1992, Sun Microsystems, Inc.
WARNING: clock gained 30 days -- CHECK AND RESET THE DATE!
Configuring the /devices directory
Configuring the /dev directory
The system is coming up. Please wait.
What type of terminal are you using?

  1) ANSI Standard CRT
  2) DEC VT52
  3) DEC VT100
  4) Heathkit 19
  5) Lear Siegler ADM31
  6) PC Console
  7) Sun Command Tool
  8) Sun Workstation
  9) Televideo 925
  10) Wyse Model 50
  11) Other

Type the number of your choice and press Return:

Figure 3-1   Booting from a Local CD

Manual Boot Query Session

2. **Assign host information.**
   The next steps will establish the hostname and IP address for the system. You will also need to indicate if the system will be installed on a network.

   a. **Assign a hostname to the system.**
      The next screen asks you to assign a hostname to your system.

```
┌─────────────────────────────────────────────────────────────────┐
│ What is the hostname for your workstation?                        │
│                                                                   │
│ Hostnames must be at least two characters in length, and may      │
│ contain letters, digits, and minus (-) signs. A hostname may not  │
│ begin or end with a minus (-) sign.                               │
│                                                                   │
│            ┌─────────────────────────────────────┐               │
│            │ Hostname _____            │               │
│            │                                      │               │
│            └─────────────────────────────────────┘               │
│                                                                   │
│ Press Return to continue.                                         │
└─────────────────────────────────────────────────────────────────┘
```

Figure 3-2   Hostname Screen

Hostnames must be unique, at least two characters in length, and cannot begin or end with a minus sign; as the screen in Figure 3-2 reminds you. Hostnames should also not begin with a numeric character or contain periods or commas. The upper character limit on hostnames is 12. You can use longer names, but some network services truncate hostnames over ten characters.

b. Specify network connection.

Once you enter a hostname, the next screen asks if the system will be connected to a network. If this is the case, scroll down to "yes" using the numeric keypad down arrow key, or use the "y" key to obtain cursor movement and confirm with a RETURN.

c. Enter an IP address for the system.

After this action, a new screen, shown in Figure 3-3, asks you to enter an IP address for the system. If you are not installing the system on a network, this session is skipped.

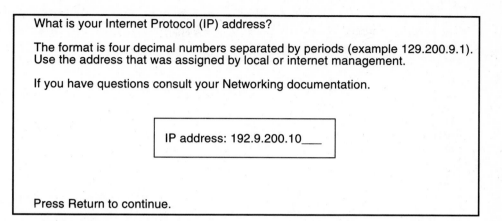

What is your Internet Protocol (IP) address?

The format is four decimal numbers separated by periods (example 129.200.9.1). Use the address that was assigned by local or internet management.

If you have questions consult your Networking documentation.

IP address: 192.9.200.10___

Press Return to continue.

Figure 3-3   Setting the Internet Protocol Address

You should already know the IP address for the system. If you do not know the IP address for this machine, stop right now. An incorrect or duplicate IP address on an existing network can really foul things up, requiring both machines to be rebooted. Find the correct IP address for this system before you continue. To continue, enter the IP address and press RETURN.

d. Confirm host information.

A confirmation screen is displayed presenting the current system information. If any of the displayed data is incorrect press RETURN. The three prior screens are redisplayed for checking and correction. If the current information is correct, use the down arrow key on the numeric keypad, the TAB key, or the letter "y" to move the cursor selection over "Yes". Then press RETURN to continue.

At this point, the name of two system processes are echoed to the screen as they are started: `rpcbind` and `sysidnis`. The `rpcbind` process maps defined port numbers for specified remote procedure calls, specifically, the naming service routines. The `sysidnis` process probes the network for current system information, using some of the RPC programs just mapped by `rpcbind`.

3. Assign name service information.

This series of steps will allow you to define the name service that the system will use. You will need to know the domain name, how to locate name servers, and the name and IP address of a name server if the server is not located automatically.

a. Specify a naming service.

`sysidnis` is also responsible for gathering the remaining system configuration information if the network probe returned incomplete data. The system in this example has not been introduced to the network or the current name service domain. Therefore, the following user-input session is necessary. Some of this data may already be in your NIS domain, resulting in a different query session from that shown below. For instance, remote install clients may be able to identify the name service and domain automatically because their server provides this information. After you have confirmed the hostname and IP address, the next screen, Figure 3-4, asks if you want to join a naming service.

```
Do you want to configure this system as a client of a name service? If so,
which name service do you want to use? If you do not want to use a name
service select `none' and consult your Install documentation.



        >NIS+ Client
         NIS (formerly yp) Client
         None - use /etc files



Use the arrow keys to select an item. (CTRL-n next, CTRL-p previous)

Press Return to continue.
```

Figure 3-4   Selecting the Naming Service

The three choices offered are: NIS+, NIS, or None. The default choice, NIS+, is the new naming service introduced in Solaris 2.x. The second choice, NIS, is the naming service currently used by most existing Sun networks. The final choice, None, disables the flag that starts the naming service daemons at boot time, defaulting to the local /etc files for network information.

Choose the naming service that is currently in use on the local network segment. If you have doubts about the spelling or syntax of the domain name, select None. It is much easier to join a naming service after the installation than trying to turn off services to a nonexistent domain. A bogus naming service selection at this juncture could also affect the outcome of the install.

b. Specify a domain name.
When you select either NIS+ or NIS, a new screen asks you to carefully input the domain name. It is very important to pay attention to the case of the domain name; for example, "eng.sun.com" is not the same as "Eng.Sun.COM". If you are installing a system on an existing network, then you are most likely running the NIS naming service. If you select a name service, a second screen is displayed, which asks if you

want the system to be bound to a particular server or to have the system locate the name server automatically each time it boots. None of the versions of Solaris 1.x software offered a choice in name server designation.

c. Specify a name service location method.
A new screen, shown in Figure 3-5, prompts you to enter a location method if you are using a name service.

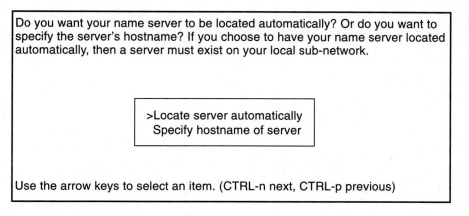

Do you want your name server to be located automatically? Or do you want to specify the server's hostname? If you choose to have your name server located automatically, then a server must exist on your local sub-network.

>Locate server automatically
Specify hostname of server

Use the arrow keys to select an item. (CTRL-n next, CTRL-p previous)

Figure 3-5   Specify Name Server Screen

Specifically choosing your name server gives more control over naming service load distribution. You may wish to designate a scheme of an NIS server for each x number of clients. On larger networks, this type of balance is necessary, and it is also more secure.

If you do not know the hostname or IP address of a name server on the local network segment, then select the first choice, to locate automatically. If you know the hostname and IP address of a slave or replica server on the local subnet, then use the second selection.

d. Specify a server name and location.
A new screen, Figure 3-6, prompts you to enter that server's name and IP address.

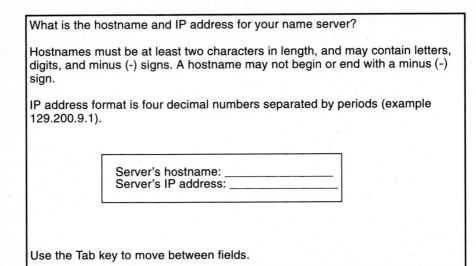

What is the hostname and IP address for your name server?

Hostnames must be at least two characters in length, and may contain letters, digits, and minus (-) signs. A hostname may not begin or end with a minus (-) sign.

IP address format is four decimal numbers separated by periods (example 129.200.9.1).

Server's hostname: _____
Server's IP address: _____

Use the Tab key to move between fields.

Figure 3-6   Entering Name Server Information

Enter the name and IP address and press RETURN.

e. Specify subnet configuration.

The next screen asks if the current network has subnetworks. Many network installations use an IP address masking scheme, called netmasks, to implement IP standard subnetting. Class B networks are most commonly subnetted. The input from this screen is used to update the `/etc/netmasks` file. If you do not use network masks, then no changes will be made to the netmasks file. If, after the system is installed, you experience problems communicating to other subnets, check to see if the network mask is properly set.

If you are sure that the network uses netmasks, then move the cursor to Yes and enter the subnet mask when prompted. If you are unsure, select no. As with the naming service, you can easily add the proper netmask value after the installation as opposed to entering the wrong one here. Most NIS domains that are running on subnetted networks include the map, `netmasks.byaddr`, which may feed the proper information to client systems while booting so this screen may be not be seen.

f. Confirm name service information.

After all of the network information has been entered, a confirmation screen displays the current system information, as shown in Figure 3-7.

```
┌─────────────────────────────────────────────────────────────────┐
│ Is the following information correct?                            │
│                                                                  │
│ Name service: NIS (formerly yp) Client                          │
│ Domain name: guitar.com                                          │
│ Server location method: Specify Hostname                        │
│ Server's hostname: henry                                        │
│ Server's IP address: 192.9.200.10                               │
│ Network is sub-netted: Yes                                      │
│ Netmask: 255.255.255.0                                          │
│                                                                  │
│                 ┌──────────────────────────────┐               │
│                 │ >No, re-enter information     │               │
│                 │   Yes, continue               │               │
│                 └──────────────────────────────┘               │
│                                                                  │
│                                                                  │
│ Use the arrow keys to select an item. (CTRL-n next, CTRL-p previous) │
│ Press Return to continue.                                       │
└─────────────────────────────────────────────────────────────────┘
```

Figure 3-7   The Confirmation Screen

Check each field carefully. If anything is incorrect, you can reenter the particular piece by going back through each of the screens, using the RETURN key. Once you are sure that everything is correct, move the cursor next to "Yes" and press RETURN to continue.

4. Set the time.

More system processes are begun, followed by a new screen that prompts for the time zone and local time. Although all of the new systems have a battery run clock, with all of the time zones available, it can be necessary to set the current time properly before the installation.

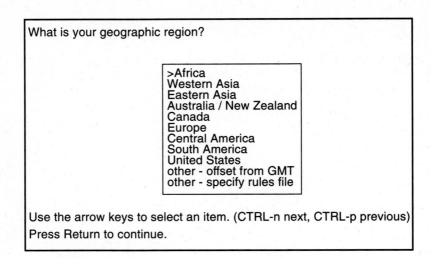

What is your geographic region?

```
>Africa
Western Asia
Eastern Asia
Australia / New Zealand
Canada
Europe
Central America
South America
United States
other - offset from GMT
other - specify rules file
```

Use the arrow keys to select an item. (CTRL-n next, CTRL-p previous)
Press Return to continue.

Figure 3-8   The Geographic Region Screen

a. Specify the timezone.

The correct time zone and time are important, but not so much that the exact time is necessary at this point. Make a close approximation so that the installed files have timestamps appropriate for most backup procedures. There are utilities that can set the system time after installation.

Use the arrow keys on the numeric keypad to toggle through the selections in the geographic region screen shown in Figure 3-8, or use a feature known as Hot-keys to obtain cursor movement to a desired selection. Hot-keys let you quickly move the cursor by typing the first unambiguous character of the listed selections. For instance, rather than scrolling down to the United States region with the down arrow key, you could instead type the single character "u," using either upper or lower case.

When you have selected the region, the timezone screen is displayed. Select the zone by using the arrow or the Hot-keys.

b. Specify the system time.

When the zone has been selected, the system prompts for the system time. A close approximation is offered and will usually suffice unless the system has a problem with the real-time clock chip on the CPU board. Use the RETURN key to scroll down though the time-setting screen.

c. **Confirm the entries.**

Again, confirmation is needed to proceed. If the information is acceptable then, confirm by moving the cursor next to "Yes" and pressing RETURN.

After the region and timezone information is confirmed, a few more system daemons are silently started. The screen quickly displays a few more messages before entering into the install program.

Example 3-1

```
ypbind done.
The system is ready
Welcome to the Solaris Install system.
```

Soon, you are placed in the Solaris 2.x Install main menu, ready to begin the install query session. To actually begin the installation, continue with "Using the Solaris 2.x Install System."

Using the Solaris 2.x Install System

After you have successfully booted from any of the previously described install media, observe the window in the center of the screen entitled "Solaris Install." Five selections are displayed, as seen in Figure 3-9: Quick Install, Custom Install, Upgrade, Exit Install, or Help. Each selection is discussed briefly.

```
┌─────────────────────────────────────────────────────────────┐
│ ▽│              Solaris Install                              │
│  ┌────────────────[ Solaris Installation ]──────────────────┐│
│  │                                                           ││
│  │                                                           ││
│  │                                                           ││
│  │                                                           ││
│  │  ⟨ Quick Install... ⟩                                     ││
│  │                                                           ││
│  │  ⟨ Custom Install... ⟩                                    ││
│  │                                                           ││
│  │  ⟨ Upgrade... ⟩                                           ││
│  │                                                           ││
│  │  ⟨ Exit Install... ⟩                                      ││
│  │                                                           ││
│  │  ⟨ Help... ⟩                                              ││
│  │                                                           ││
│  │                                                           ││
│  │                                                           ││
│  │                                                           ││
│  │                                                           ││
│  │                                                           ││
│  │                                                           ││
│  │                                                           ││
│  │                                                           ││
│  │                                                           ││
│  │                                                           ││
│  │ <Return> Select; <Tab> Next; <F1> Help                    ││
│  └───────────────────────────────────────────────────────────┘│
└─────────────────────────────────────────────────────────────┘
```

Figure 3-9   The Solaris Install System Main Menu

- **Quick Install** - The Quick Install is an easy way to install Solaris 2.x on your system, but it lacks flexibility. This selection configures the system with a predefined disk partition arrangement, regardless of how it may currently be defined. Disk partition sizes are determined by an algorithm based on capacity. You have no control over distributing free disk space and are not able to preserve any file systems. The default software is a predefined set of packages consisting of the End User cluster, defined on the installation CD. The packages contained in the End User cluster are sufficient to operate most general-purpose workstations.

- **Custom Install** - The Custom Install selection is the most flexible option, allowing you to install standalone, dataless, and server systems. This option is the choice of experienced system administrators, because it allows for the preservation of selected filesystems and provides alternatives to predefined software clusters. Some different types of custom installations will be discussed shortly.

- **Upgrade** - Use the upgrade option to upgrade systems already installed with a previous version of Solaris 2.x, such as upgrading from the Solaris 2.1 to Solaris 2.2 operating system, or from Solaris 2.2 to Solaris 2.3. The upgrade option attempts to save most of your system-specific files, such as /etc/hosts, /etc/passwd, before the upgrade occurs. It returns those files to the system after the upgrade completes. If you are upgrading a system from Solaris 1.x or older SunOS 4.x operating system, this option will not even be available.

- **Exit Install** - If you do not wish to install or desire to perform disk maintenance, you can abort the Solaris Install system at any point by returning to the topmost menu and selecting Exit Install. You will be prompted to confirm this action in a pop-up menu before you obtain the shell prompt. Once the shell prompt is displayed, nearly all of the normal system utilities are available in this state, as you are running Solaris 2.x from the 300 megabyte CD-ROM. Of course, response time is much slower than normal.

  Solaris 1.x install programs were limited by either the size of the local memory or the size of swap space. A minimum number of UNIX utilities were available. The new CD-ROM boot environment is a very powerful tool for situations that require the system to be in a state that allows access both to the local disks and to networking utilities.

  To reenter the install program, type suninstall from the shell command prompt.

- **Help** - You may use the help option at any point by pressing the "F1" function key. A system of help menus is included with the 2.x version of the Solaris Install system. Cursor movement within the help screens is the same for all screens throughout the install program. There is even a help screen for cursor movement.

Quick Install

If you are unfamiliar with Solaris installations, you may want to use the Quick Install method. More experienced administrators have discovered that the Quick Install tends to leave large amounts of free disk space in the wrong partitions, often requiring some postinstallation work. Even with this shortfall, the Quick Install is a fast, proven method of getting Solaris 2.x up and running with the least amount of user intervention.

1. **Select Quick Install option.**
   To begin a Quick Install, press RETURN while the cursor is over the Quick Install selection in the main menu.

2. **Select software configuration.**
   A new screen appears, Figure 3-10, showing the four predefined software clusters that may be installed. Each selection's total size requirements are shown, indicating the total amount of disk space needed to install that cluster, not including system swap

space. In Figure 3-10, the amount of disk space required to install the entire distribution of Solaris 2.2 is 287.14 megabytes, while the End User System Support only requires 147 MB.

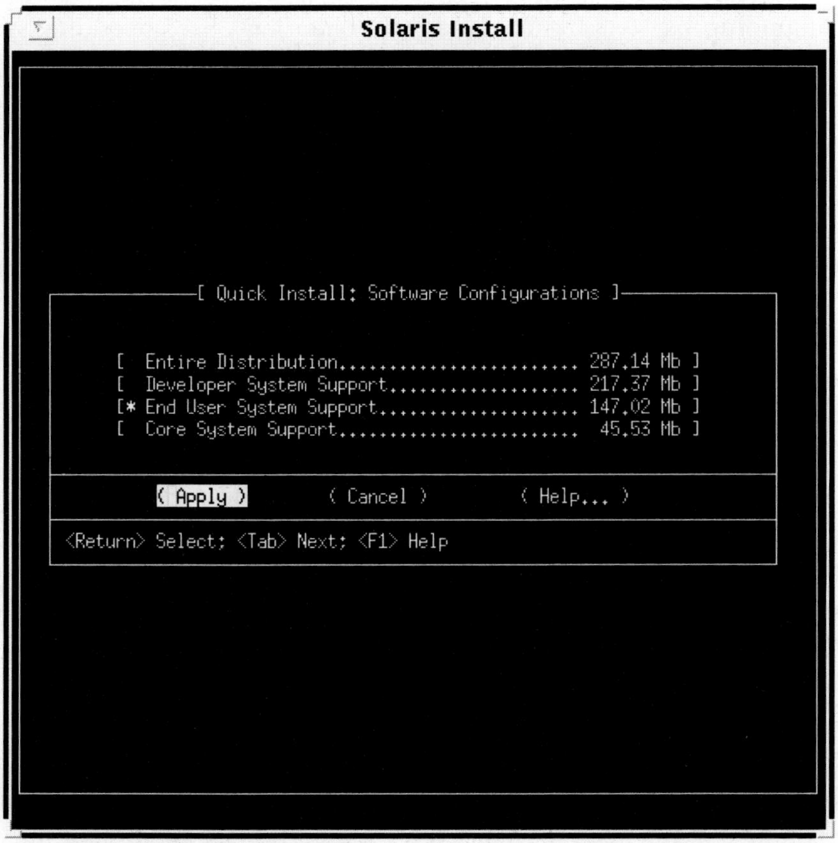

```
┌─────────────────────────────────────────────────────────────┐
│ ▽              Solaris Install                               │
├─────────────────────────────────────────────────────────────┤
│                                                             │
│                                                             │
│        ┌─[ Quick Install: Software Configurations ]──┐       │
│        │                                             │       │
│        │  [  Entire Distribution................ 287.14 Mb ] │
│        │  [  Developer System Support........... 217.37 Mb ] │
│        │  [* End User System Support............ 147.02 Mb ] │
│        │  [  Core System Support................  45.53 Mb ] │
│        ├─────────────────────────────────────────────┤       │
│        │    ( Apply )      ( Cancel )      ( Help... )│       │
│        ├─────────────────────────────────────────────┤       │
│        │ <Return> Select; <Tab> Next; <F1> Help       │       │
│        └─────────────────────────────────────────────┘       │
│                                                             │
└─────────────────────────────────────────────────────────────┘
```

Figure 3-10   The Quick Install Software Selection Menu

If you want to install a software cluster other than the End User System Support, you must make that selection while in this screen. You cannot select more than one software cluster.

Note – To gain cursor movement in the Quick Install software selection menu, use the TAB key. Once the cursor is placed over the Entire Distribution selection, use the down or up arrow keys to move the cursor over the desired choice. To select that cluster, press the RETURN key or the space-bar. An asterisk will then mark that selection to be installed.

When you have chosen the software you desire, again use the TAB key to move the cursor over Apply and press RETURN. The final Quick Install screen, Figure 3-11, is displayed.

If you choose a configuration that does not fit on the current disk, a warning describes the problem and informs you to try again, prohibiting any further action. The Quick Install prompts you only once before writing a new label and making new filesystems, completely overwriting anything on the current disk.

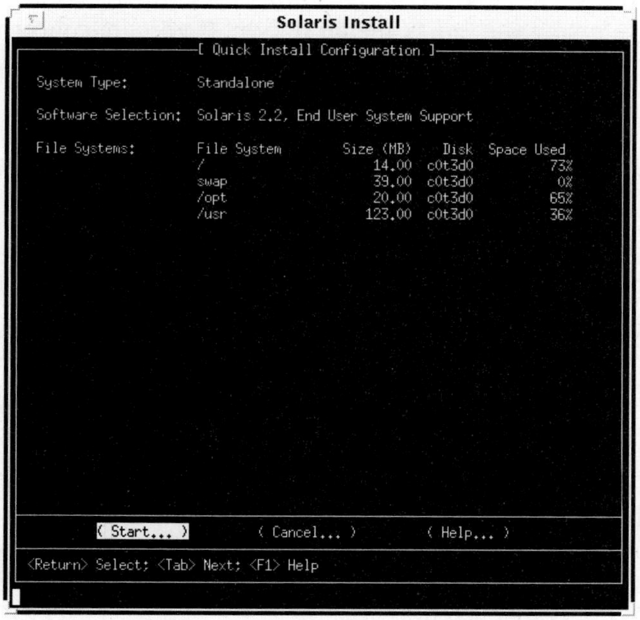

```
┌─────────────────────────────────────────────────────────┐
│ ▽                     Solaris Install                    │
│          ─────[ Quick Install Configuration ]─────       │
│  System Type:       Standalone                           │
│                                                          │
│  Software Selection:  Solaris 2.2, End User System Support│
│                                                          │
│  File Systems:      File System    Size (MB)   Disk   Space Used│
│                     /                 14.00  c0t3d0      73%    │
│                     swap              39.00  c0t3d0       0%    │
│                     /opt              20.00  c0t3d0      65%    │
│                     /usr             123.00  c0t3d0      36%    │
│                                                          │
│                                                          │
│     ( Start... )        ( Cancel... )      ( Help... )   │
│  <Return> Select; <Tab> Next; <F1> Help                  │
└─────────────────────────────────────────────────────────┘
```

Figure 3-11   The Quick Install Final Screen

Should you decide to abort before starting the actual Quick Install, the screen shown in Figure 3-11 is your last chance. This screen shows the disk configuration selected for a 207 megabyte disk. Study the final Quick Install screen carefully. If you find anything amiss, abort the installation by moving the cursor over the Cancel selection at the bottom of the screen and pressing RETURN. You are then returned to the topmost screen of the Solaris Install menu.

Observe the size and space used by the /usr file system in Figure 3-11. The /usr partition on this particular standalone system has been given 123 megabytes of disk space. Only 36 percent of that space will be used when the installation has completed. The other 64 percent will be free space, but in the /usr filesystem. It is good to have extra disk space available in the /usr filesystem, especially if you plan to install additional unbundled software packages from vendors who do not yet support the /opt convention. However, with utilities like the Software Manager Tool, swmtool, system packages that are not installed by Quick Install can be easily obtained from a local CD device or by using NFS.

Any extra disk space could be more useful in the root partition or even in a separate /var partition. Of course, you do not have the option of changing the partition arrangement when using the Quick Install option. If you are concerned about setting explicit disk partition sizes, then do not use Quick Install; use the Custom Installation option, discussed next.

3. Start the installation.
The last step is to move the cursor over the Start selection and to press RETURN. This will start the installation.

Custom Standalone Installation

For the Custom Standalone Installation example, assume that a SPARCstation IPC with an internal 207 Mbyte SCSI disk has already booted into the Solaris install system. This system type was chosen because it is one of the most common configurations; the entire release of Solaris 2.x does not fit on a 207 Mbyte disk, making it an ideal candidate for customization.

1. Select Custom Install option.
To begin a custom standalone installation, move the cursor over Custom Install in the Solaris Install main menu and press RETURN. The Custom Install Configuration menu shown in Figure 3-12 is displayed.

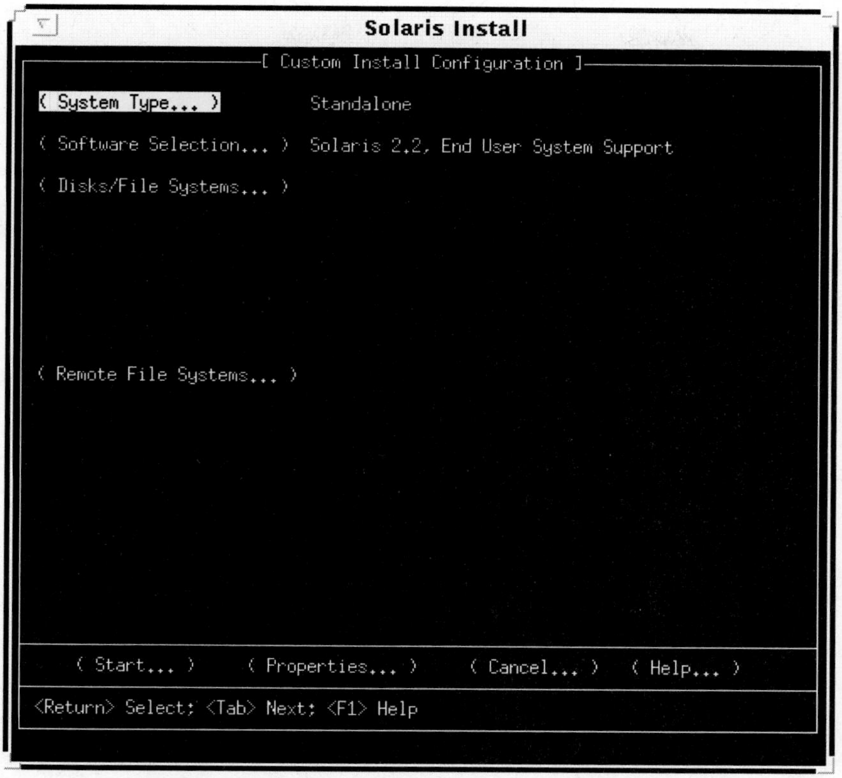

```
 ▽                        Solaris Install
                    ─[ Custom Install Configuration ]─
  ( System Type... )          Standalone

  ( Software Selection... )   Solaris 2.2, End User System Support

  ( Disks/File Systems... )




  ( Remote File Systems... )





      ( Start... )      ( Properties... )      ( Cancel... )    ( Help... )
  <Return> Select; <Tab> Next; <F1> Help
```

Figure 3-12   The Custom Install Main Menu

Cursor movement is controlled by using the TAB key, as in other Solaris Install screens. Notice that the Custom Install screen defaults to a Standalone system type, so no selection is necessary.

2. Select system type.

Since this system is to be a standalone system, rather than diskless client or server, the system type will not need to be changed for this example. Changing the system type is described in the Server Installation section, later in this chapter.

3. Select software.

Press the TAB key to highlight the Software Selection field. The default Software Selection for a standalone machine is the End User System Support cluster.

a. To select a different software cluster.

To edit this selection, press the RETURN key. The Software Configuration menu shown in Figure 3-13, with four predefined software selections, is displayed.

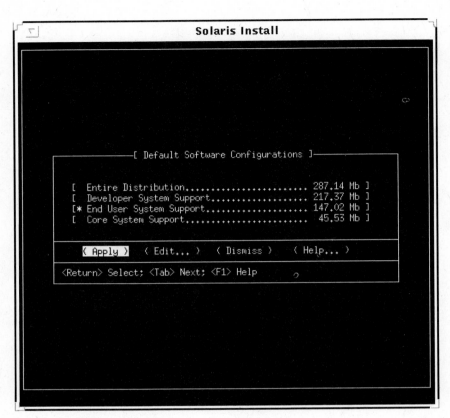

Figure 3-13 *Software Configuration Menu*

From the software configuration menu, select one of four options: Entire Distribution, Developer System Support, End User System Support, or Core System Support. The asterisk next to the End User selection indicates that it is currently selected. If the End User cluster is your desired cluster, press RETURN while the cursor is over Apply. When your selection is applied, the previous screen is displayed.

To select Entire Distribution, continue to press the TAB key until the Entire Distribution field is highlighted. At this point, press RETURN, or the SPACE bar; notice that the asterisk selecting the End User cluster is now next to the Entire Distribution selection.

b. To view packages.

To view the packages that are included in any of the predefined clusters listed in the top part of the menu, use the TAB key to move the cursor over the Edit field at the bottom of the screen. Press RETURN, and the Edit Software Configuration screen is displayed as shown in Figure 3-14. The current status of selected software packages is determined by the column immediately preceding the package name. Packages displayed in this screen can be in one of the following states:

- + (required)
- * (selected)
- - (partially selected)
- empty (not selected)

```
 ▽                       Solaris Install
                   ─[ Edit Software Configuration ]─

       Editing: End User System Support

        ┌─────────────────────────────────────────────────────┐
        │ 4.1* Heterogeneous Install Software...........  0.00 MB ▒│
        │    Archive Libraries.........................  0.00 MB │
        │  - Audio.....................................  0.57 MB │
        │    Automated Security Enhancement Tools......  0.00 MB │
        │    Basic Networking..........................  0.00 MB │
        │  * Binary Compatibility......................  1.16 MB │
        │  + Core Architecture, (Kvm)..................  0.66 MB │
        │  + Core Architecture, (Root).................  2.21 MB │
        │  + Core SPARC................................ 21.95 MB │
        │    Direct Xlib...............................  0.00 MB │
        │  * Documentation Tools.......................  1.06 MB │
        │  + Extended System Utilities.................  1.49 MB │
        │  + Framebuffer (bwtwo, CG3) support..........  0.22 MB │
        │    Framed Access Command Environment.........  0.00 MB │
        │    GS (cg12) OS Support Files................  0.00 MB │
        │    GT Device Drivers.........................  0.00 MB │
        │    GT Run-time support software..............  0.00 MB │
        │  + GX (cg6) OS Support Files.................  0.09 MB │
        │    Header Files..............................  0.00 MB │
        │  * Install Software..........................  2.29 MB │
        │  * Interprocess Communications...............  0.04 MB │
        └─────────────────────────────────────────────────────┘

             * = Selected    + = Required    - = Partially Selected

        ( Done )        ( Reset )        ( Space... )        ( Help... )

     <Return> Popup Menu; <Space> Select; <U/D Arrow> Scan List; <F1> Help
```

Figure 3-14 The Edit Software Configuration Screen

The Edit Software Configuration screen shows all of the clusters and packages that are selected under the End User System Support. The list is actually much longer than the screen allows. To view the full complement of packages, scroll with the down arrow key.

Each of the packages marked as partially selected is itself a cluster of packages. For instance, if you scroll down the list until the partially selected OpenWindows Version 3 entry is highlighted, you can view or zoom in on its contents by pressing

RETURN, using the down arrow key to highlight Zoom In, and again pressing RETURN. The resulting screen, shown in Figure 3-15, shows all of the OpenWindows packages that make up the total OpenWindows cluster.

```
┌────────────────────────────────────────────────────────┐
│                    Solaris Install                      │
│              ─[ Edit Software Configuration ]─           │
│                                                          │
│  Editing: End User System Support/OpenWindows Version 3  │
│ ┌──────────────────────────────────────────────────────┐│
│ │ + OpenWindows Window Drivers.....................  0.22 MB││
│ │ * OpenWindows binary compatibility...............  5.92 MB││
│ │   OpenWindows demo images........................  0.00 MB││
│ │   OpenWindows demo programs......................  0.00 MB││
│ │   OpenWindows include files......................  0.00 MB││
│ │ * OpenWindows nonessential MIT core clients......  1.81 MB││
│ │ * OpenWindows online handbooks...................  2.49 MB││
│ │   OpenWindows online programmers man pages.......  0.00 MB││
│ │   OpenWindows online user man pages..............  0.00 MB││
│ │ * OpenWindows optional fonts..................... 11.93 MB││
│ │ * OpenWindows required core package.............. 41.64 MB││
│ │   OpenWindows sample source......................  0.00 MB││
│ │   OpenWindows static libraries...................  0.00 MB││
│ │                                                      ││
│ │                                                      ││
│ │                                                      ││
│ └──────────────────────────────────────────────────────┘│
│                                                          │
│      * = Selected    + = Required    - = Partially Selected│
│                                                          │
│  ( Done )      ( Reset )      ( Space... )     ( Help... )│
│ <Return> Popup Menu; <Space> Select; <U/D Arrow> Scan List; <F1> Help│
└────────────────────────────────────────────────────────┘
```

Figure 3-15   Editing a Partially Selected Cluster

Of the 13 OpenWindows packages, only 6 are currently selected, and only 2 are required. The required packages contain a number of kernel drivers necessary for operation and the binary compatibility software for running Solaris 1.x-based software. If you are planning to use NFS to obtain the windowing system on your standalone machine, then you can deselect the entire OpenWindows cluster except for the required packages.

Helpful Hint – This action could be the key to gaining enough disk space to allow other bundled or unbundled software packages to be installed on a machine with a limited amount of disk space.

---

c. To edit the packages added.

To actually edit the software to be installed, use the down arrow key to highlight the selection to be added or removed. Use the spacebar to toggle between selected and not selected by observing the asterisk. When you are satisfied with the selections made, use the TAB key to highlight the "Space..." field at the bottom of the screen.

View the current space requirements by pressing RETURN. Figure 3-16 shows the space requirements for the current installation.

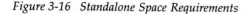

```
                          Solaris Install


                  ┌─[ File System Space Requirements ]─┐
                  │ File System      Minimum   Suggested   Configured │
                  │ ┌───────────────────────────────────────────────┐ │
                  │ │ /                 9.22 MB   11.52 MB    0.00 MB │ │
                  │ │ swap             16.00 MB   32.00 MB    0.00 MB │ │
                  │ │ /opt              7.97 MB    9.96 MB    0.00 MB │ │
                  │ │ /var              1.82 MB    2.28 MB    0.00 MB │ │
                  │ │ /usr             36.20 MB   45.25 MB    0.00 MB │ │
                  │ │ /usr/openwin     55.33 MB   69.16 MB    0.00 MB │ │
                  │ └───────────────────────────────────────────────┘ │
                  │ Totals:          126.53 MB  170.17 MB    0.00 MB │
                  │──────────────────────────────────────────────────│
                  │        〈 Dismiss 〉        ( Help... )           │
                  └──────────────────────────────────────────────────┘
```

Figure 3-16   Standalone Space Requirements

d. To record space requirements.

After you have selected the software packages you desire, record the amount of megabytes suggested by each partition, as shown in Figure 3-16. You will use these requirements in the disk configuration screen. It is important to note here that /opt, /var, and /usr/openwin are listed as separate partitions here. You may choose to have /var as a part of the / partition, or /usr/openwin as part of the /usr partition. This screen breaks down partitioning needs of all major partition areas.

e. Confirm software selection.
Press RETURN to return to the Edit Software Configuration menu. From there, depending on how deep you were, keep selecting Done until you are at the Custom Install Configuration menu. It is now time to configure the disk.

4. Select disk and filesystem configuration.
Enter the Disks/File Systems configuration from the Custom Install Configuration menu by pressing RETURN while its selection is highlighted. Upon the first entry into the Disks/File Systems section, the Disk Editing Properties screen is displayed, Figure 3-17.

```
┌─▽──────────────────── Solaris Install ──────────────────────┐
│                                                             │
│                                                             │
│       ┌──────────[ Disk Editing Properties ]──────────┐     │
│       │                                               │     │
│       │  Initial disk configuration:  [* Automatic          ] │     │
│       │                               [  Disk label (existing) ] │     │
│       │                               [  None               ] │     │
│       │                               [  Redo current initial c ] │     │
│       │                                               │     │
│       │         Size Editing Units:   [* MBytes      ]     │     │
│       │                               [  Cylinders  ]     │     │
│       │                               [  Blocks     ]     │     │
│       │                                               │     │
│       │   Display start/end cylinders?  [ ]  No       │     │
│       │                                               │     │
│       │  Display mount point size hints?  [*]  Yes     │     │
│       │                                               │     │
│       ├───────────────────────────────────────────────┤     │
│       │    ( Apply )      ( Dismiss )     ( Help... )  │     │
│       │ <Return> Select; <Tab> Next; <U/D Arrow> Scan Choices; <F1> │     │
│       └───────────────────────────────────────────────┘     │
│                                                             │
└─────────────────────────────────────────────────────────────┘
```

Figure 3-17 Disk Properties Screen

a. Select configuration method.

This screen determines how the partitions will be sized; the editing units and other information on the disk will be displayed in the session about to occur.

- If you want the install program to automatically size the necessary partitions for you, then select the default, Automatic.
- If you already partitioned your disk with `format` or other means, then select Disk Label (existing).
- To start from scratch and define the partitions yourself, select None.
- Use Redo current initial configurations if you need to go back and partition the disk after you had once done it before.

Automatic disk configuration will be chosen for the current installation example. Select Apply on the Properties screen. The Local Disks and File Systems screen, Figure 3-18, is displayed. The screen shows the available disks in the current configuration, a single 207-Mbyte drive. If your system has more than one disk connected, they will appear as a selection on this menu.

```
                        Solaris Install
 ┌─────────────────────────────────────────────────────────────┐
 │                                                               │
 │                                                               │
 │                                                               │
 │              ─[ Local Disks & File Systems ]─                 │
 │                                                               │
 │         Disk    Size     Status                               │
 │      ┌──────────────────────────────────────────────────┐    │
 │      │ c0t3d0   198 MB - unconfigured                    │    │
 │      │                                                   │    │
 │      │                                                   │    │
 │      └──────────────────────────────────────────────────┘    │
 │                                                               │
 │          ( Done )        ( Space... )      ( Help... )        │
 │      ─────────────────────────────────────────────────────   │
 │      <Return> Popup Menu; <U/D Arrow> Scan List; <F1> Help    │
 │                                                               │
 │                                                               │
 └─────────────────────────────────────────────────────────────┘
```

Figure 3-18   Selecting an Unconfigured Disk

b. Select the boot disk.

Select the disk you would like to designate as the boot disk by using the down arrow key to highlight your choice. When the choice is highlighted, press RETURN and observe the pop-up menu with three choices. Press RETURN while the cursor is over Configure Disk.

Any disk can be your boot disk, but remember that the command to boot from a disk that is not aliased in the boot PROM can become long and difficult to type. If you chose something other than the disk in the PROM, you must update the PROM after installation.

Note – Traditionally the c0t3d0 disk is used as the boot disk on most desktop and deskside systems. Target three translates to the Solaris 1.x device /dev/sd0 and is also the default boot device in many systems' EEPROM.

```
┌─┐                    Solaris Install
│▽│
│    ┌─────[ Configuring File Systems on Disk (c0t3d0) ]─────┐
│    │ Slice  Mount Point          Size (MBs)                │
│    │   0    /                     13                       │
│    │   1    swap                  32                       │
│    │   2                         198                       │
│    │   3                           0                       │
│    │   4                           0                       │
│    │   5    /opt                   9                       │
│    │   6    /usr                 114                       │
│    │   7                           0                       │
│    │                                                       │
│    │ Unallocated Space: 27 MBs                             │
│    ├───────────────────────────────────────────────────────┤
│    │ ( Apply )  ( Props... )  ( Space... )  ( Dismiss ) ( Help... ) │
│    │ <Return> Commit: <Tab> Next Field: <F1> Help          │
│    └───────────────────────────────────────────────────────┘
```

Figure 3-19   Default 207-Mbyte Disk Partitioning

c. Select partitioning for the boot disk.

Figure 3-19 shows the default layout for a 207-Mbyte disk, a common device in many SPARC systems. The partitions are as follows:

- slice 0 - root filesystem. The 13-Mbyte allocation is barely enough space for the default kernel, drivers, and modules, not to mention any mail or printer spooling.
- slice 1 - swap. Swap is calculated on-the-fly by doubling the amount of installed RAM. The system used in this example has 16 megabytes of installed memory, hence the 32-megabyte swap size.
- slice 2 - whole disk. The third partition is equivalent to partition "c" in previous versions of the Solaris 1.x or older SunOS 4.x operating system. The whole disk partition is used primarily for the install program.
- slices 3 and 4 - not configured

- slice 5 - /opt. /opt has been given 9 megabytes as a result of the current software packages selected, particularly the SUNWpex package, necessary for XGL runtime applications, and SUNWxilrt, the X Imaging libraries, necessary for a new tool called ImageTool. Many systems do not need the SUNWxglrt package installed locally unless XGL applications are to be executed. You might want to keep the SUNWxilrt package around because ImageTool is a handy utility. Other packages that may be installed into the /opt directory are the bundled compiler tools, SUNWbtool; the on-line diagnostic package, SUNWdiag; and the bundled on-line Solaris AnswerBook, SUNWabe. Many of these packages occupy large amounts of disk space. Consider using NFS resources to supply these utilities.
- slice 6 - /usr. The current size for the /usr partition is 114 megabytes, including the OpenWindows drivers and programs. Only 27 megabytes of free disk space are left for a home filesystem where user files are typically stored. Most systems with disks of this size are destined to use an NFS-mounted home directory because of the lack of space.
- slice 7 - not configured

The partition arrangement shown in Figure 3-19 is suitable for most systems with a single 207-Mbyte disk. However, the system may experience problems with this arrangement if the user ever needs to print a large file or if email spooling is local. Both of these activities require temporary space in the /var directory. There are workarounds for both events after the install, but why not make room for these activities during the installation?

The options are to increase the size of the root partition, create a separate /var partition, or leave the root partition the way it is and NFS-mount the spooling directories during postinstallation procedures. Increasing the size of the root partition is the least difficult option if you have the disk space, but system processes stop abruptly when the root filesystem becomes full. It is less severe to the system when other file systems overflow. The more obvious choice is to create a separate /var partition.

This particular system will use a remote home directory, but mail and print spooling will occur locally. The disk space currently earmarked for /export/home will instead be given to the /var partition to accommodate this spooling activity.

The next two steps describe how to edit the filesystem configuration to achieve the configuration shown in Figure 3-20.

```
┌─┐                    Solaris Install
│▽│
│
│
│
│        ┌─[ Configuring File Systems on Disk (c0t3d0) ]──────┐
│        │                                                    │
│        │  Slice  Mount Point        Size (MBs)              │
│        │    0    /                  20                      │
│        │    1    swap               32                      │
│        │    2                       198                     │
│        │    3                       0                       │
│        │    4    /var               10                      │
│        │    5    /opt               21                      │
│        │    6    /usr               114                     │
│        │    7                       0                       │
│        │                                                    │
│        │  Unallocated Space: 0 MBs                          │
│        │                                                    │
│        │ ┌──────────────────────────────────────────────┐  │
│        │ │ ( Apply )  ( Props... )  ( Space... )  ( Dismiss ) ( Help... ) │
│        │ │ <Return> Select; <Tab> Next; <F1> Help        │  │
│        │ └──────────────────────────────────────────────┘  │
│        └────────────────────────────────────────────────────┘
```

Figure 3-20   An Edited 207-Mbyte Disk

d. To change the root partition.

Use the TAB key to position the cursor over the field that you wish to change. To change the size of the root slice to 20 megabytes, TAB over until the Size field is highlighted, then type in the size you want.

e. To add a new /var partition.

Use the TAB or RETURN key to move the cursor over the mount point field next to an undefined partition. Type in the mount point /var, then use the RETURN key to move the cursor under the Size column. Enter the desired size for the /var partition while observing the Unallocated Space monitor in the middle of the screen. Attempt to use or find a use for any unallocated space.

Modify other partition sizes in a similar manner, depending on the specific software needs of the machine. This system is now nearly ready to begin the actual installation.

f. Confirm disk partitioning.

Once you are satisfied with the disk partitioning, move the cursor to highlight Apply and press RETURN. The Local Disks and File Systems screen appears once again but this time the status field shows the different filesystems that have been configured on the disk. Use the TAB key to position the cursor over Done and press RETURN. The Custom Install Configuration menu is once again displayed.

5. Select remote mounts.

The final step in configuring this system is to set up the remote mount for its home directory. This step is not required at this point as it can be done during the post-installation procedures.

6. Begin the installation.

Start the installation from the main Solaris Install window by positioning the cursor over Start and pressing RETURN. A pop-up menu asks you to confirm the selection as shown in Figure 3-21. Press the TAB key once to highlight "Continue with Install" and again press RETURN.

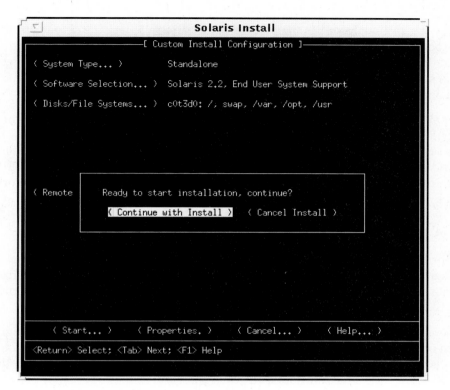

```
 ╔═════════════════════════════════════════════════════════╗
 ║                    Solaris Install                      ║
 ╟─────────────[ Custom Install Configuration ]───────────╢
 ║                                                         ║
 ║  ( System Type... )       Standalone                    ║
 ║                                                         ║
 ║  ( Software Selection... )  Solaris 2.2, End User System Support
 ║                                                         ║
 ║  ( Disks/File Systems... )  c0t3d0: /, swap, /var, /opt, /usr
 ║                                                         ║
 ║                                                         ║
 ║          ┌─────────────────────────────────────────┐   ║
 ║  ( Remote│  Ready to start installation, continue? │   ║
 ║          │ ( Continue with Install )  ( Cancel Install )
 ║          └─────────────────────────────────────────┘   ║
 ║                                                         ║
 ║                                                         ║
 ║                                                         ║
 ║                                                         ║
 ║  ( Start... )   ( Properties. )   ( Cancel... )   ( Help... )
 ║ <Return> Select; <Tab> Next; <F1> Help                  ║
 ╚═════════════════════════════════════════════════════════╝
```

Figure 3-21 The Standalone Install Confirmation Screen

The system responds by clearing the screen and begins to create filesystems in all of the previously configured partitions. The system is actually running `fsck` for partitions that were marked to be preserved and `newfs` for all new partitions. On an average system, this should take three to five minutes. However, if you have a 2-gigabyte disk, this will take considerably longer.

After all of the filesystems have been created, a new screen displays an installation monitor which determines the amount of time elapsed and remaining until completion. A console window also appears in the upper left corner of the screen to capture any error messages that occur during the install. This window can be checked periodically for such events, but it will generally remain empty.

A normal standalone installation takes approximately one hour, depending on whether the Solaris 2.x medium is a locally mounted CD, remotely mounted CD, or remotely mounted UFS image. The UFS image usually takes the least amount of time. Check the postinstallation instructions to find out what needs to be done after the install has completed.

Server Installation

The following section describes the process of installing a Solaris 2.2 server system. Many of the procedures are identical to a standalone install, specifically in the software and disk configuration sections. A few additional steps are necessary to configure a server machine, such as selecting the client architecture and allocating necessary filesystems for diskless client root and swap areas.

A server system must have sufficient disk space not only for the operating system that the server will boot from and use but also for the operating system files needed by each diskless or dataless machine. Server systems should also be more powerful in terms of speed and memory than the clients they serve. One client with more raw power than its server can make it hard on the other diskless systems vying for the same network resources.

Shared vs. Nonshared Files

The majority of the system executable files can be shared across all architectures, but certain kernel-specific files cannot be shared. The kernel-specific files are kept in separate directories under the /export/root and /export/exec/kvm paths. Non-kernel-specific files are stored under the /export/exec/sparc.

Each client's root directory uses 10 Mbytes of disk space when minimally configured. If you plan on supporting ten clients, then the server needs 100 Mbytes or more. Each client also needs a place for swapping, minimally as much memory as is installed on the client and ideally twice the size of installed RAM.

Since systems that run Solaris 2.x require a minimum of 16 Mbytes of installed RAM, the swap area for ten clients, then based on minimum RAM, is already 320 megabytes. Both of these areas are not only architecture specific, but system specific also. So, for ten minimally configured clients the server must have over 400 megabytes of disk space just for diskless root and swap areas.

Also consider where email and print spooling will occur for each client. A large /var partition can be configured on the server and NFS-mounted by each client, or spooling can occur in each client's root directory. Either method is acceptable as long as space is reserved in advance.

If you reserve 4 Mbytes for email spooling per each client and a few megabytes for print spooling, then a server of ten diskless systems must increase the /export/root partition or create a /var partition with 100 Mbytes of free disk space. You can understand how quickly a server's disk space can be used by its clients.

1. Select Custom Install.

To begin a server installation, move the cursor over the Custom Install in the Solaris Install main menu and press RETURN. The Custom Insall Configuration menu is displayed.

2. Select the server system type.

To select the server install, press RETURN while the cursor is over the System Type selection in the Custom Install Configuration screen. A new screen, Choose System Type, is displayed, as shown in Figure 3-22.

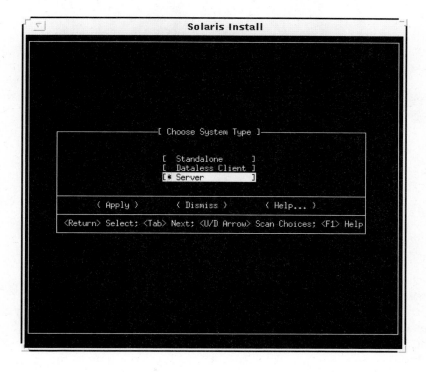

Figure 3-22 Choosing the Server System Type

From this screen, use the TAB key to move the cursor over the Standalone selection. When the Standalone selection is highlighted, use the down arrow key to highlight the Server selection and press the SPACE bar. The asterisk that was next to the Standalone selection moves next to the Server selection. Again use the TAB key to move the cursor over Apply, and confirm by pressing the RETURN key.

The Custom Install menu is displayed. The screen shows a new item in the upper right corner, the Server Params field.

3. Select the server parameters.

Use the TAB key to highlight this selection and press RETURN to view the Server Parameters screen, shown in Figure 3-23.

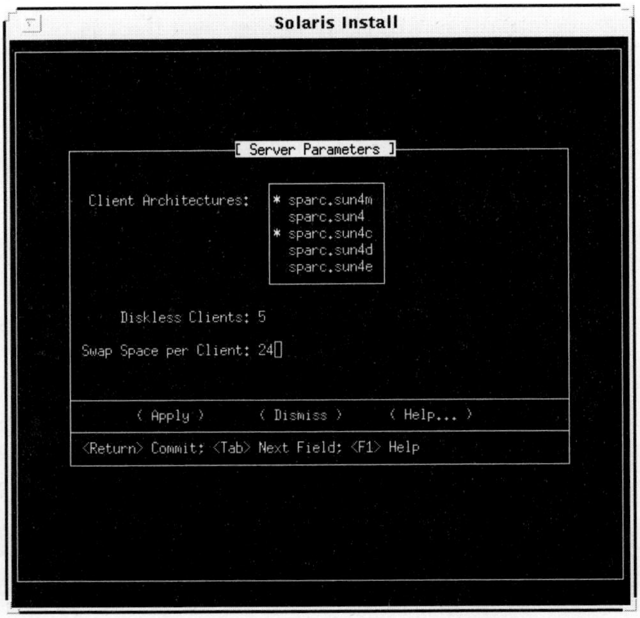

Figure 3-23   The Server Parameters Screen

a. Select the client architectures.

You select client architecture types from the Server Parameters screen. You should already know the kernel architecture of the diskless clients supported by a server. In the example shown in Figure 3-23, the server supports five diskless machines. Three of the clients are SPARCstation 1 series systems that belong to the `sparc.sun4c` family. Two other systems are SPARCstation 10s, belonging to the `sparc.sun4m` family.

Use the TAB key to move the cursor into the Client Architecture section of the screen. Use the arrow key to highlight the client architecture type you wish to select and press RETURN. An asterisk will be shown next to the selection. Use the TAB key to move to the Diskless Clients selection, when you have completed choosing the client architectures.

b. Select the number of clients.

Here you configure the number of diskless clients that will be supported by this server. The disk configuration screen uses this number to reserve client root space. If you plan on configuring more clients than the initial install, then enter that number here. Or, you can manually reserve the space while in the disk configuration menu. The server being installed will support five diskless clients.

c. Select the amount of swap space.

Use the TAB key to move the cursor over the next field, Swap Space per Client.The install program will also automatically reserve swap space based on the amount of Swap Space per Client size. The default swap space per client is 24 megabytes. You may need more or less depending on the type of diskless clients you support. For the systems in this example, 24 megabytes of swap per client is sufficient space so it will not be changed. Be aware that changing the swap space per client affects the size allocated to the /export/swap filesystem in the Disk menu.

When you have completed the Server Parameters screen, move the cursor using the TAB key, to highlight Apply, and press RETURN.

4. Select server software.

You are returned to the Custom Install Configuration screen. The cursor is highlighting the Software Selection field. Press RETURN. The Software selection screen, shown in Figure 3-24, is displayed.

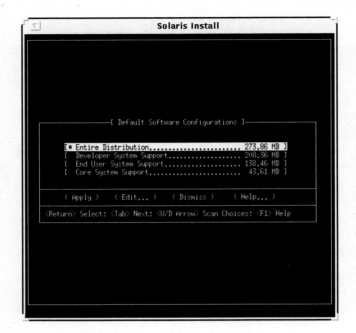

Figure 3-24 Selecting Server Software

The software you select for installation from this menu is what will be available to the diskless and dataless systems that are supported by this server. To be safe, err on the side of installing more system software than is necessary. It is difficult to install additional packages after the system is running, especially with the space requirements of server systems. You might be able to get by without installing the manual pages or windowing system, but doing so makes it more difficult on the administrator, requiring additional set up after the installation. You might as well keep everything together on the same server when possible.

a. To edit a particular software configuration.
   Move the cursor to highlight the item. Press the TAB key to highlight the Edit selection; that particular cluster is expanded into its components. From there use the arrow keys to control cursor movement and press RETURN to select and deselect components. When you have selected the software packages to install, apply your selections as before, highlighting the Apply selection and confirming with RETURN.

   Back to the Custom Install screen you go, this time selecting the Disks/File Systems. The Local Disks & File Systems main menu, shown in Figure 3-25, is displayed.

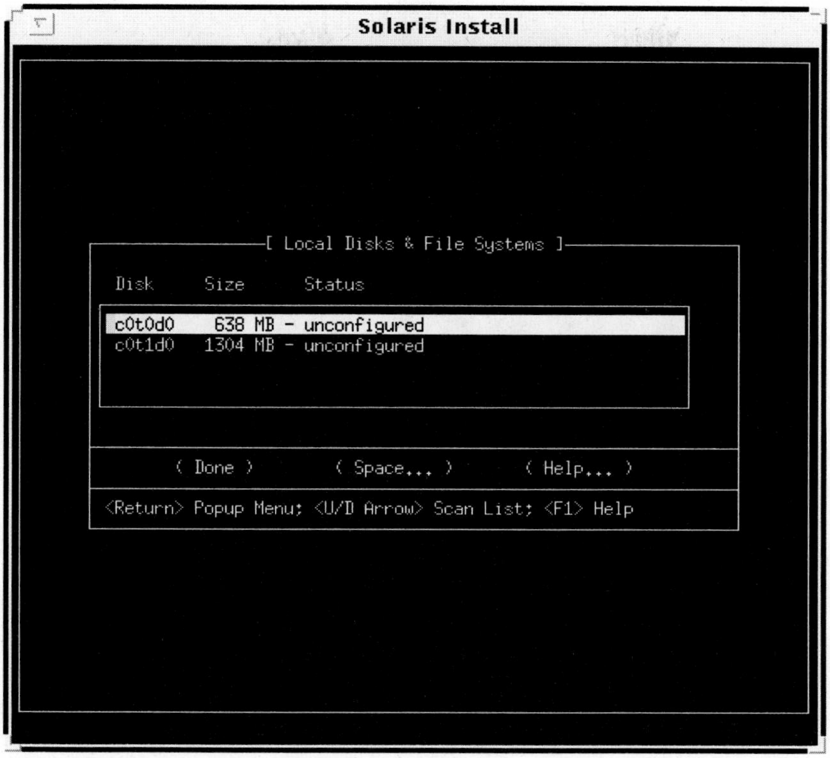

```
┌─────────────────────────────────────────────────────────┐
│ ▽                    Solaris Install                     │
├─────────────────────────────────────────────────────────┤
│                                                         │
│                                                         │
│                                                         │
│                                                         │
│          ──────[ Local Disks & File Systems ]──────      │
│                                                         │
│        Disk      Size      Status                        │
│      ┌────────────────────────────────────────────┐     │
│      │ c0t0d0    638 MB – unconfigured            │     │
│      │ c0t1d0   1304 MB – unconfigured            │     │
│      │                                            │     │
│      │                                            │     │
│      └────────────────────────────────────────────┘     │
│      ───────────────────────────────────────────────    │
│           ( Done )       ( Space... )      ( Help... )   │
│       <Return> Popup Menu; <U/D Arrow> Scan List; <F1> Help │
│                                                         │
│                                                         │
│                                                         │
└─────────────────────────────────────────────────────────┘
```

Figure 3-25 Disks & File Systems Main Menu

5. Configuring disks and filesystems.

The first disk you select in this menu will be configured as the server's boot disk. There are two disks in this server configuration, one 669-megabyte disk and one 1.3-gigabyte disk. The 669-megabyte disk will be used as the boot disk, and the 1.3-gigabyte disk will be used for the diskless client areas.

a. Select the boot disk.

Select the boot disk by pressing RETURN. A pop-up menu is displayed with three choices: Configure Disk, Unconfigure Disk, or Dismiss. To configure the selected disk, again press RETURN. A new screen called Disk Editing Properties, shown in Figure 3-26, is displayed.

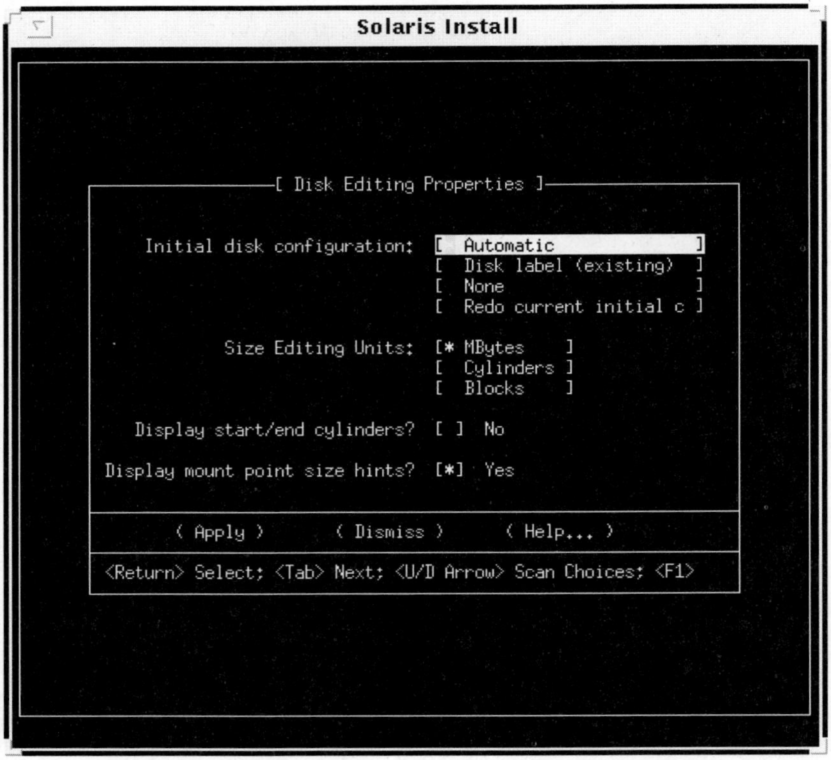

```
┌─────────────────────────────────────────────────────────────┐
│ ▽                    Solaris Install                         │
├─────────────────────────────────────────────────────────────┤
│                                                             │
│                                                             │
│           ──[ Disk Editing Properties ]──                   │
│                                                             │
│   Initial disk configuration:  [  Automatic          ]      │
│                                [  Disk label (existing) ]    │
│                                [  None                ]      │
│                                [  Redo current initial c ]   │
│                                                             │
│          Size Editing Units:   [* MBytes    ]               │
│                                [  Cylinders ]               │
│                                [  Blocks    ]               │
│                                                             │
│   Display start/end cylinders?  [ ]  No                     │
│                                                             │
│   Display mount point size hints? [*]  Yes                  │
│                                                             │
│  ──────────────────────────────────────────────────        │
│       ( Apply )      ( Dismiss )      ( Help... )            │
│  <Return> Select; <Tab> Next; <U/D Arrow> Scan Choices; <F1> │
└─────────────────────────────────────────────────────────────┘
```

Figure 3-26   The Disk Properties Menu

b. Select editing properties.

Under the Initial disk configuration section are four choices: Automatic, Disk label, None, and Redo current initial configuration.

- To instruct the install program to determine the initial disk configuration, select Automatic.
- If you have already written a disk label to this disk or are reinstalling a system that you wish to preserve existing partitions, select Disk label.
- To define your own initial disk partition arrangement, select None.
- Use Redo current initial configuration when you have once defined the disk configuration and want to check or change something that you forgot.

The server being installed in this example will use the Automatic method.

The Size Editing field permits three choices, the default being MB or megabytes. This selection is used in the next screen, when the actual partition sizes are displayed. To see the partition sizes displayed in values other than megabytes, make that choice under this field.

To monitor the start and end cylinders for the configured partitions, change the Display start/end cylinders by means of the SPACE bar or the RETURN key. This selection is used as a monitoring tool and has no real effect on the installation.

The final selection in this menu is another tool that offers size hints for necessary filesystems. Again this selection has no effect in the installation but can aid in making intelligent choices.

When finished selecting the disk properties, use the TAB key to highlight Apply and press RETURN. The filesystems for the selected disk are displayed, as shown in Figure 3-27.

```
┌─┐                          Solaris Install
│ ⌐│
├──────────────────────────────────────────────────────────────┤
│                                                                │
│                                                                │
│        ┌────[ Configuring File Systems on Disk (c0t0d0) ]────┐ │
│        │ Slice  Mount Point         Size (MBs)               │ │
│        │   0    /                   21                       │ │
│        │   1    swap                127                      │ │
│        │   2                        638                      │ │
│        │   3    /export             120                      │ │
│        │   4                        0                        │ │
│        │   5    /opt                60                       │ │
│        │   6    /usr                219                      │ │
│        │   7                        0                        │ │
│        │                                                     │ │
│        │ Unallocated Space: 88 MBs                           │ │
│        │                                                     │ │
│        ├─────────────────────────────────────────────────────┤ │
│        │ ( Apply )  ( Props... )  ( Space... )  ( Dismiss ) ( Help... ) │
│        ├─────────────────────────────────────────────────────┤ │
│        │ <Return> Select; <Tab> Next; <F1> Help              │ │
│        └─────────────────────────────────────────────────────┘ │
│                                                                │
└────────────────────────────────────────────────────────────────┘
```

Figure 3-27   Configuring the Server's Boot Disk

c. Select boot disk filesystems.

There is not much that you need to do in this menu unless you wish to configure additional space in any of the displayed filesystems. The root partition looks a bit small, as does /opt. The server being installed in this example will also be used as a mail host for its clients, so an additional /var partition will be configured.

Notice that no filesystems are configured for the diskless client root and swap areas. The install program has already twiddled with the other installed disk, reserving the space it thinks is necessary for those client areas.

d. To check the space requirements.

To determine the minimum amount of disk space necessary, you can move the cursor over the Space selection at the bottom of the screen. The Space Requirements screen is displayed, as shown in Figure 3-28.

```
┌─┐                      Solaris Install
│ ▼ │
│
│    ┌─[ File System Space Requirements ]──────────────────┐
│    │ File System          Minimum    Suggested   Configured        │
│    │ /                     13.56 MB    16.95 MB    21.00 MB         │
│    │ swap                   0.00 MB   127.00 MB   127.00 MB         │
│    │ /var                   3.72 MB     4.65 MB     0.00 MB         │
│    │ /opt                  48.44 MB    60.55 MB    60.00 MB         │
│    │ /usr                  73.78 MB    92.22 MB   219.00 MB         │
│    │ /usr/openwin         101.41 MB   126.76 MB     0.00 MB         │
│    │ /export                0.00 MB     0.00 MB   120.00 MB         │
│    │ /export/swap         138.00 MB   172.50 MB     0.00 MB         │
│    │ /export/exec           1.22 MB     1.53 MB     0.00 MB         │
│    │ /export/root          94.89 MB   118.61 MB     0.00 MB         │
│    │ Totals:              475.01 MB   720.76 MB   547.00 MB         │
│    └──────────────────────────────────────────────────┘
│         ( Dismiss )              ( Help... )
```

Figure 3-28   Current Disk Space Requirements

The /var partition is mentioned here but not in the previous screen. Also notice that the /usr and /usr/openwin filesystems are displayed separately in minimum and suggested columns, but are totalled together under the /usr configured requirements. The OpenWindows packages will be installed under /usr unless specifically configured otherwise.

Also notice the minimum required space for the /export filesystem. The current configuration is reserving 120 megabytes for /export. This space is not necessary and can be used instead as additional home directory or application space. To apply this space elsewhere follow the next step, after dismissing the current screen.

e. To change the boot disk filesystems.
Change the mount point column from /export to /apps, as shown in Figure 3-29. A proper use of all disk resources should result in 0 MB's of Unallocated Space, also shown in Figure 3-29. After the root disk has been configured, configure the second disk as the diskless client area.

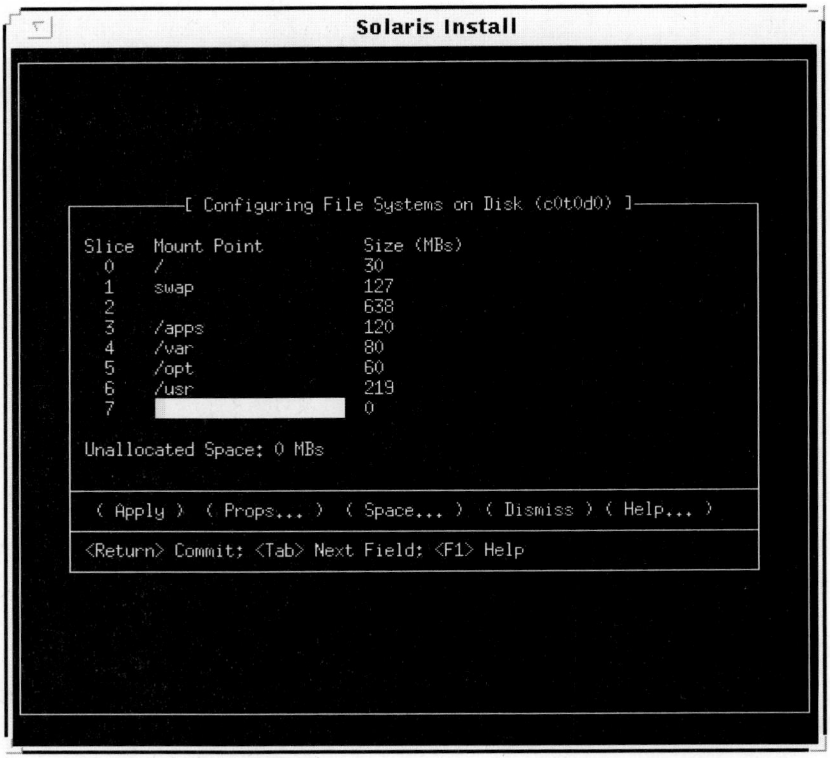

```
┌─────┐                    Solaris Install
│  ⌐  │
│
│
│
│
│                ─[ Configuring File Systems on Disk (c0t0d0) ]─────────
│               │
│               │  Slice  Mount Point        Size (MBs)
│               │    0    /                   30
│               │    1    swap                127
│               │    2                        638
│               │    3    /apps               120
│               │    4    /var                80
│               │    5    /opt                60
│               │    6    /usr                219
│               │    7    ▓▓▓▓▓▓▓▓▓▓▓▓▓▓       0
│               │
│               │  Unallocated Space: 0 MBs
│               │
│               │ ──────────────────────────────────────────────────────
│               │  ( Apply )  ( Props... )  ( Space... )  ( Dismiss ) ( Help... )
│               │ ──────────────────────────────────────────────────────
│               │  <Return> Commit; <Tab> Next Field; <F1> Help
│                └─────────────────────────────────────────────────────
│
│
│
└──────────────────────────────────────────────────────────────────────
```

Figure 3-29 Updated Boot Disk Configuration

f. Confirm the root disk layout.

To confirm the current layout, move the cursor over the Apply selection and press RETURN.

g. Configure the second disk.

Select the second disk using the down arrow key, and press RETURN on the Configure Disk pop-up menu choice. The disk properties screen is skipped this time because it was set once. Instead the Configuring File Systems screen appears for the selected disk, as shown in Figure 3-30.

```
 ┌─┐                    Solaris Install
 │ ⬎ │
```

```
        ┌─[ Configuring File Systems on Disk (c0t1d0) ]─┐
        │  Slice   Mount Point        Size (MBs)        │
        │    0    ████████████████    0                 │
        │    1                        0                 │
        │    2                        1304              │
        │    3    /export             120               │
        │    4    /export/swap        150               │
        │    5                        0                 │
        │    6                        0                 │
        │    7                        0                 │
        │                                               │
        │  Unallocated Space: 1034 MBs                  │
        │                                               │
        │  < Apply >  < Props... >  < Space... >  < Dismiss > < Help... > │
        │  <Return> Commit; <Tab> Next Field; <F1> Help │
        └───────────────────────────────────────────────┘
```

Figure 3-30   Editing the Server's Second Disk

On the second disk, only two partitions are configured, /export and /export/swap. It is interesting to note that when the /export filesystem was removed from the previous disk, it was actually moved to this disk. Unless a separate /export/root filesystem is designated, the install program will attempt to place both the /export/root and /export/exec directories in a partition called /export.

The current server installation requires more disk space in both the /export/root and /export/swap partitions, which is done as a safeguard to allow for additional diskless systems on this server. A large amount of disk space is left. We will increase /export and /export/swap.

In addition to increasing the size of the client's root and swap areas, we will create two home directory partitions, /export/home1 and /export/home2.

To edit the second disk parameters, use the TAB key to move around the screen, highlighting the area that you wish to edit. Enter the mount point and size for the partitions you desire, commit the current table as before by highlighting the Apply selection. Figure 3-31 shows the edited second disk screen.

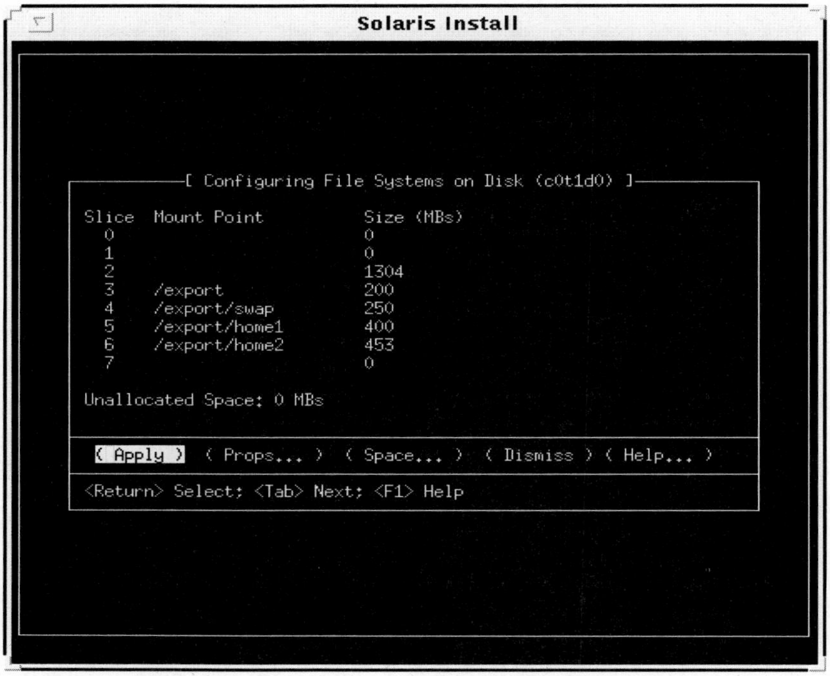

```
┌─────────────────────────────────────────────────────────────┐
│▽│                    Solaris Install                         │
│─────────────────────────────────────────────────────────────│
│                                                               │
│                                                               │
│                                                               │
│          ┌──[ Configuring File Systems on Disk (c0t1d0) ]──┐  │
│          │                                                  │  │
│          │ Slice  Mount Point        Size (MBs)             │  │
│          │   0                        0                      │  │
│          │   1                        0                      │  │
│          │   2                        1304                   │  │
│          │   3    /export             200                    │  │
│          │   4    /export/swap        250                    │  │
│          │   5    /export/home1       400                    │  │
│          │   6    /export/home2       453                    │  │
│          │   7                        0                      │  │
│          │                                                   │  │
│          │ Unallocated Space: 0 MBs                          │  │
│          │                                                   │  │
│          │──────────────────────────────────────────────────│  │
│          │ ( Apply )  ( Props... )  ( Space... )  ( Dismiss ) ( Help... ) │
│          │──────────────────────────────────────────────────│  │
│          │ <Return> Select; <Tab> Next; <F1> Help            │  │
│          └──────────────────────────────────────────────────┘  │
│                                                               │
│                                                               │
│                                                               │
└─────────────────────────────────────────────────────────────┘
```

Figure 3-31   Updated Second Disk Screen

6. Accept the disks' configuration.

Once you have committed both disks, the Local Disks & File Systems screen is displayed. The Status field after each disk shows the filesystems currently configured on that disk. If acceptable, move the cursor over Done and press RETURN. The topmost Custom Install Configuration Menu, Figure 3-32, is displayed.

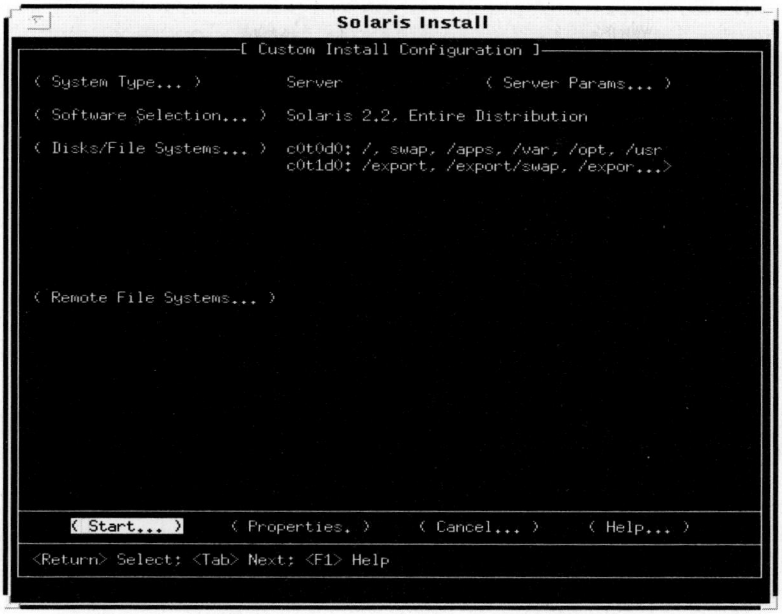

Figure 3-32   Starting the Server Installation

7. Define remote filesystems.

Notice the Remote File Systems selection in the middle of the figure. Use this selection to configure existing NFS mounts to the system being installed. Remote filesystem mounts configured under this option will affect the server only, not any of the diskless machines. Usually, server systems do not NFS-mount resources over the network.

8. Start the server installation.

To begin the server installation, place the cursor over Start and press RETURN. You are immediately prompted for confirmation. To confirm, highlight Yes, and start the installation by pressing the TAB key one last time, and then press RETURN.

The system starts creating filesystems and soon displays a new screen that monitors the progress of the installation. Also, a console window that captures any system messages during the install is displayed.

When the installation is complete, diskless and dataless clients can be added to the server by means of the Administration Tool or the screen-based `ttyhstmgr`. Details for accomplishing such feats are discussed in Chapter 4, Admintool.

After Installation

The steps performed on a Solaris 2.x machine after installation depend on the system type. Standalone workstations tend to require administrative tasks that enable remote mounting of shared network resources. Server systems must have shared applications installed and must make those resources available to other machines on the network. Other server types, such as the NIS+ root server, need to generate name service maps before they can be used throughout the NIS+ domain.

In addition to the network functions and file sharing, several tunable system parameters can be changed to gain the best performance for a particular machine type. Many of these parameters were once hard-coded into objects that were linked into the Solaris 1.x kernel. In the Solaris 2.x model, changing system parameters is accomplished by editing the /etc/system file and rebooting.

Root Password

Newly installed systems prompt for a root password upon the first boot. You may choose not to enter a root password at this time by pressing RETURN twice upon encountering the root password screen, shown in Figure 3-33. This action places no root password on the system, which is a security risk.

What is your root password?

A root password may contain any number of characters, but only the first eight characters in the password are significant. For example, if you enter `a1b2c3d4e5f6' as your root password, then `a1b2c3d4' could also be used to gain root access. If you do not want a root password, press RETURN.

You will be asked to type the root password twice. (It will not appear on the screen as you type it.)

If you have questions consult your Install documentation.

Root password: <RETURN>

Press Return to continue.

Please re-enter your root password. <RETURN>

Press Return to continue.

Figure 3-33 The Root Password Screen

Automounter Files

The files that enable the automounter, `/etc/auto_master` and `/etc/auto_home`, contain entries that start the automounter and cover the `/home` and `/net` directories on every new Solaris 2.x installed system. The contents of these files explain the action taken by the automounter.

```
# cat  /etc/auto_master
# Master map for automounter
#
+auto_master
/net            -hosts          -nosuid
/home           auto_home
```

Figure 3-34 The `/etc/auto_master` File

The first uncommented line in Figure 3-34 instructs the automounter to check with the name service map called `auto_master`. If the map does not exist, then nothing happens. If there is a map with this name, its contents will be honored before any local files are used. Solaris 1.x releases used a similar naming scheme for this action in the `/etc/auto.master` file and `auto.master` map. To check if an `auto.master` map already exists in the NIS domain, use the command below.

```
% ypcat -k auto.master
no such map in server's domain
```

If the system responds as shown above, then no map exists in the current domain. If the system returns entries that are similar to the contents of the `/etc/auto_master` file, then those entries can be used by changing the name of the name service line in the local `/etc/auto_master` file to **+auto.master**.

Diskless or Dataless Client Support

The Solaris 2.2 install process does not create diskless clients on server systems, as was done in Solaris 1.x. Instead, you must add each client manually by using the GUI-based `admintool` or the screen-based `ttyhstmgr`. Either way is a means to the same end. The procedure for adding diskless clients is shown in the Chapter 4, Admintool.

Admintool 4 ≡

Administering a large network installation can be very difficult. Early networking schemes depended on convoluted mechanisms to share information among servers. As networks grew larger, it became obvious that some sort of service would need to be created to allow for the sharing of network data. The Network Information Service (NIS) was created to help with this task. Instead of using scripts to duplicate the data on all hosts, the administrator can make changes with shell commands and visual editors to files stored on one server, then propagate name service changes throughout the network from this location. In addition, this service allowed for data to be stored on selected servers for client lookup, instead of copying it to every host. Unfortunately, in large domains, the propagation step could take so long that special schedules and procedures needed to be established so that the information could stay in sync.

The NIS+ naming service has improvements that cut down on the amount of time tied up in the data propagation. Fewer servers are needed to support the name service and, most importantly, only the changes are sent out, instead of resending all the data.

Even with these naming services to help with the load, a certain amount of information always must be stored locally, so some procedures still require manual editing of local configuration files. The Administration Tool, or `admintool`, allows most of the manual processes to be handled in a GUI. This means that an administrator will not have to remember long and convoluted commands or cryptic table formats in order to complete local tasks.

There will always be times when manual intervention is necessary, so the first part of this chapter presents background information and the manual processes required to administer terminals, modems, and printers. The second part of the chapter details the specifics of using `admintool`.

The Manual Process

This section covers the Service Access Facility (SAF) and the LP subsystem. The last part includes the commands necessary to initialize a printer manually. Some familiarity with the manual process is necessary, but most administrators will use admintool to manage most of these systems.

Service Access Facility (SAF)

The Service Access Facility provides a new set of software programs that help manage printers, modems, and terminals. Most tty devices can be administered with this package. These devices are better administered with admintool, but line-by-line instructions are included to provide an in-depth picture of admintool functions.

Two primary commands are associated with SAF: sacadm and pmadm.

sacadm adds, removes, and monitors the status of port monitors. This is the upper level of SAF administration. Port monitors are daemons that allow access to tty devices. Two port monitors, ttymon and listen, are included with the generic system. ttymon is a STREAMS-based TTY port monitor that can be used to set baud rates and other important characteristics for tty devices. listen is the network listener daemon; it "listens" for service requests from the network and starts up services in response to those requests.

pmadm adds a service, removes it, or associates it with a particular port. This is the lower level of the SAF package. Each port can only have one service associated with it, but one service can be running on many ports.

The service access controller, sac, is the process that usually starts these two processes. When a system enters multiuser mode, the inittab file starts sac after the rc* scripts are run.

Many files are checked for configuration information once sac has been started. The first file is /etc/saf/_sysconfig, the system configuration script. Any configuration changes made in this file are passed down to all of the port monitors and services. By default this file is empty.

The next file that is checked is /etc/saf/_sactab. The syntax of each entry is

pmname:pmtype:flags:retrys:command

where *pmname* is the name of the port monitor, *pmtype* is the type of port monitor (usually listen or ttymon), *flags* lists flags for the port monitor, *retrys* is the number of times the monitor can fail before being placed in a failed state, and *command* is the command line that starts the port monitor.

The port monitor for ttya and ttyb on most systems is started by this line:

```
zsmon:ttymon::0:/usr/lib/saf/ttymon         #
```

Each port monitor may have an /etc/saf/*pmname*/_config file, which is the
configuration script for the port monitor, *pmname*. Several port monitors do not have an
/etc/saf/*pmname*/_config file associated with them, but each port that is to be
associated with a port monitor should have an entry in the appropriate
/etc/saf/*pmname*/_pmtab file. For the example above, in /etc/saf/zsmon/_pmtab
are:

```
ttya:u:root:reserved:reserved:reserved:/dev/term/a:I:\
:/usr/bin/login::9600:ldterm,ttcompat:ttya login\: ::tvi925:y:#
ttyb:u:root:reserved:reserved:reserved:/dev/term/b:I:\
:/usr/bin/login::9600:ldterm,ttcompat:ttyb login\: ::tvi925:y:#
```

These lines define the characteristics for the ttya and ttyb ports. The actual syntax of the
entries can be significantly different for each port monitor, so it is best to check the
specific port monitor documentation to understand the syntax. The */_pmtab files are
best administered by using the appropriate port monitor administrative command,
ttyadm for ttymon and nlsadmin for listen. Each port monitor is required to have an
administrative command.

sac is started with a -t flag, which sets the frequency with which the port monitors are
polled. The frequency is measured in seconds, so the default setting of -t 300 polls every
5 minutes. Messages from sac are stored in /var/saf/_log. In most cases, entries are
added to this file during booting. A port monitor can be in any of the states listed in
Table 4-1.

Table 4-1   States for Port Monitors

State	Meaning
enabled	Running and accepting connections.
disabled	Running but not accepting connections; can be used to leave a message to port users rather than shutting down the whole thing.
starting	In process of starting.
failed	Unable to start and/or remain running.
stopped	Has been manually terminated.
notrunning	Port monitor is not running.

Port Monitor Administration

The sacadm command administers port monitors (see sacadm(1m)). This use includes enabling, disabling, starting, and stopping the port monitors. The scripts, /etc/saf/pmtag/_config and /etc/saf/_sysconfig, used to configure the port monitors, can also be administered through this command. Status requests of the port monitors and requests to print the configuration scripts can be made by any user, but the administration commands must be run by root. The options for this command are listed in Table 4-2.

Table 4-2   Options for sacadm

Option	Meaning
-a	Add a port monitor; requires -p, -t, -c, and -v options.
-c *string*	Execute the command string to start a port monitor; use with the -a option.
-d *pmtag*	Disable the port monitor named *pmtag*.
-e *pmtag*	Enable the port monitor named *pmtag*.
-f *dx*	Specify flags to be included in the _sactab entry for a new port monitor; d = do not enable, f = do not start.
-g	Print out, install, or replace the per-port monitor script; requires the -p option to specify a port monitor.
-G	Print out, install, or replace the per-system configuration script.
-k *pmtag*	Stop the port monitor named *pmtag*.
-l	Print out information about the port monitors; use -p to specify a port monitor.
-L	Same as -l, but in a condensed form using ":" as the field separator.
-n *count*	Set the restart count to *count*; if set to 0, the port monitor will not restart if it fails.
-p *pmtag*	Select a specific port monitor named *pmtag*.
-r *pmtag*	Remove the port monitor named *pmtag*; shut down running port monitors.
-s *pmtag*	Start the port monitor named *pmtag*.
-t *type*	Specify a port monitor *type*.
-v *ver*	Specify the version number of a port monitor.
-x	Read the database file (_sactab) or the administrative file for a port monitor.
-y *comment*	Include this command in the _sactab entry for the port monitor; use with -p.
-z *script*	Specify the name of a file that contains a configuration script; use with -g or -G.

Adding a port monitor by using this command can be done, but in most cases it is easier to use admintool to complete this function. The sacadm command is most useful for obtaining information and administering port monitors on the spot.

Tty ports can be monitored with ttymon, usually run with sac. ttymon. It sets terminal baud rates and connects users or programs to the appropriate, required services. This monitor runs constantly on any Sun workstation with hardware ports for ttya and ttyb.

The ttyadm command is used with pmadm or sacadm to send specific administrative commands to ttymon. It allows bidirectional communications to be set, as well as providing other options necessary to set up a tty device, such as a modem or printer.

Requests for a service made over the network are monitored by listen. For instance, a system with an attached printer would normally have this monitor running to handle remote requests. The nlsadmin command is used with pmadm or sacadm to send specific administrative commands to the network port monitor. It can also provide reporting for any listener processes running on a system, if invoked with the -x option.

Service Administration

Administration of the services attached to each port is accomplished by using pmadm. It provides for the addition, removal, enabling, or disabling of either all ports associated with a service or only one service on one port. Like sacadm, it allows for reporting and for administration of the per-service configuration scripts. Many of the options that may be used with this command are identical to the options for sacadm. Table 4-3 lists those options that are different.

Table 4-3   Options for pmadm

Option	Meaning
-f xu	Specify flags to be included in the port monitor administrative file; u = do not enable, x = do not start.
-i id	Specify the identity for a particular service, which must be in the passwd file.
-s svctag	Specify the service tag; use with -p for one service on one port.

LP Subsystem

The change in the printing subsystem is the most visible change for most users involved in the transition from older versions of the operating system. The way that a remote print job is handled and monitored is significantly different.

One of the first changes is that there is no longer a /etc/printcap file to help with the printer setup. This information is now stored in /etc/lp. Table 4-4 identifies the major parts of this directory. Many of these files and directories are consulted when a printer is configured.

Table 4-4 `/etc/lp` *Filesystem*

Name	Function
Systems	Defines remote systems that the local system can print to.
alerts	Directory of files to consult in response to alerts.
classes	Directory of printer classes.
default	Lists the local system default printer.
fd	Directory of filters for the printers.
forms	Directory of forms for the printers.
interfaces	Directory of interface program files for local printers.
logs	Links to `/var/lp/logs` and contains some of the logged information.
model	Contains the standard printer interface program printers; one directory is created for each printer; this is linked to `/usr/lib/lp/model`.
printers	Directory listing all known printers, including both local and remote.
pwheels	Print wheel or cartridge files.

LP Commands

A significant change for most users is that the `lpstat` command only lists activity on the local system. Users can still use the `cancel` and `lp` commands to access remote printers, but they will only be able to tell that the job was queued on the local system. Table 4-5 lists the common commands that most users will need to know.

Table 4-5 *User-level* `lp` *Commands*

Name	Function	
lp	Equivalent to `lpr`.	
	`-c`	makes copy
	`-d` *dest*	where *dest* specifies printer to do the printing
	`-H`	immediate, that is, prints this request next
	`-m`	sends mail after the files have been printed
	`-n`	specifies number of copies
	`-q`	sets priority level from 0 (high) to 39 (low)
	`-w`	writes a message on the user's terminal
cancel	Cancels `lp` request; can cancel by job, printer, or user.	
lpstat	Gets status from local system.	

As with earlier versions of the printing software, the System Administrator can still make several status changes to the printer, but these are now commands rather than options. For instance, a printer can be enabled so that the queue is cleared at the same time as it is rejecting new queuing requests—a good way to clean out a full queue or disk partition. Table 4-6 lists the commands that most System Administrators should be familiar with.

Table 4-6   LP Administrator Commands

Name	Function
accept	Allows queuing.
reject	Prevents queuing; -r gives reason for rejection.
enable	Allows printing if local; allows transfer if remote.
disable	Deactivates printing or transmission; -W waits until current job is done.
lpsched	Starts the print service; done through rc scripts during boot.
lpshut	Shuts down the print service, interrupting current jobs.
lpmove	Moves requests between LP destinations or moves all requests to *dest2* and rejects any new requests for *dest1*.
lpadmin	Configures the LP print service.
lpsystem	Defines remote systems with the print service; listed in /etc/lp/Systems.
lpusers	Sets printing queue priorities. -d sets system-wide priority -q sets highest priority level for all users not explicitly added -u removes any explicit priority level -l lists current priority levels assigned to users
lpfilter	Administers filters.
lpforms	Administers forms.

The lpmove command is a nice addition to this service, because it lets the System Administrator move whole queues from one printer to another without having to do many manual tasks. This is invaluable for helping to keep things in order when a printer needs to be taken off-line for an extended amount of time.

Note – lp does not make a copy of the file but creates links to the file, so the file that you are trying to print should be quiescent until it has completed printing. The command has a -c option, which creates a copy instead of relying on links. This is more like the way lpr behaved in previous versions.

Normally, a printer should be started with admintool, as described in the next section. The steps included below show the commands that must be entered to start up a printer on ttyb.

1. Set up the printer port.

```
# chown lp /dev/term/b
# chmod 666 /dev/term/b
```

2. Set up printer files.

```
# lpadmin -p <name> -v /dev/term/b -T <type> -I <input-file-type>
# cd /usr/lp/fd
# sh
# for f in `ls | sed `s/.fd$//'`
 > do
 > lpfilter -f $f -F $f.fd
 > done
```

3. Start up the printer.

```
# accept <name>
# enable <name>
# lpadmin -p <name> -D <description>
# lpadmin -d <name>
```

The last command sets the default printer for the local system.

4. Start the port monitor.

```
# sacadm -a -p tcp -t listen -c "/usr/lib/sag/listen tcp" -v `nlsadmin -V`\
  -n 9999
# lpsystem -A
  00020203c091c8010000000000000000
```

The result of the `lpsystem` command is the TCP/IP address for the server and is used to define the port monitor. Make sure to change this number if you move the system to a different IP address.

```
# pmadm -a -p tcp -s lp -i root -m `nlsadmin -o /var/spool/lp/fifos/listens5`\
    -v `nlsadmin -V`
# pmadm -a -p tcp -s lpd -i root -m `nlsadmin -o /var/spool/lp/fifos/listensBSD`\
 -A `\x00020203c091c8010000000000000000` -v `nlsadmin -V`
# pmadm -a -p tcp -s 0 -i root -m `nlsadmin -o /usr/lib/saf/nlps_server\
 -A `\x000ACE03c091c8010000000000000000` -v `nlsadmin -V`
# pmadm -a -p tcp -s lp -i root -m `nlsadmin -o /var/spool/lp/fifos/listens5`\
 -v `nlsadmin -V`
```

admintool

Many implementations of SVR4 rely on the `sysadm` interface to perform administrative tasks, but objects of that interface are limited to files on the local machine and are, for the most part, network deficient. The `sysadm` interface is not included in the Solaris release. Instead, local and network-wide administration can be accomplished with the GUI-based System Administration Tool, `admintool`.

`admintool` is a distributed application that allows selected users to manipulate files and databases not only on local machines but on remote machines as well. `admintool` can be very beneficial in the Solaris environment. It saves an administrator from logging in to every machine to perform routine tasks and works especially well with the NIS+ naming service structure. A special daemon called `admind` performs administrative tasks on behalf of users that are privileged members of the UNIX group *sysadmin*, GID 14.

Note – If you have already have a UNIX group that occupies GID 14, then consider moving its members to a different group ID number. The `admind` process reserves GID 14 as the *sysadmin* account and cannot be changed.

Manipulation of remote systems cannot be done without the initial creation and addition of members to this group. Users who are added to the *sysadmin* group thereby have permission to change many administrative files on any machine, which is great for administrators who know what they are doing, but can be disastrous when access is given to users who know just enough to wreak havoc. Usually, only system administrators are members of this group.

A logical assumption is that `admintool` is run as the superuser, root. However, `admintool` should only be run as root during the initial setup procedure or when the information to be modified is stored locally. In all other cases, `admintool` is launched by administrators who are logged in as themselves or by specified members of the *sysadmin* group. When done properly and when the group database is known network wide, access to remote machines is accomplished within the tool.

Before `admintool` can be invoked, the following Solaris bundled software packages must be installed both on the machine launching `admintool` and on any remote machine that is to be modified by `admintool`. These packages are automatically included on systems that select the End User Cluster, the Developers Cluster, or the Entire Distribution at installation time. They can also be added after the installation by means of `pkgadd` or the `swmtool`.

- `SUNWadmap` contains the application portion, including the `admintool` itself

- `SUNWadmfw` contains the developer tools for building distributed administrative applications

- `SUNWadmr` contains the required libraries and scripts for `admintool` and related programs to execute

Setting Up the Administration Tool Security

First, determine the users that are to be included in the *sysadmin* group. Use existing user account or login names as they appear in the first field of the `/etc/passwd` file or password database if a naming service is active. There is no need to create a special user account for `admintool` because the `admind` process can alter files that are owned by root.

Create the *sysadmin* group by placing the selected users into the group file or database. In the following example, four administrators are included in the *sysadmin* group; their login accounts are bobn, davep, nathan, and laurab. The *sysadmin* group entry for this imaginary system administration team would be similar to the following line:

```
sysadmin:*:14:bobn,davep,laurab,nathan
```

Setting Up admintool When Using NIS+

To set up the *sysadmin* group in an NIS+ domain, you must manually enter a line similar to the one above into the master root server's group database. You can do this with command-line programs or by using the admintool itself, if launched from the NIS+ root server.

Setting Up admintool When Using NIS

Setting up the *sysadmin* group in an NIS domain is accomplished by adding the group and any members to the NIS master's group data file and rebuilding the map. Even though admintool is specifically targeted to the NIS+ naming service, there are many advantages to setting up this group in an NIS domain. You can still manipulate remote services on system files that are not included in any name service database, such as printers and serial devices, without root access. Do not avoid admintool just because your network is running NIS.

Setting Up admintool for Local Files

To set up admintool security on systems that use local files for network information, you must manually add the *sysadmin* group to each machine's /etc/group file before local entries can be manipulated remotely. Also, edit each machine's /etc/passwd file to include the user accounts of every member of the *sysadmin* group. This procedure in itself may take a while to accomplish and may be another factor in the decision to take the name service plunge.

Detailed instructions for setting up the *sysadmin* group for NIS+, NIS, and /etc files can also be found by pressing the Help button of the admintool base window and then selecting the "How to Set up Administration Tool Security" section within the help viewer.

Starting the Administration Tool

The Administration Tool is launched from the command line of a shelltool or cmdtool from a system that is already running OpenWindows. Remember that admintool is started as an authorized member of the *sysadmin* group, while under the environment of that user.

Figure 4-1 shows the main admintool window, in this case from the Solaris 2.3 release.

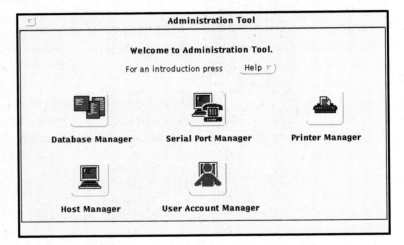

Figure 4-1   The Administration Tool Base Window

Five icons in the admintool base window launch subtools that perform the following functions:

- Database Manager—manages NIS+ databases or local network files
- Serial Port Manager—manages serial login ports, modems, or direct connections
- Printer Manager—sets up and maintains local or remote printing services
- Host Manager—adds or deletes hosts, sets up and maintains diskless, dataless, and installation clients
- User Account Manager—sets up and maintains user accounts

Unlike icons within the workspace of OpenWindows that require double-clicking, icons in the Administration Tool only need to be clicked on once to launch that particular tool. Double-clicking on an admintool icon may cause multiple instances of the same tool, which is allowed but may be confusing.

Many of these tools, such as the Database Manager and Host Manager, perform functions that cross over administrative boundaries. Each tool can update local or remote hosts databases or files. The level of detail for a particular host is greater in the Host Manager than in the Database Manager.

The same idea applies to the User Account Manager and Database Manager. User accounts that are manipulated under the Database Manager require less detail than those created or modified under the User Account Manager, even though they edit the same files.

The Manager functions of `admintool` are discussed in detail in the following sections.

Database Manager

The Database Manager of `admintool` is especially designed for a large network installation that is maintained by a group of system administrators using the NIS+ naming service. This is the ideal arrangement, since changes to NIS+ databases by authorized users of `admintool` are automatically updated on the NIS+ root server and thereby propagated throughout the domain. With this arrangement, it no longer necessary to log in remotely and deal with race conditions between administrators vying for file access on the local NIS master server.

If you currently maintain a large installation under the NIS naming service, then use `admintool` only to set up diskless, dataless, and installation clients on local servers. Network-wide database changes must then be done on the NIS master and propagated throughout the network by means of the NIS `Makefile` and `yppush` commands. There is no real use for the Database Manager in the NIS domain, unless you like to view the contents of NIS databases.

The current implementation of `admintool` does not create credentials for the hosts or the users within the NIS+ namespace. The `nisclient` script must be used to create these to use the full advantages of NIS+. This script is discussed in the NIS+ section of Chapter 6, "Using the Network."

To launch the Database Manager, click once on its icon in the main Administration Tool window. Figure 4-2 displays the results of this action.

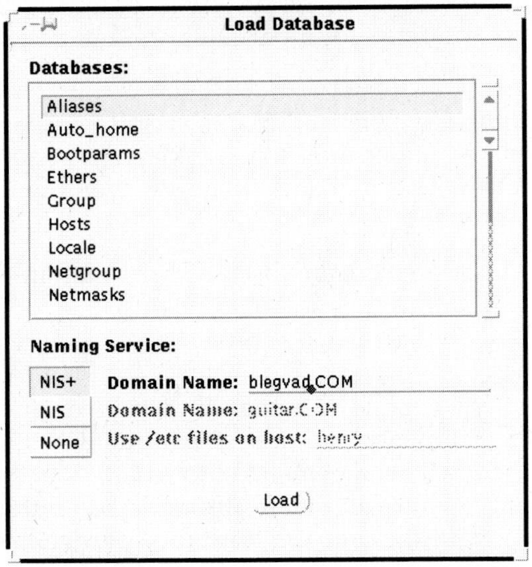

Figure 4-2   Loading a Database with Database Manager

The Database Manager and Local Files

If you are updating the /etc files on a system, click once on None. If the files you wish to edit are on a remote system, enter the remote machine name in the space next to the phrase "Use /etc files on host:." Select the desired database and click on the Load button. After you have loaded a database into the Database Manager, a new window, shown in Figure 4-3, displays a scrolling list of the contents of that database. The main Load Database window is dismissed after a database is loaded, unless you pinned it up by clicking on the pushpin in the upper left corner. To load a different database, bring up a new Load Database window by pulling down the menu under the File button.

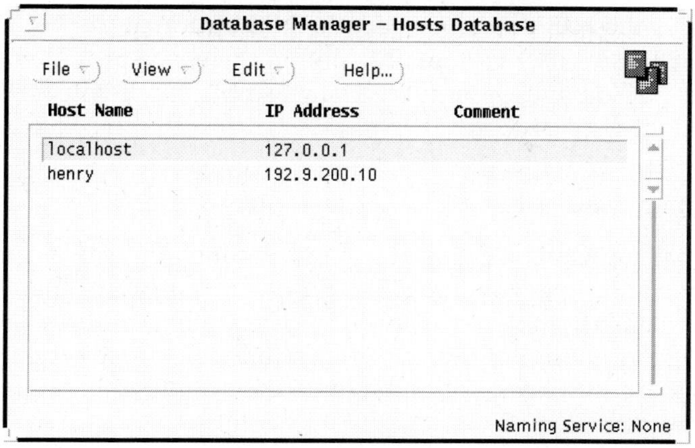

Figure 4-3   The Hosts Database—No Naming Service Selected

Select the desired activity for the loaded database. For instance, to add a single host to the database shown in Figure 4-3, click once on the Edit button and enter the host name, IP address, and any other information desired. The Host Name and IP Address fields must contain valid data, but the Aliases and Comment fields are optional. Figure 4-4 shows the Add Entry pop-up window for adding a single host.

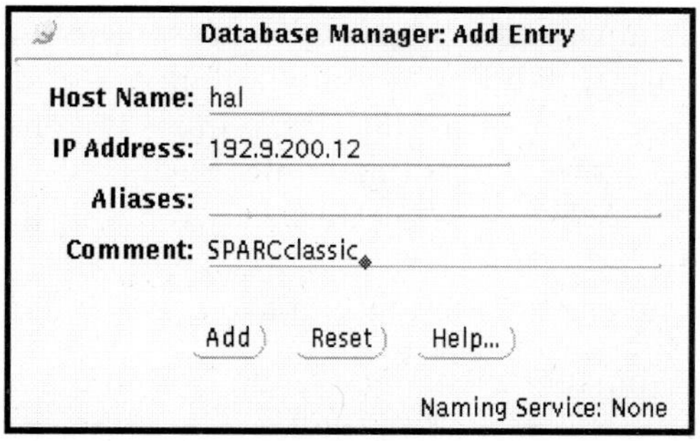

Figure 4-4   Add Entry Pop-up Window for Hosts Database

After the entry has been added, click on the Add button. While the process is running, the Add button is gray and the phrase "Adding to the Database" is displayed in the lower left corner of the Add Entry pop-up window. After a short time, the Database Manager's scrolling list is updated with the new information, and the Add Entry window remains visible but is now devoid of information.

The Database Manager and NIS

If your network uses the NIS domain, select the NIS button at the bottom of the Load Database window and specify the domain name in the space provided. Remember that you cannot change NIS databases with the Database Manager. You can only view the contents of NIS databases.

The Database Manager and NIS+

By default, the Database Manager looks for an NIS+ domain, using the current domain name of the system running `admintool`. To edit one of the NIS+ databases in the current domain, select the database that you want to update in the scrolling list by double-clicking on that entry or by highlighting the entry and clicking on the Load button at the bottom of the Database Manager. You must have the permissions set properly to allow remote access to the name space.

Upon entering the Database Manager, select the NIS+ naming service and proper domain name in the space provided. Select the database to be manipulated and perform the same functions as above. Upon completion, changes made to the particular database are automatically propagated to the root server and then to all other NIS+ replica servers. No other action is necessary.

Serial Port Manager

The Serial Port Manager is new in the Solaris 2.3 release; use it to enable, modify, or delete services on serial ports, including terminal, modems, and high-speed serial network connections. Quite a number of steps are required to enable a login port from the command line of a UNIX System V-based machine. Each of these commands requires arguments that are quite long. This tool is clearly a winner in that regard. Services on serial devices can be easily configured one at a time or in batch mode, something not attainable via command-line arguments without the use of a complex shell script.

To activate the Serial Port Manager, click once on its icon in the main Administration Tool window. Serial devices that are attached to the local system are polled and placed in the resulting Serial Port Manager's scrolling list, as shown in Figure 4-5. To change a serial device connection on a remote machine, enter the hostname of that machine in the Goto field at the top of the tool and press RETURN. If the proper group setting are enabled, the scrolling list displays the serial devices that are attached to that machine.

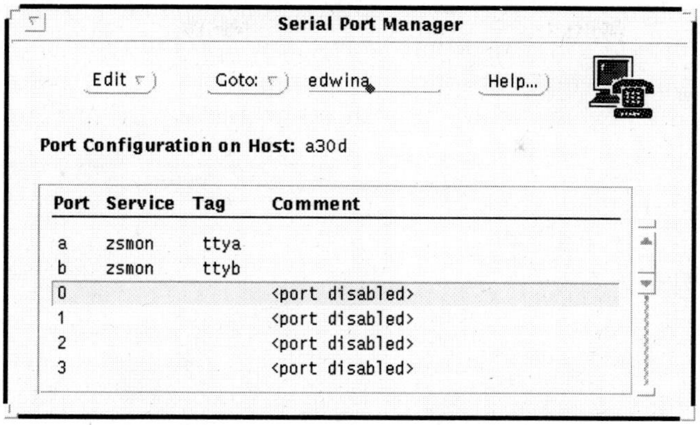

Figure 4-5   The Serial Port Manager

Most systems have at least two serial ports, named A and B, which are built into the main CPU board. Additional serial devices are obtained through add-on option cards such as SBus or VME cards. In the Solaris 2.1 and 2.2 releases, serial option cards were only available as unbundled options. In the Solaris 2.3 and later releases, serial device drivers for SMCC add-on cards are included as part of the base OS and are automatically configured at boot time when attached. In either case, devices should be present in the Serial Port Manager's scrolling list and, if not, you should reboot the system with the reconfigure option after verifying that the hardware is functional.

Configuring a Terminal Port

To configure a single terminal port, select the device from the scrolling list with the SELECT mouse button. When highlighted, click on the Edit button in the top-left corner of the Serial Port Manager tool to obtain the Modify Service window, shown in Figure 4-6.

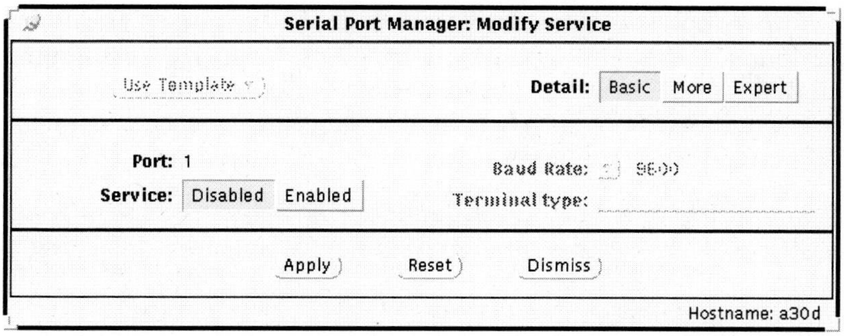

Figure 4-6   The Modify Service Window

Three buttons, labeled Detail:, in the upper right corner of the Modify Service window, enable different levels of detail about the port or ports that are currently selected. By default, the basic amount of information is reported. To obtain the most amount of information during the current session, click on the button labeled Expert. The Modify Service window is then expanded to one similar to that shown in Figure 4-7.

<table>
<tr><td colspan="2" align="center">**Serial Port Manager: Modify Service**</td></tr>
<tr><td>Use Template ▽</td><td>**Detail:** Basic | More | Expert</td></tr>
<tr><td>**Port:** 0
Service: Disabled | Enabled</td><td>**Baud Rate:** ▽ 9600
Terminal type:</td></tr>
<tr><td>**Options:** ⬚ Initialize Only
⬚ Bidirectional
⬚ Software Carrier</td><td>**Login Prompt:** login:▲
Comment: /dev/term/0
Service Tag: 0
Port Monitor Tag: ▽ ttymon0</td></tr>
<tr><td>**Expert Options:** ✔ Create utmp entry
⬚ Connect on Carrier</td><td>**Service:** /usr/bin/login
Streams Modules:
Timeout (secs): ▽ Never</td></tr>
<tr><td colspan="2" align="center">Apply)   Reset)   Dismiss)</td></tr>
<tr><td colspan="2" align="right">Hostname: a30d</td></tr>
</table>

Figure 4-7   The Expert Modify Service Window

Enable the service for the selected port by clicking on the Enable button. The MENU mouse button can be used to pull down the pop-up menu under the Use Template button in the upper left corner of the Modify Service window.

The pop-up window shows the five templates available: Terminal – Hardwired; Modem – Dial-In Only; Modem – Dial-Out Only; Modem – Bidirectional; and Initialize only – no connection. Highlight the hardwired terminal selection in the pop-up window and release the MENU mouse button. Now, select the baud rate of the selected port using a similar pull-down action over the Baud Rate arrow.

Next, enter the terminal type. The /etc/termcap file contains a list of terminal types and characteristics. Nearly every terminal type known to mankind is contained in this file.

The center of the Expert Modify Service window contains other options, such as initialize only, bidirectional, and software carrier buttons. You can enable a custom login prompt for this device by editing the Login Prompt field. You can also place a description such as physical location into the comment field. You can change the Service Tag or the Port Monitor Tag, used as arguments to sacadm and pmadm.

The bottom portion of the Expert Modify Service window contains the expert Options; you can modify such things as the service to be activated, additional streams modules to use, and initialize a time-out period on the port to automatically close the connection.

After you have modified any of the basic or expert options, many of which need not be touched for standard serial ports, press the Apply button at the bottom of the window. This action begins the actual port initialization and may take a minute or so to complete.

Select the modem template to initialize single or bidirectional modem. The procedure is similar to that for a hardwired port.

Printer Manager

Use the Printer Manager to install local or remote printing capabilities for one or many machines. Several common printer types are available from which to choose. The Printer Manager probably provides the easiest way to set up local and remote printing capabilities on a Solaris system, as the command-line alternatives can be quite cumbersome.

Administrators who belong to the *sysadmin* group can add, modify, or remove print services for any Solaris machine on the network that knows about that group. As with remote manipulation of serial devices, the Printer Manager is not dependent on a name service database and can, therefore, be used to modify machines remotely.

Adding a Printer with admintool

To launch the Printer Manager, position the cursor over the Printer Manager icon in the main admintool window and click the SELECT mouse button. After a short period, the Printer Manager base window is displayed. Figure 4-8 shows a Printer Manager base window and also shows the pull-down menus under the Edit button. To manipulate print services on a remote machine, enter the remote machine name in the Goto field at the top-center of the window and click on Goto.

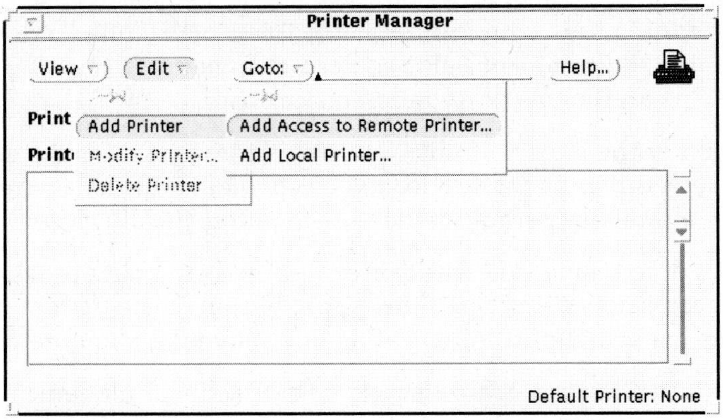

Figure 4-8   The Printer Manager Tool

Remote print services are enabled by placing the cursor over the Edit button and pressing the SELECT mouse button. A new window, shown in Figure 4-9, lets you enter specific information such as the name of the printer, the server to which it is attached, and any other comments, such as physical location, that you would like to associate with this printer. The Print Server OS button defaults to BSD, which means that the remote printer is attached to a system that uses the lpr print spooler. Select the System V button if the remote print server is a System V-based system that uses the lp printer subsystem.

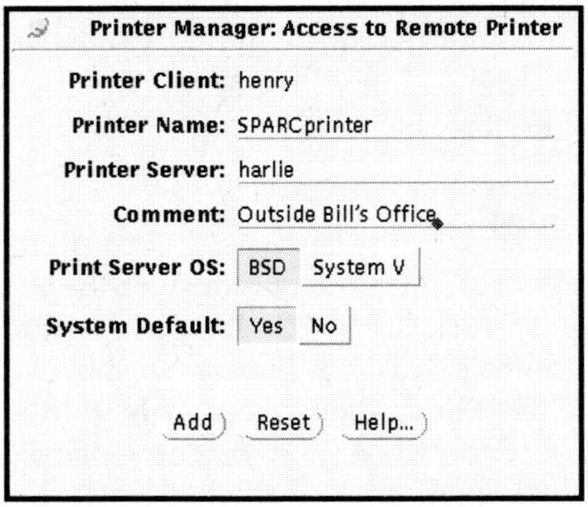

Figure 4-9   Enabling Access to a Remote Printer

After you provide the detailed information, move the mouse cursor over the Add button of this tool and press the SELECT mouse button. When the process is complete, the Access to Remote Printer window remains open, but contains blank entries. Printer Manager tool should contain an entry in its scrolling list for the printer just added.

Host Manager

Use the Host Manager to add, delete, or modify standalone, diskless, dataless, and installation clients on the network. Realistically, the Host Manager is one of the many ways to edit the local /etc/hosts file or NIS+ database. If you are simply adding standalone systems to the network, an easier method is to use the Database Manager, since it requires less detailed information than the Host Manager while editing the same object. If you are adding or removing diskless, dataless, or installation clients on a network, then the Host Manager is the preferred tool. The only other way of adding these machine types is to use ttyhstmgr, a tty-based tool that runs in a shelltool or cmdtool. There is no command-line interface to add or remove diskless clients in the Solaris 2.x software as there was in previous versions of SunOS and Solaris 1.x software.

Dataless clients are systems that use some combination of a local disk and NFS server to obtain base operating system functionality. Dataless systems can be configured to get the root, swap, and /usr partitions locally, but they mount mail and perhaps a home directory from a local server. Many variations are possible, depending on the needs of the user and resources that are available. Diskless clients are systems that rely entirely on a server for booting and running the Solaris environment.

Launching the Host Manager

Launch the Host Manager by clicking on its icon in the main admintool window. The Host Manager:Select Naming Service window, shown in Figure 4-10, is displayed. What you select at this point depends on the action you are about to perform, the size of your hosts database, and whether the naming service will be updated. If you have a domain with a large hosts database, then you may wish to accelerate entry into the Host Manager by pulling down on the Show button and selecting the option to show one host or no hosts. Otherwise, the Host Manager places all known hosts in the database into the scrolling list, possibly taking several minutes to complete.

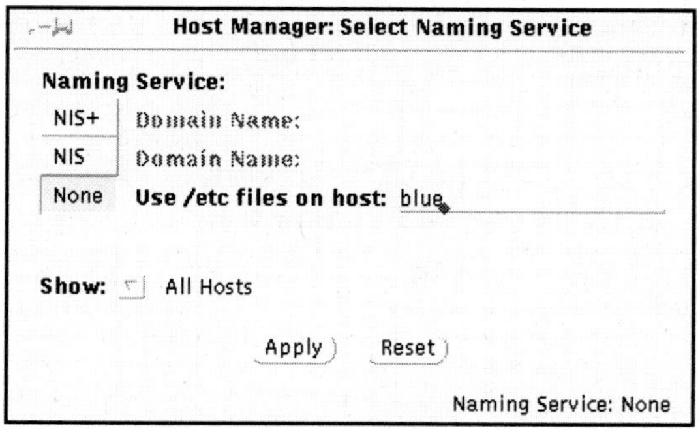

Figure 4-10 Host Manager: Select Naming Service Pop-up Window

NIS+

Choose NIS+ if the NIS+ naming service is currently running and you want to update the NIS+ hosts database. The Domain Name entry should contain the current domain name. If not, you can change it by typing over current entry in the space provided.

NIS

The Host Manager and the NIS naming service are rarely used together. You cannot update any NIS name service databases with the Host Manager, so do not select this combination. Even if NIS is selected, any attempt to add or remove systems with the Host Manager will be denied. A pop-up message informs you of the problem; click on the pop-up's OK button to return to the Host Manager main window.

None

When you select None, or no naming service, you are choosing to edit only the /etc files on the machine that is specified in the field following this choice. When the Host Manager is first launched, the default host is the machine name that is running the Host Manager. To edit the /etc files on a system other than those of the default host, enter that system's hostname in the space provided. As with all remote manipulation by admintool, the remote host must be running the Solaris 2.x release, have the proper administrative packages installed, and know which users are members of the *sysadmin* group. If these requirements are met, you can make changes to remote systems, but you must make the change on one system at a time.

User Account Manager

Use the User Account Manager to accomplish almost any task having to do with user accounts. When used with a naming service, user accounts can be created on remote machines anywhere on the network. When used with the local files, home directories are placed on the local machine and the user account files, /etc/passwd and /etc/shadow, are updated appropriately.

As with other Administration Tools, the User Account Manager works best in a distributed environment in which the NIS+ naming service is active. The User Account Manager does not offer any advantages in the NIS realm, but can be used to obtain and view information about accounts that are in the NIS passwd databases. Much of the User Account Manager's information is obtained in the /etc/shadow file, not available in the NIS realm.

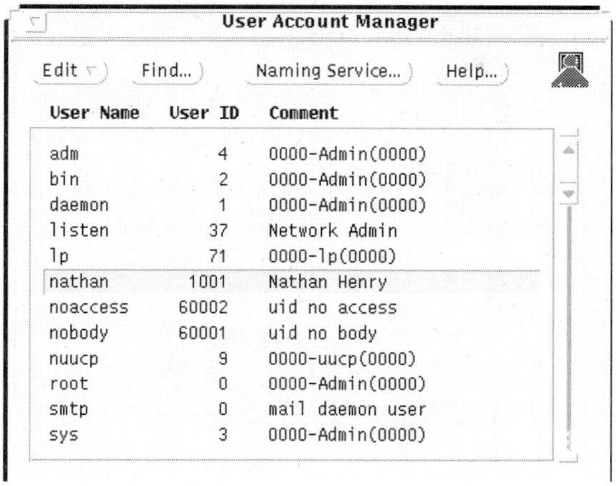

Figure 4-11   The User Account Manager

Launch the User Account Manager by clicking once on the SELECT mouse button while the cursor is over the User Account Manager icon in the main admintool window. As with other tools launched from admintool, a pop-up window requires that you enter the name service selection, one of NIS+, NIS, or local files on a certain host.

To view a user account from the User Account Manager, locate the user name in the scrolling list; either double-click on that user or highlight the entry, and use the pull-down menu under the Edit button, as shown in Figure 4-11.

When the user account is selected, a larger, more detailed window is displayed, from which you can set many parameters, as shown in Figure 4-12.

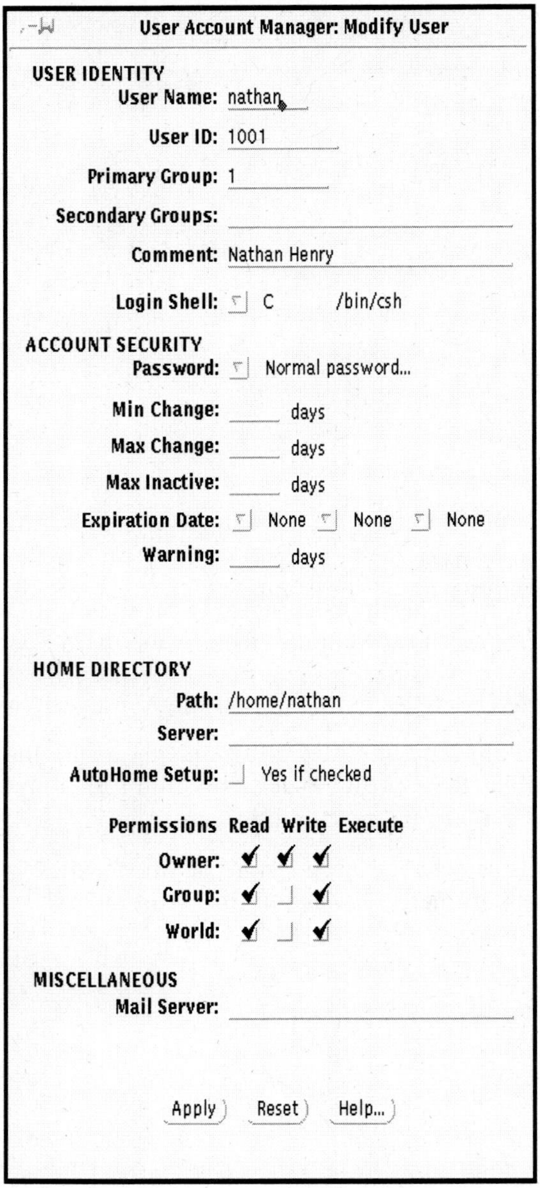

```
 ,-⊌           User Account Manager: Modify User

USER IDENTITY
           User Name: nathan

             User ID: 1001

       Primary Group: 1

     Secondary Groups:

            Comment: Nathan Henry

         Login Shell: ▽  C        /bin/csh

ACCOUNT SECURITY
            Password: ▽  Normal password...

          Min Change: _____ days

          Max Change: _____ days

         Max Inactive: _____ days

      Expiration Date: ▽  None ▽  None ▽  None

            Warning: _____ days




HOME DIRECTORY
                Path: /home/nathan

              Server:

      AutoHome Setup: ⌐  Yes if checked


        Permissions  Read  Write  Execute
              Owner:  ✔   ✔    ✔

              Group:  ✔   ⌐    ✔

              World:  ✔   ⌐    ✔

MISCELLANEOUS
          Mail Server:




            Apply )   Reset )   Help... )
```

Figure 4-12 *The Modify User Window*

The fields in the Modify User window can be divided into four sections:

- User identity — those things that identify the user: the login or user name; the user identification number, commonly known as the UID; the primary group to which the user belongs; the comment field, which will be placed in email message headers; and the base login shell that the user uses upon successful login.

- Account security — security information: password status, which indicates the login access of the account (normal account with password or a locked account); min change, which lists the minimum number of days required between password changes; max change, which lists the maximum number of days before a password must be changed; max inactive, which lists the number of days an account may be unused; expiration date, which displays the number of days left until the account expires; and warning, which lists the number of days at which to start warning the user about an expiring password.

- Home directory — the location of a home directory whether local or remote, automounted or not, and the permissions that apply to that home directory.

- Miscellaneous — for example, you can designate an email server if spooling is not accomplished on the local machine. If spooling is local, no action is necessary.

The Solaris 2.x release provides more control over user accounts than do previous versions of SunOS and Solaris 1.x software. Password aging and account expiration are among the new features that may be of great assistance to your particular site. Because these features are new, they cannot be applied to NIS domains. Password aging and the like are controlled by the /etc/shadow file, not resident in the Solaris 1.x release. If you want to use these features, you must use local files of a Solaris 2.x machine. Password aging is not yet functional under NIS+.

Another useful feature of the User Account Manager is the Copy User function. Use this when you are creating new accounts that are similar to one that currently exists. While it is not difficult to edit fields within the Modify User window, reducing the amount of typing can be helpful, especially when many accounts need to be added at a single sitting. You might even like to create a template user account to use as a starting point. If you decide to do this, be sure that you lock it down so that unauthorized entry is avoided.

The Copy User function can be found under the Edit button on the main User Account Manager window. Use the pull-down technique to summon the pop-up menu under the Edit button. Be sure you have highlighted the correct source account to be copied.

Administration Tool Summary

The Solaris `admintool` can be of great assistance in both large and small networked environments. It is a good step in the right direction, allowing both local and remote administrative tasks to be completed from a single instance of the tool. Many UNIX purists argue that GUI-based tools are for wimps and that command-line programs are the way to go, but some of these commands are more than even the purists want to handle.

Boot and Shutdown Files 5 ≡

This chapter discusses some of the files and their contents that changed between the SunOS 4.1 and the Solaris 5.x operating systems. Most of the files that are discussed control the booting process and are key to understanding the system software.

rc Scripts and inittab

In the older versions of the SunOS operating system, most of the processing that occurred after the kernel was loaded was started by scripts called /etc/rc*. These scripts did the single-user setup and established all networking and any other connections that were necessary for operation. The Solaris 2.x environment uses the same sort of idea, but several directories contain scripts that can either start or stop a process or a selected group of processes. Also, one file initiates all the processes after booting the system or changing the *run state*. The term "run state" is new in Solaris 2.0 release, but is only an expansion of the multiuser and single-user levels that the systems were booted into under earlier versions.

The following run states are part of the default installation:

level 0	power down
level 1	single user
level 2	multiuser – no networking
level 3	multiuser with networking
level 4	unused
level 5	interactive reboot (boot –a)
level 6	reboot
level s	single user startup only

The only new run states are level 2 and the system-administrator-definable level 4. An example showing the use of level 4 is described after the discussion of the `rc` scripts and `/etc/inittab`.

The advantage to the new run states is that the processing of a system can be altered by changing `init` states (also called *run levels*). You can change from normal multiuser to single user and back again without having to go through the shutdown process. The `init` command has been altered under Solaris 5.0 and later versions of the operating system (see `init(1M)`). Many of the scripts in the new structure include the commands to start processes and to kill them, so depending how you call them, you can make changes to the state of your system beyond boot, boot to single user, and shutdown.

rc Scripts

The `rc` directory structure is one of the enhancements to the new operating system. As the manager of a system, you can add scripts to start and stop many processes, controlling both the initiation and the termination of these processes. In the SunOS 4.x environment, you could have created a special script to shut down any special processes, but there was no standard way to easily stop or start a single process.

Now, when the server is shut down, databases and other critical functions can be terminated in a controlled fashion before the server software is terminated. Of course, under crash conditions this controlled termination won't help much, but will save lengthy processes that must be run manually before the server is shut down.

A generic system has a directory called `/etc/init.d`, which contains the following files:

ANNOUNCE	buildmnttab	inetsvc	rpc	ufs_quota
MOUNTFSYS	cron	lp	sendmail	uucp
PRESERVE	devlinks	mkdtab	standardmounts	volmgt
README	drvconfig	nfs.client	sysetup	
RMTMPFILES	gsconfig	nfs.server	sysid.net	
acct	gtconfig	perf	sysid.sys	
autoinstall	inetinit	rootusr	syslog	

Each of these files can contain instructions to start and to stop processes. For instance, the `sendmail` script can either do some quick setup and start `sendmail`, or can kill the `sendmail` daemon. This script and many of the others can be run with either a start or stop option. Running these scripts from `/etc/init.d` if you just want to stop or start one process is a good idea. To stop the line printer daemon, for example, use the command:

```
/etc/init.d/lp stop
```

These files are hardlinked into other `rc` directories. There are five `rc` directories in the generic system, but you can add one more if you need it. The names of the `rc` directories are related to the run state that the system should enter when these scripts are run. So, the scripts for the single-user startup are in `/etc/rc1.d`, multiuser scripts are in `/etc/rc2.d` and `/etc/rc3.d`, and so forth. All the files in these directories should be linked to the files in the `/etc/init.d` directory, so that process for starting or stopping a local printer is the same for all run states.

Each of these files located in the `/etc/rc?.d` directories is hard-linked to `/etc/init.d` and is given a letter and a number as part of the local name. The initial letter "S" identifies a script as start-up; the letter "K" identifies the script for the shutdown or killing process. The next part of the new name is a number from 01 – 99. The number indicates the order in which a process will be killed or started when the `init` level is changed. The scripts are run in ascending numerical order; for instance, S80lp is run before S88sendmail. When run states are changed, the kill scripts are run first, followed by the start scripts.

> **Warning** – Be very careful when changing or adding scripts to these directories. Improper installation can, at the minimum, keep certain process from running, but if it is badly done, you can significantly damage the data on the server.

/etc/inittab

The first file that is consulted after the kernel is loaded is `/etc/inittab`. Each entry in this file uses the syntax—

id:rstate:action:process

—in which *id* is a unique identifier for that entry, *rstate* lists the run states that use this entry, *action* can be one of the items listed in Table 5-1, and *process* is the command to be executed.

Table 5-1   Actions in `/etc/inittab`

Action	Description
boot	Command to be run by `init` only during a reboot. Eject CDs or tapes or perform other reboot housecleaning.
bootwait	Command will be run when going from single user to multiuser.
initdefault	Level when `init` is first run; must be defined; *never* set to 6!
off	Terminate the process.
once	Start the process, but do not wait for completion; no restart if it is running; good for starting database programs.
ondemand	Like `respawn`, but use for a, b or c pseudo-states.

Table 5-1   Actions in /etc/inittab (Continued)

Action	Description
powerfail	Execute after power fail signal.
powerwait	Same as powerfail, but no processing is done until the command completes.
respawn	Restart the process if it has died; continue use for gettys and other process that you always want to have running.
sysinit	Run before console.
wait	Start process and wait for termination; used for process that must complete before anything else is done.

Any line without an rstate value is checked whenever this file is consulted by an init command. The generic file is shown in Figure 5-1. Since there are no rstate values for the first two lines, they are run whenever init reads this file.

```
ap::sysinit:/sbin/autopush -f  /etc/iu.ap
fs::sysinit:/sbin/rcS                      >/dev/console 2>&1 </dev/console
is:3:initdefault:
p3:s1234:powerfail:/sbin/shutdown -y -i0 -g0 >/dev/console 2>&1
s0:0:wait:/sbin/rc0 off                    >/dev/console 2>&1 </dev/console
s1:1:wait:/sbin/shutdown -y -iS -g0        >/dev/console 2>&1 </dev/console
s2:23:wait:/sbin/rc2                       >/dev/console 2>&1 </dev/console
s3:3:wait:/sbin/rc3                        >/dev/console 2>&1 </dev/console
s5:5:wait:/sbin/rc5 ask                    >/dev/console 2>&1 </dev/console
s6:6:wait:/sbin/rc6 reboot                 >/dev/console 2>&1 </dev/console
of:0:wait:/sbin/uadmin 2 0                 >/dev/console 2>&1 </dev/console
fw:5:wait:/sbin/uadmin 2 2                 >/dev/console 2>&1 </dev/console
RB:6:wait:/sbin/sh -c `echo "\nThe system is being restarted."'
            >/dev/console 2>&1
rb:6:wait:/sbin/uadmin 2 1                 >/dev/console 2>&1 </dev/console
sc:234:respawn:/usr/lib/saf/sac -t 300
co:234:respawn:/usr/lib/saf/ttymon -g -h -p "`uname -n` console login: "
            -T sun -d /dev/console -l console -m ldterm,ttcompat
```

Figure 5-1   Generic inittab File

The first line invokes autopush, which uses the file /etc/iu.ap to configure a list of streams modules that should be pushed onto the stream when a device is opened (see autopush(1M)). In particular, this file specifies the modules for /dev/console and /dev/contty, which should be made available before the rest of the file is processed.

The second line starts the processes necessary to put the system into single-user mode. The /sbin/rcS script sets up enough of an environment to start the system running, then runs all the startup scripts in /etc/rcS.d. The line is executed whenever this file is consulted.

The third line sets the default run level to 3. This is the first line that is searched for when init is run during booting. You can change this to another run level, but remember that the server, if left unattended, will always boot to the level set in this line.

Helpful Hint – Interesting things can happen if this line is set to run level 6, reboot. Make sure not to do this or the system will constantly reboot.

If line three is deleted, then a run level must be entered during the boot process from the system console. You might delete the line for test systems that are continually rebooted to get into different states. However, the init command should take care of this case, unless for some reason a system must be shut down to reset hardware before a reboot.

The entry identified as p3 is consulted when init powerfail is run. It runs the shutdown script.

The next six lines start rc scripts. There is one line for each run state. Notice that the command to start run state 2 is executed for both run state 2 and 3, so to reach run state 3, you must go through run state 2. This procedure keeps the number of scripts associated with run state 3 to a reasonable level.

The lines labeled of, fw, RB, and rb are used during shutdown and reboot. Several of these use a new command called uadmin (see uadmin(1M)). This command can be used manually to shut down a system. It requires a command and a function option. The options are defined in Table 5-2 and Table 5-3.

Table 5-2   Command Options for uadmin

Value	Command	Description
2	shutdown	Kill all user processes, flush the buffer cache, unmount root, and shut down the system.
1	reboot	Stop system immediately; no further processing.
4	remount	Remount the root filesystem.

Table 5-3   Function Options for uadmin

Value	Function	Description
0	halt	Halt the processors and turn off the power.
1	boot	Reboot the system by using /kernel/unix.
2	iboot	Interactive boot.
3	sboot	Single-user reboot of /kernel/unix.
4	siboot	Single-user interactive boot.
5	panic	Multiuser reboot after crash dump.

Use command option 2 most of the time to gracefully shut down your system. Options "2 0" are used by run state 0, "2 1" are invoked in run state 6, and "2 2" are used when starting run state 5.

The last two lines for init states 2, 3, and 4 start sac and ttymon with respawn, to make sure that the processes stays running. sac starts the port monitors, and the ttymon command spawns the login on the console. These last two lines are used only when going into one of the multiuser states.

If changes are made to this file, init -q reexamines the file without forcing a reboot or an init state change.

init Pseudo-States

init allows for three options, a, b, and c, that can be used to start processes. The options are useful for adding a record to a log or starting a script or process that you only want to start occasionally.

For example, the following entry could be added to /etc/inittab:

```
ab:a:once:cat /usr/demo/SOUND/sounds/rooster.au >/dev/audio
```

After that entry, whenever the command init a is run on a system with an audio chip, you will hear a rooster. This is not a useful example for your home directory server that is running in the computer room, but it illustrates what can be done with the pseudo-states.

New Run State

You can add most additional processing by including a linked file in the appropriate /etc/rc?.d directory. This file should include the commands to start and to shut down the process. Pseudo-states can also be included to control special processes. Under some conditions, however, the pseudo-states or additions to the default init states are not enough.

In the example below, init 4 is used to create a state that is single user with some networking. This state could be useful on any system where mount access to a remote filesystem is desired during single-user operation. In particular, this state could be useful during software installs.

To create the state, remove the "4" from the "234" entries on the last two lines of /etc/inittab and add the following lines:

```
s4:4:wait:/sbin/rc4 >/dev/console 2>&1 </dev/console
14:4:wait:/bin/sh >/dev/console 2>&1 </dev/console
```

The first line runs the `rc` script for level 4, and the second runs a shell on the console. The latter is very important to do since no tty processes are running at this init state. Next, in /sbin create a file, rc4, that resembles the following file.

```
#!/sbin/sh
if [ -d /etc/rc4.d ]
then
      for f in /etc/rc4.d/K*
      {
            if [ -s ${f} ]
            then
                case ${f} in
                    *.sh)          .      ${f} ;;          # source it
                    *)             /sbin/sh ${f} stop ;;   # sub shell
                esac
            fi
      }

      for f in /etc/rc4.d/S*
      {
            if [ -s ${f} ]
            then
                case ${f} in
                    *.sh)          .      ${f} ;;          # source it
                    *)             /sbin/sh ${f} start ;;  # sub shell
                esac
            fi
      }
fi
if [ $9 = 'S' -o 9 '1' ]
then
            echo 'Networking started.'
fi
```

The simplest way to create the file is to copy /sbin/rc3 and to change all instances of rc3 to rc4. For this example, no additional files need to be added to /etc/init.d, but if a new process was being started, a file to start and stop the process should be inserted into this directory.

Next, enter these commands:

```
# mkdir /etc/rc4.d
# ln -s ../sbin/rc4 /etc/rc4
# cd /etc/rc4.d
# ln -s ../init.d/MOUNTFSYS S01MOUNTFSYS
# ln -s ../init.d/inetinit S69inet
```

After all of these changes are made, an init 4 command from single user allows the system to mount partitions from systems that are defined in the /etc/hosts file.

Kernel Configuration

In the Solaris 2.x release, the kernel is dynamically configured. This means that except for a static core, all the rest of the running kernel is made up of modules that have been loaded. These modules can be loaded at boot time, whenever a device or driver is first used or when you manually load it. The option to unload these modules is also available. With this software, it is no longer necessary to reboot a system in order to modify the running kernel.

The static kernel core is named /kernel/unix (see kernel(1M)). It provides necessary system services such as I/O management, virtual memory, and scheduling. During booting, this file is loaded into memory. The loadable kernel modules consist of drivers, filesystems, STREAMS modules, and other programs. The actual running kernel is a combination of the static core with all of the currently loaded modules.

The kernel modules are located in /kernel and /usr/kernel. The first directory contains the machine-dependent modules, and the second contains the modules that are shared among SPARC implementations. Table 5-4 lists the contents of these directories.

Table 5-4   Directory Structure for Kernel Modules

Directory	Appropriate Modules
/kernel	Machine-dependent code
/kernel/drv	Loadable device drivers
/kernel/exec	Modules used to execute processes
/kernel/fs	Filesystem modules
/kernel/misc	Miscellaneous system-related modules
/kernel/sched	Operating system schedulers
/kernel/strmod	STREAMS-loadable modules
/kernel/sys	Loadable system calls
/kernel/unix	Statically loadable portion of the kernel
/usr/kernel	Modules shared among SPARC implementations
/usr/kernel/drv	Loadable device drivers
/usr/kernel/fs	Filesystem modules
/usr/kernel/misc	Miscellaneous system-related modules
/usr/kernel/sched	Operating system schedulers
/usr/kernel/sys	Loadable system calls

Many of the modules in the drv directories have *<driver>*.conf files associated with them (see driver.conf(4)). These files contain information about the module and its configuration. This file should be included with the driver if necessary, so little is to be done with them from a systems administrator's viewpoint.

With boot -a you can use another core image or another file instead of /etc/system for kernel configuration. This command could be useful while testing a kernel or configuration file. The system prompts for the kernel name, system file name, default directory for the kernel modules, the device instance file name, the type of the root filesystem, and the physical name of the root partition. The physical name of the swap partition might also be required. Default values are displayed; you can select them by just pressing RETURN. This is also a good method for rebooting a system that has a corrupted /etc/system file. In this case, if a backup file does not exist, /dev/null could be entered as the system file name, to initialize the system with no special loading. Since the system file is delivered without any entries, using /dev/null as the system file name would mimic a generic boot.

The device-instance file is a new feature of this OS (see path_to_inst (4)). It retains the mappings between the actual physical device and its instance number which is encoded in its minor number. This prevents names like sd10 from being reconfigured each time the system is booted.

Helpful Hint – Do not try to manually alter this file. These names are listed each time the system is rebooted so they can be checked by using dmesg.

You can manually administer the kernel modules by means of modload, modunload, and modinfo. Use the file /etc/system to control the modules that are loaded during boot, but since most drivers are dynamically loaded, this file should not require many changes unless parameters in the kernel need to be changed from their default values. These commands and the file are discussed in more detail below.

Kernel Configuration Commands

Run /usr/sbin/modinfo to see which modules are currently loaded. The command lists the module ID, starting text address, size of test, data and bss (uninitialized data) in bytes, any module specific information, the revision of the module, and a name and description for each module. The module specific information is defined by the type of module; for instance, it is the system call number for system calls (see modinfo(1M)) but is unused for many modules.

```
harlie 5: modinfo
  ID  Loadaddr   Size   Info  Rev   Module Name
   1  ff0cd000   3c98     1    1    specfs (filesystem for specfs)
   2  ff0d7000   132c     -    1    swapgeneric (root and swap configuration)
   3  ff0df000   17ba     1    1    TS (time sharing sched class)
   4  ff08d000    49c     -    1    Ptem (pty hardware emulator)
   ...
  65  ff389000   12df    15    1    TS_DPTBL (Time sharing dispatch table)
  66  ff221e00    19d    16    1    redirmod (redirection module)
  67  ff398000    d87    17    1    bufmod (streams buffer mod)
  68  ff3a3000    888    18    1    pckt (pckt module)
```

Use the -i *module_number* option to list the information for a selected module.

Use /usr/sbin/modload *module* to manually load a module (see modload(1M)). Use the -p option to load a module from /kernel or /usr/modules. For instance, to load the floppy driver (/kernel/drv/fd), you could use either of the following commands—

```
# modload -p drv/fd
# modload /kernel/drv/fd
```

—or simply accessing the drive automatically loads the module.

The following command unloads a module:

```
# modunload -i module_ID
```

This action does not always remove the module from memory. To force an unload and clear all unloadable modules from memory, use -i 0. This option requires that the module is reloaded from the disk image, so could be useful if you have replaced a loaded module. Note that the module ID zero unloads all of the modules that it can, but any module that is being used is not unloaded. A reboot may be required to reload some modules. For instance, the first two modules in the list above (specfs and swapgeneric) cannot be unloaded if the system is to stay operational, so there is no way to unload them except through a reboot.

/etc/system

Use the /etc/system file to control the loading of modules during booting. In generic form the file consists of nothing but comments. The supported options are discussed below.

exclude — prevents the named module from being loaded.

include — allows this module to be loaded. include is the default state, so it need not be added to the file.

`forceload` — loads the device during boot, but this loading does not mean that the module will stay loaded. If a device is accessed through `/etc/inittab` during booting, it is sometimes necessary to forceload the driver to make sure that it is accessible.

`rootdev` — changes the physical pathname of the device where the boot program is located.

`rootfs` — changes the type of filesystem that root is. By default this is set to `ufs`.

`moddir` — changes the path to the modules location. The default value is:

```
moddir: /kernel /usr/kernel
```

Helpful Hint – Make sure to include these two entries in the path if you need to alter it, or you will have problems loading all of the modules.

Use the `set` command to adjust kernel parameter values. For example:

```
set maxusers=40
```

Many parameters are discussed in the sections on kernel parameters in *SunOS 5.x Administering Security, Performance, and Accounting.*

Filesystem Mounting

Two files are now used to manage the mounting of local filesystems. The primary file is `/etc/vfstab`. This is the replacement for `/etc/fstab` (from the SunOS 4.x release). Filesystems on CDs and diskettes are mounted automatically by the volume manager in Solaris release 2.2 and later. This process depends on the definitions in `/etc/vold.conf`. Both of these files can be used to control the mounting of local and remote filesystems.

/etc/vfstab

The `/etc/vfstab` file is checked by `fsck` during the boot process and by the `mount` command. The file can list local filesystems, remote filesystems, and swap areas. Each entry in the file must contain the following data:

- device to mount
- device to `fsck`
- mount point
- filesystem type
- `fsck` pass
- mount at boot
- mount options

If there is no appropriate information, a "–" must be included. Each entry must have all seven fields filled in order for the system to function properly. For instance:

```
#Device              device          mount     FS    fsck mount   mount
#to mount            to fsck         point     type  pass at boot options
#
/dev/dsk/c0t3d0s0    /dev/rdsk/c0t3d0s0 /       ufs   1    yes     -
/dev/dsk/c0t3d0s2    -               -         swap  -    no      -
<server>:/usr/local  -               /usr/local nfs  -    yes     -
```

With the implementation of the faster version of fsck, the fsck pass value is not as important to the setup as it was in earlier releases. The new version of fsck will run a filesystem check only if the filesystem is suspect. Under most conditions, the disk will have been labeled as being consistent; the program will report this and go to the next partition. Normally, the only time that a full filesystem check will be run is after a system crash.

The Volume Manager

New in the Solaris 2.2 environment is a process called the *volume manager*. If a CD or a diskette is inserted into a drive, this software automatically determines if this is a device to be controlled. If it is and if it has a filesystem on it, then the rmmount command (see rmmount(1)) is run to automatically mount the device. This feature is very convenient if you are loading files from CD or are transferring files on diskette.

Currently, there is a bug with the volume manager and diskettes without a filesystem: The diskette is not correctly identified and must be ejected manually. To work around the problem, you can kill the volume manager process, /usr/sbin/vold, and use the diskette as /dev/diskette. Alternatively, you can edit /etc/vold.conf to ignore the diskette. One problem with killing or disabling the volume manager permanently is that the eject command depends on the volume manager, so it is less convenient to eject media.

Any medium that does not have a filesystem on it should be available through /vol. For instance, a CD could be found as:

```
# ls -1 /vol/dev/aliases
lrwxrwxrwx  1 root           32 Jun 14 20:00 cdrom0 ->
                                /vol/dev/rdsk/c0t6/unnamed_cdrom
```

Since this process does not seem to work for floppy devices, the vold process can be left running if you comment out the following lines in /etc/vold.conf and restart vold.

```
      # @(#)vold.conf 1.15 93/01/18 SMI
      #
      # Volume Daemon Configuration file
      #

      # Database to use (must be first) db db_mem.so

      # Labels supported
      label dos label_dos.so floppy
      label cdrom label_cdrom.so cdrom
->    #label sun label_sun.so floppy

      # Devices to use
      use cdrom drive /dev/dsk/c0t6 dev_cdrom.so cdrom0
->    #use floppy drive /dev/diskette dev_floppy.so floppy0

      Actions
->    #insert /vol*/dev/fd[0-9]/* user=root /usr/sbin/rmmount
      insert /vol*/dev/dsk/* user=root /usr/sbin/rmmount
->    #eject /vol*/dev/fd[0-9]/* user=root /usr/sbin/rmmount
      eject /vol*/dev/dsk/* user=root /usr/sbin/rmmount
      notify /vol*/rdsk/* group=tty /usr/lib/vold/volmissing -c

      # List of file system types unsafe to eject unsafe ufs hsfs pcfs
```

Now, the volume manager is prevented from trying to mount the diskette automatically.

Another configuration file associated with this process is /etc/rmmount.conf. Both of these files are well documented, see rmmount.conf(4) and vold.conf(4), so they are not discussed in great detail here. Under normal circumstances you may need to add a new device, like a second tape or cd drive, to vold.conf, but that should be the only change these files need.

Additional Boot Files

The files discussed below are important to the configuration of the system that is booting. The information in them is used while the system is initializing.

/etc/nodename

The /etc/nodename file is new and, like /etc/hostname.<*interface*>, identifies the name of the system that is being booted. The name in this file is used by RFS to identify the system. If the hostname of the local system is changed, this file must be updated as well as /etc/hosts and /etc/hostname.<*interface*>.

/etc/nsswitch.conf

The contents of the /etc/nsswitch.conf file identifies the name service to use for information. The search path for each database can be established in this file. Three copies of this file are included in the generic system, one based on each of the three name services that can be selected during the install process.

/etc/nsswitch.files is configured not to use any of the name services and makes the system dependent on local files for information. This is a good file to use for the first system installed or for a system that is not being hooked up to a network.

/etc/nsswitch.nis is configured to look for data in NIS and then in local files if the NIS data is not available. The local files are looked at first for the following databases: passwd, group, automount, aliases, and services. Netgroup data only is to be looked up in NIS.

/etc/nsswitch.nisplus is configured to look for data in NIS+ and then in local files if the NIS+ data is not available. The local files are looked at first for the following databases: passwd, group, automount, aliases, services, and sendmailvars. Netgroup and publickey data is only to be looked up in NIS+. Be sure to follow the instructions in this file to use DNS with NIS+.

Either of these files can be copied to /etc/nsswitch.conf to establish the name service for the local system. The changes will take effect the next time the name service is consulted. Within the file, each database is listed with a list of sources and conditions. The allowed sources are DNS (only valid in hosts entry), files (local files only), NIS, and NIS+. For the passwd and group maps, a compat option allows for the +/- syntax that was popular in the earlier releases. The +/- allows a user to specify the logins allowed and disallowed while still using the database.

Table 5-5 lists other conditions that can be specified.

Table 5-5   Values for /etc/nsswitch.conf

Value	Meaning
success	Entry was found.
unavail	Source not responding.
notfound	Source available but no entry was found.
tryagain	Source busy.

With each condition, one of two actions can be specified. The action "continue" indicates that the next source in the list should be consulted; the action "return" forces the search to end. For instance, in both of the nis* configuration files, the entry [NOTFOUND=return] is used. This entry specifies that the next source is used only if the previous name service is unavailable. It will not proceed to the next selection if the first name service returns a "not found" error. Thus, the data in the namespace (either NIS or NIS+) will be the data that is used unless the name service does not respond. The default action is to continue for all conditions except `success`.

Most installations will be able to use one of these files with few changes; however, the options can be mixed to best use whatever namespace data is available. For instance, to restrict login access to an NIS+ system without removing the lookup capability, change the passwd entry and add the `passwd_compat` line as follows:

```
passwd:compat
passwd_compat:nisplus
```

With this change, the following entries in the local password file will work:

```
+@<netgroup>:x:0:0:::
+:x:0:0:::/bin/false
```

The first entry allows any user in the listed netgroup to log in to the local system. The second entry keeps all other users in the password file from completing a login. The data from the password file is still available, but `/bin/false` prevents unauthorized users from gaining access.

Cold Start File

If NIS+ is the selected name service for the local system, then the cold start file is consulted during the boot process. The section on NIS+ discusses the ways of installing this file and other issues. The file `/var/nis/NIS_COLD_START` identifies the name server that should be used for information requests. It contains information necessary to allow a client to bind directly to a special server by using an authenticated secure RPC request. Previous versions of the software did not provide this service directly, so it was hard to increase the level of security for the name service.

Useful Commands

The `pwconv` and `sys-unconfig` commands are useful for some specialized system administration tasks. The general user population will probably never use these commands, but they can help streamline processes for those involved with day-to-day support tasks. Both commands must be run as root.

pwconv

The pwconv command updates and creates /etc/shadow from information from /etc/passwd. In Solaris 2.x releases, the encrypted password is stored in a file called /etc/shadow. Use the pwconv command to create the shadow file after full entries have been entered into the passwd file. For instance, a password entry from the local name space could be added to the password file (this will include the encrypted password). After the pwconv command is run, the shadow file will include the new entry, and an "x" will be put in place of the password in /etc/passwd. The shadow file is protected so that normal users cannot gain easy access to other users' encrypted passwords. Using pwconv should increase the level of security.

sys-unconfig

The sys-unconfig command removes many of the configuration files and resets others to a generic configuration. Use this command if the hostname on a system needs to be changed. The hostname for each system is now stored in six files on the local system, so in most cases it is easier to run /usr/sbin/sys-unconfig, rather than attempt to change all of the files manually. The program reboots the system, and after the kernel is loaded, you must enter the following information to reconfigure the system: hostname, domain name, time zone, IP address, subnet mask, and root password. Since the host information, in particular, is stored in several files now, this command makes it much easier to rename a system.

Using the Network

6 ≡

This chapter explains how to set up and maintain a network of systems running the Solaris environment. Included in this discussion are working models of simple network topology, implementation of NFS resources such as shared application and home directory servers that use the NFS automounter, network naming services, timeshare systems, and shared printing resources.

No single network topology works for every situation. Models vary, depending on the type of work performed, resources available, and, of course, overall cost. Some of the following examples may not apply to every network environment. Our intent is to provide models and procedures for implementing specific machine usage on many networks that currently use the Solaris distributed computing environment.

Building the Network

In the building of a network of workstations and servers, there is a natural separation of workgroups, usually determined by the physical location of the machines and the type of work being performed on those machines. Not only should the accounting department's files not be accessible by engineering, these systems may need to be isolated onto separate networks, depending on the amount of files that are shared across the network. Often the building configuration can be used to develop a generalized network layout, but the network load that each organization generates must be estimated in order to assign a reasonable number of hosts per network.

The Internet numbering scheme allows up to 254 distinct network nodes per segment. Addresses .0 and .255 are used for broadcasts, but all of the numbers in between are usable. On larger networks, the 10 megabit/second Ethernet transport medium may become the bottleneck, especially when there are many systems with high processing power. Solutions for the bandwidth problem are becoming available, but in the meantime, one way to increase throughput is to reduce the node count per network.

Although the network has physical boundaries, network administrators can implement logical boundaries within the physical realm. Divisions of a corporation can be divided by both physical and logical boundaries by using a namespace (like DNS, NIS, or NIS+). The physical boundary of the network is somewhat finite, whereas the logical structure of a network can be forever changing.

The example of Bigco Inc. illustrates how to allocate and use network resources.

The Backbone Network

The network structure of Bigco uses four different IP address ranges. The first is called the bigco backbone, a network that is the data path for company-wide communications. The only systems that reside on the backbone are machines that provide some kind of service, such as routers, mail servers, and the company-wide name service master. No production type systems should be located on this network. It may seem wasteful to use an entire IP range of 255 nodes for only a few machines, but the company backbone network must have the bandwidth to transfer large amounts of data to and from each of its slave networks. This arrangement allows for future expansion for both local and remote networks.

Think of the backbone network as the motherboard of the network, to which all other networks connect. If possible, the backbone network should be built on a transport medium that is greater than the standard 10 megabit per second Ethernet wire. Fiber optic FDDI or a faster copper network, using CDDI, is preferred. Fiber is more expensive, not only for each interface card connection but also for the cable itself. CDDI and other faster network possibilities can often use the existing cable infrastructure and offer less expensive interface cards. In either case, the backbone network should be able to handle large amounts of data and should not be the bottleneck.

If the corporation is spread out in various parts of a city, or in multiple cities, then wide-area solutions such as leased lines should be used.

Systems on the Backbone Network

Figure 6-1 illustrates the machines that are resident on the backbone network. Each of these systems runs some version of the Solaris operating system, and some offer more than one type of network service. The name service master server contains network information for the entire bigco domain. Notice the three different subdomains, each on a separate network and named appropriately *corp*, *eng*, and *ops*. Each subnetwork has multiple router machines so that communications between the networks and the backbone can occur even if one of the routers is not working properly.

Each system on the backbone is discussed, along with the procedures used to implement the specific functions it performs. Many of the router systems perform duplicate functions, so their procedures are discussed only once.

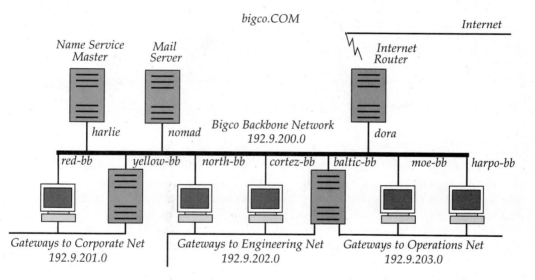

Figure 6-1   The Backbone Network of Bigco

The Corporate Network

The corporate domain is a single network segment that is connected to the company backbone through two internetwork router systems. All the systems in the corporate network obtain their routing information from these two routers. The corporate network is illustrated in Figure 6-2.

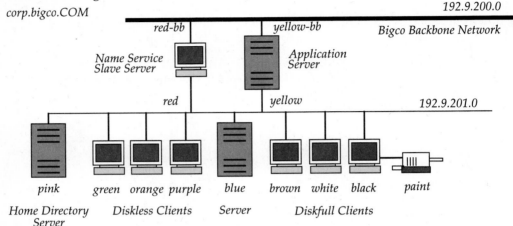

Figure 6-2   A Section of the Corporate Network

The corporate domain is usually a large group of users with similar, standard computing needs. In this environment, it is effective to have home directory and mail services centralized on servers. This environment is also a good environment for taking advantage of diskless and dataless systems to ease system administration overhead. One problem with the diskless and dataless systems is that since all or many of the filesystems are remotely mounted, this configuration is network intensive.

Gateways to the Corporate Network

The gateway systems to the corporate network perform two different services. The first system, red, is both a router and a name service slave or replica server, depending on which name service is used. These two services seem to work well together because NIS client systems cannot obtain NIS data through routers. So, there must be at least one NIS server on every local network segment. The easiest way to satisfy the requirement is to make the router also the name server. NIS+ does not have this limitation, but to be safe, an NIS+ replica server should also placed on every network segment if possible. The NIS+ implementation uses broadcasts to locate the "closest" NIS+ server, so a replica does not have to be installed on the local net, but it is a good idea.

The second gateway system for the corporate network, yellow, is also an application server, providing applications in the form of NFS-shared directories to machines within the corporate domain. The application server itself should be a machine with relatively good performance and should contain an adequate amount of RAM and swap space. Since the application server itself does not execute applications, it can run either Solaris 1.x or Solaris 2.x software.

The Engineering Network

The systems on the engineering network perform functions different from those of systems on the corporate network, so the network services are different. The majority of the systems are general purpose workstations that use a variety of applications. Figure 6-3 illustrates the network.

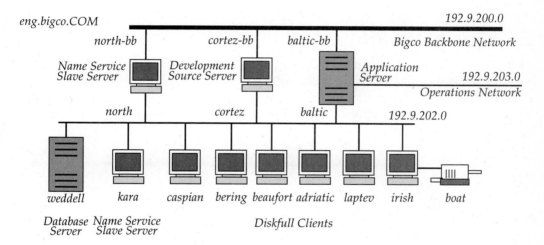

Figure 6-3   A Section of the Engineering Network

Gateways to the Engineering Network

Three gateways connect the backbone to the engineering network through the machines north, cortez, and baltic, known on the backbone as north-bb, cortez-bb, and baltic-bb. Baltic is a system that is similar to the application server on the corporate network. Not only is baltic connected to the engineering network and the company backbone, it is also a gateway system for the operations network, so it provides applications to both networks.

Workstations on the Engineering Network

The workstations on the engineering network all contain local home directories. This arrangement can be quite challenging, especially in maintaining automounter maps. Normally, systems are set up to use the automounter, which means that a server will automount home directories from itself. If it is necessary to restrict login access to a server, it is possible not to use the automounter or to use only part of the information to keep users from remote hosting or using the server as a computing resource.

Server Systems on the Engineering Network

Server systems on the engineering network, other than those previously discussed, are a database server, responsible for tracking bugs found in the software development process, and the source development server, which shares the source code to all systems within the engineering domain.

The Operations Network

The operations network is similar to the other two domains in bigco.COM. Its gateways serve the same purposes as those in the other networks. Applications can be NFS-mounted from baltic-ops or from a remote application server called yellow. Notice that the names of the router machines contain information about where they are connected. Figure 6-4 illustrates the network.

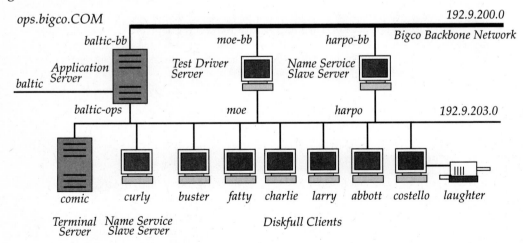

Figure 6-4   A Section of the Operations Network

Network Services

Having discussed the layout or architecture, we now review many of the network services and provide examples of each type of system.

NFS Servers

The NFS system, Sun's distributed computing filesystem, is used as an extension of local disk space on networked systems. NFS server systems store resources on their local disks and share specified directories through a series of commands. NFS client systems attach to, or mount, NFS-shared directories by means of the `mount` command or by way of the automounter.

NFS server systems usually have more computing power than the clients they serve. The logic behind this is clear. Server systems usually handle requests from more than one client system simultaneously. If the client systems generate network traffic faster than the server can handle it, the result is a network-bound NFS server and unhappy users of those clients.

Any machine can share NFS resources if the shared directory is on a local disk filesystem. Filesystems that are mounted on an NFS-shared directory on a server system are not exported to clients mounting that resource. For example, if a server is configured to mount the man pages from a remote system on `/usr/man`, that directory could not be exported by the local server to the clients mounting `/usr`. The clients would need to be able to mount `/usr/man` from another host. The only system that can share a filesystem is the system that has the disks containing the filesystem physically attached to it.

Sharing NFS Resources

All NFS utilities are installed as part of the Core system meta-cluster of Solaris packages. There are no specific packages to install before a system can use NFS services. Special add-on products can act as NFS accelerators to boost performance over the wire, but every Solaris system includes basic NFS functionality for both servers and clients.

NFS resources can be shared from the command line or through entries in special files that are executed during the change from `init` state 2 to `init` state 3. To facilitate NFS mounting, the server system must also be running the daemon processes `nfsd` and `mountd`. Both daemons are RPC-based programs that run silently, responding to client-side requests. Details on how to start these processes are discussed below.

6

When an NFS resource is shared from the command line, references to it are erased when the system reboots. To make exported NFS directories available after rebooting, enter the *share line* into the server's `/etc/dfs/dfstab` file. The share line is nothing more than the command-line syntax for sharing a resource. Adding share lines to the `/etc/dfstab` file is preferred, as it paves the way for use of many more NFS administrative commands.

▼ Setting Up an NFS Server

1. Edit the `/etc/dfs/dfstab` file.
Enter the `share` command for the resource, including any specific options, into the `/etc/dfs/dfstab` file of the server system. The `share` command syntax is as follows:

share -F *fstype* **-o** *options* **-d** *"Description" /absolute/directory/path*

For instance, to share the OpenWindows executables, usually located in the `/usr/openwin` directory, place the following line in the `/etc/dfs/dfstab` file of the server system:

share -F nfs -o ro -d "OWV3.2" /usr/openwin

The share line in the example is interpreted as follows: Share the resource, an NFS filesystem type, using the read-only option; the description of the resource is called OWV3.2; and the shared directory path is `/usr/openwin`.

Similarly, to share a writeable NFS resource, such as a network scratch pad, enter the following share line:

share -F nfs -o rw -d "Scratch area" /export/scratch

The difference between the two share lines is the option, the description, and, of course, the absolute directory path to the resource.

Other options can be used here to control access to the filesystem. The `access={name}` option can be used to limit the hosts or groups of hosts that can mount the filesystem. The name(s) specified after `access=` can either be systems from a hosts map or file, or a group of systems specified in the netgroup map or file. However, hosts and netgroups cannot be mixed on the same share line.

```
share -F nfs -o ro,access=pinkgroup:goldgroup -d "Applications"\
   /export/local
```

The previous example grants read-only access to an applications filesystem for the netgroups *pinkgroup* and *goldgroup*. The share line has a length limit. Thus, netgroups are important for keeping the share line short in a large environment.

Diskless client servers, dataless client servers, and install servers need to export their filesystems without granting root access to all hosts. To achieve this, use the `root={name}` option. This option allows the root user on the listed hosts to be able to make changes to the mounted filesystem. Normally only the system that has the disks containing the filesystem physically attached can make changes as root.

One insecure method for granting root access is the `anon=0` option. This option grants root capabilities to any root user on the system that mounts the filesystem. Use the `anon=0` option to allow access to files that need to be changed more quickly than the changes can be propagated through a name service. One example of this might be a heavily used install server.

```
share -F nfs -o rw,anon=0 -d "Solaris 2.3" /export/sol2.3
```

Again, this option is insecure and should be used only in a trusted environment.

2. Execute the NFS server startup script.
Once the share line is in place, two network daemons must be started before NFS mounting can occur. If the system is already sharing NFS resources, these daemons are most likely running. Otherwise, they must be started manually.

There are three different ways to start these daemons: reboot the system after the `/etc/dfs/dfstab` file contains a share line; change the system to `init` state 2 and then back up to `init` state 3; or execute the NFS server startup script, as shown below:

```
# /etc/init.d/nfs.server start
```

Each of the three ways listed above eventually executes the contents of the NFS server script, but only does so when the `/etc/dfs/dfstab` file contains a share line for an NFS-type filesystem.

3. Check the share status.

After the server startup script has been executed, check the status of the server system by again using the `share` command, this time with no arguments.

```
# share
/usr/openwin -ro OWV3.2
/export/scratch -rw Scratch area
```

The output returned from `share` displays the shared directories and options for the current machine. There are other methods of checking the NFS share status while logged into the server.

One method is to execute the `dfshares` command. When this command is executed without any arguments, it polls the local system for share information.

```
# dfshares
RESOURCE                SERVER  ACCESS  TRANSPORT
thyme:/usr/openwin      thyme   ro      -
thyme:/export/scratch   thyme   -       -
thyme:/export/sol2.3    thyme   anon=0  -
```

Another method is to execute the `exportfs` command, a carry-over from earlier versions of the operating system. As with `share`, when `exportfs` is executed without arguments, all locally shared directories are displayed.

```
# exportfs
/usr/openwin -ro
/export/scratch
```

Another method of obtaining local NFS share status is to execute `showmount`, also born in the BSD realm. The `showmount` command requires the `-e` argument to list the locally exported directories and can also be used to check the shared directories on remote machines, a feature not available with either `share` or `exportfs`.

```
# showmount -e
/usr/openwin (everyone)
/export/scratch (everyone)
```

Once satisfied that resources have been properly shared, you may begin to mount the exported directories on NFS client systems by following the actions described below.

Mounting NFS Resources

The act of attaching NFS resources to a client machine is known as *mounting*, similar to the manner in which local disk filesystems are attached. The major difference is that local mounts can be performed only on filesystems. Remote mounts are performed on NFS-shared directories, which are either part of or complete partitions.

Before you can mount any NFS resource from the command line, you must know three items: the NFS server's hostname or IP address, the absolute directory path to the resource on the server, and the mount point where the resource will be attached.

If you know the hostname of the server system, use showmount to obtain other information about the shared resources, as described above. showmount also verifies that the NFS server is running the proper RPC services before attempting the actual mount operation. A mount point is usually an empty directory on the client machine in which the logical connection is made. Many times the name of this directory mount point can be a clue to the type of resources found therein.

1. Check the remote resource from a client.

Use showmount -e *server* to determine the resources that are exported by a remote server:

```
# showmount -e blue
/usr/openwin (everyone)
/export/scratch (everyone)
```

This output confirms both network access to the server and properly registered RPC programs. If the output from the showmount command returns a message such as "RPC program not registered," then check to see if the server is running the nfsd and rpc.mountd daemons by viewing the process status, using ps. If the daemons are not running, use the /etc/init.d/nfs.server script, as shown above, or reboot the server.

2. Mount the NFS resource.

Mounting is accomplished by a series of command-line arguments. There are several different ways to mount NFS resources. The most common uses the following syntax:

```
# mount <options> server:/exported/directory /mount_point
```

To mount the /usr/openwin resource shared in the above example, the command line is:

```
# mount -o ro blue:/usr/openwin /usr/openwin
```

The contents of the /usr/openwin directory on the NFS server, blue, are now mounted on the client's /usr/openwin directory as a read-only resource.

3. Use the NFS resource.

Files resident under the NFS mount point can be invoked as though they were local. If a resource is shared and mounted read-only, then, obviously, writes are disabled. If the resource is shared with read-write access, then users who have been granted permission can update or create files under the NFS mount point. The superuser, root, cannot write to directories under an NFS mount unless granted specific permission in the share line on the server.

4. Unmount the NFS resource

Once the resource is no longer needed, you can unmount it.

```
# umount /usr/openwin
```

One reason to unmount filesystems that are not used regularly is that they will always incur some background checking even when the resource is not in use. If resources need to be available but will not be used frequently, the automounter can mount and unmount them automatically. Refer to the section "The Automounter" on page 155.

Permanent NFS Mounts

NFS resources can be placed into the /etc/vfstab file for permanent mounting upon entry into init state 3. On standalone machines, the /etc/vfstab entries are of local or UFS type. NFS mounts use a slightly different format because not all of the fields apply.

The syntax for /etc/vfstab entries is as follows:

```
device     device     mount   FS     fsck    mount     mount
to mount   to fsck    point   type   pass    at boot   options
```

Some of the fields in the /etc/vfstab file have no meaning for NFS type mounts but still must contain the single character "-" as a placeholder. Using these constraints and the syntax shown above, the /etc/vfstab entry for a system mounting the /usr/openwin resource from the server blue at boot time is:

```
blue:/usr/openwin - /usr/openwin nfs - yes ro,bg
blue:/export/scratch - /export/home/extra nfs - no rw,bg
```

From left to right, the first line means: The device to mount is the /usr/openwin directory on the server blue. Attach the shared directory to the mount point /usr/openwin. It is an NFS-type mount, and skip the fsck pass at boot time. Mount the resource each and every time init state 3 is reached, read-only, and if the server is not available when first checked, place the mount operation into the background and proceed with the boot process.

There is no device on which to perform filesystem checks, hence the "-" character in the second and fifth fields. The last field in the vfstab entry, mount options, can contain the same type of placeholder. If this is the case, then the default permissions on the NFS-mounted directory allow for both read and write access, and they also allow for set user ID upon execution, which can open the door for severe security problems.

Another alternative for permanent NFS mounts is to use the automounter. The automounter adds the convenience of having the filesystems available when needed, but it also unmounts filesystems when they are not in use, thus reducing overhead.

The Automounter

The NFS automounter provides a method for users to access networked resources without first becoming the superuser, root, and invoking the `mount` command. A system process controls mounting under designated directories when they are accessed. Automounted resources that remain inactive after a time-out period are disconnected until referenced again. This makes the automounter more network-efficient than NFS resources that have been mounted by means of the `/etc/vfstab` method.

The automounter is implemented differently in versions of the Solaris software older than 2.3. In the earlier versions, a single executable called `/usr/lib/nfs/automount` was responsible for all automounter activity. In the Solaris 2.3 environment, the automounter has been divided into two different executable files: the executable `/usr/sbin/automount`, which determines the directories that must be monitored for access, and the daemon `/usr/lib/autofs/automountd`, which actually does the mounting of the directories. The daemon checks the automounter maps or local files to determine which directories to mount. In this version of the software, the `/usr/lib/autofs/automountd` also services requests from the volume manager `vold`.

The automounter is started because of the existence of the `/etc/auto_master` file and because the entries contained in that file determine which resources to mount. The generic `/etc/auto_master` file on a Solaris 2.2 system contains the following entries:

```
# Master map for automounter
#
/net -hosts -nosuid
/home auto_home
```

The first noncommented entry in the `/etc/auto_master` file instructs the automounter to take control of the `/net` directory for NFS mount points. When you change the working directory to `/net/<hostname>`, the NFS mounts will be attached there.

Translated into layman terms, these lines mean: When you change directories to `/net/<hostname>`, mount all of the NFS-shared resources shared by that system under the path `/net/<hostname>`, where *hostname* is the name of an NFS server, and do not allow setuid programs to execute over the NFS mount.

So, to mount an NFS resource from a known server, as in the example above, simply use the following command:

```
% cd /net/blue/usr/openwin
```

The second line of the default `/etc/auto_master` file means: When attempting to change directories to `/home`, consult the `auto_home` map, which can be a local file or name service map of the same name.

Types of Automount Maps

The automounter relies on a set of maps to determine what it will mount and where. These maps are usually named `auto_name`. The `/etc/nsswitch.conf` file is prepared to reference any map starting with *auto*. To preserve compatibility with previous versions of automounter, if an `auto_name` map is not found, then the system searches for an `auto.name` map. This is only true for non-NIS+ networks because NIS+ uses the "`.`" as a delimiter for naming.

As noted above, the `auto_master` map is the parent of all maps. It supplies pointers to other maps. There are special, included, direct, and indirect maps in addition to the master map.

Special and Included Maps

There are two types of special maps. The first type of special map is the `-hosts` entry previously discussed. The second is a `-null` map entry, which excludes a specific directory in a map.

Any map can include other maps. For example, source files may be made available via `auto_src`. However, there may be a need to keep the development and final versions of source code maps under different control. In this case, an `auto_src` map might look like the following:

```
+auto_devsrc
+auto_fixedsrc
```

This example references both maps. In earlier releases, include maps were created to control the source of the map. A map could be controlled locally or could come from NIS. This function is now controlled by the `/etc/nsswitch.conf` in all releases of Solaris software.

Direct Map

A direct map lists a full pathname for the mount point and specifies a filesystem to mount at that point. The standard naming convention is to call the map `auto_direct`. This is not a mandatory name and the convention of using `auto.direct` for non-NIS+ networks can be used here. The direct map entry is called from the master map with the following entry:

```
/-  auto_direct
```

The direct map itself contains one entry for each specific mount point needed. This map is usually good for mounting such directories as `/usr/openwin`, `/usr/man`, `/usr/local`, or `/opt`. A sample map might look like the following:

```
/usr/openwin        blue:/usr/openwin
/usr/man            blue:/usr/man
/usr/local          blue,pink:/export/local
```

The last line of the example references two different servers as the source of these files. If one mount fails, the other source is tried. In the Solaris 2.3 environment, both mounts are attempted simultaneously, and the first system to respond is used. This technique is effective in balancing load on servers.

Indirect Maps

A master map lists the parent directory name for a set of mounts and lists an indirect map as the pointer. An indirect map lists the specific keys for the set of mounts and the system that these mounts can come from. In the example of the default entries that is included in the Solaris 2.x release, an entry with the `/home` directory is tied to the `auto_home` map.

In UNIX, accessing a directory by its full name, starting with /, is a direct reference. An indirect reference specifies the path relative to a specific starting point. Indirect maps work the same way. The specific starting point is the pathname listed in the `auto_master` map. Each entry in the indirect map is then a subdirectory under that starting point. For example, given the standard `auto_master` map and the following `auto_home` map, changing directory to `/home/stuff` mounts `purple:/export/home/stuff` to `/home/stuff` on the client system and makes `/home/stuff` the current working directory.

```
stuff       purple:/export/home/&
```

The ampersand, `&`, means to substitute the key value on the left wherever the ampersand appears. For example, —

```
prodmktg    &:/export/home/&
```

— could be expanded to `prodmktg:/export/home/prodmktg`.

Name Services

Rather than making sure every system has a local copy of the same host information, you can place each system's host name and IP number in the name service database files. Name service client systems obtain the information stored on name servers via series of underlying protocols that are started at boot time. A name service provides a single point to change network-wide information. When naming services are not used, every system on the network must find a way to stay current with dynamic network information, a difficult task on large networks.

There are large differences between administering NIS (Network Information Service) and NIS+ (Network Information Service Plus); several dependencies apply.

Network-wide maps allow for user mobility, remote copy of files, and mail services, but only when selected to do so. On Solaris 1.x systems, NIS-wide passwd data is made available by placing the "+" character at the end of the local system's /etc/passwd file. On Solaris 2.x systems, a new file, called /etc/nsswitch.conf, controls where and in what order name service data is to be found. The "+" character is no longer used in the same manner. Specifically, the nsswitch file must be set up to use the NIS compatibility mode in order to use the "+@*name*" for referencing netgroups from the /etc/passwd file.

Solaris 2.x systems can use either NIS or NIS+ naming services, or both at the same time, for most configurations, although running both is not really useful. In addition, DNS is available for host information. Configuring and managing each naming service is described below.

Name Service Master

A name service master is the focal point for network-wide information, such as host names, IP addresses, Ethernet numbers, password and group account entries, automounter maps, rpc services, and other data. Host names that are assigned unique IP addresses provide a means for basic communication between systems.

Name Service Replica or Slave

The name service slave or replica server does not need large amounts of free disk space. There must be room enough to house a complete copy of the name service databases, which varies depending on the size of the network and the amount of name service information stored. NIS+ also requires extra space for the log files. You can check the space requirements by observing the amount of space consumed on the master or root server. Then, adjust the slaves accordingly.

NIS+

NIS+ is designed for Solaris 2.x systems, although Solaris 1.x systems can run as clients on NIS+ domains. There are several advantages to using NIS+ instead of NIS. Two of the most important advantages are that a System Administrator no longer has to log in to a central server to make changes and these changes are propagated automatically instead of requiring that a whole new version of the table be sent out. NIS+ works well with the GUI-based Administration Tool, but not all NIS+ data can be administered this way. NIS+ also contains a more enhanced level of security than does NIS.

Automatic propagation does not mean instantaneous updates for the data on all of the servers. Many of the lookup commands include a -M option to force the lookup on the master. This option allows anyone to make sure that the change is on the master. The `nisping` command displays the last update times for all of the servers of a directory. If the times are identical, then the namespace is up-to-date on all systems. This process can cause confusion if system administrators forget to let the update occur before they implement the change on the client. The update is much faster than the `ypmake` process used in NIS, but in large domains it can take time.

One of the major new NIS+ concepts is the idea of an NIS+ principal. A principal is any user or workstation whose credentials are stored in the namespace. This means that each user is a principal and, as that principal, can work within the namespace from anywhere within the defined network. The host principals are only for the root account on each host. For example, if permissions are given to the principal hostname.corp.bigco.com., anyone who can log in as root on that host can make changes to the namespace. Alternatively, giving access to user.corp.bigco.com. allows that user to make changes if logged in to an NIS+ client anywhere in the defined namespace.

Helpful Hint – Understanding this difference is important when deciding how to set up the administration group for a domain directory.

 Warning – Each principal must be uniquely identified, so you cannot have a hostname and a username that are the same within the namespace.

Two directories, `org_dir` and `groups_dir`, will exist within the domain directory after the setup is complete. Each domain directory is made up of three parts. In this case, the main domain directory is `corp.bigco.com`. In this top directory is `groups_dir.corp.bigco.com.`, which will not be used or consulted by most of the users. It simply is the directory structure that defines who can administer the namespace. Also in the top directory is `org_dir.corp.bigco.com.`, where the passwd, hosts, and other generic namespace tables reside. Each namespace has at least these three directory structures. You will add more directories to the namespace as you add more domains and, if necessary, create a separate directory for information storage.

> **Warning –** Be careful if you add custom tables to `org_dir`. Currently, 16 predefined tables can be created in `org_dir`. Future releases could define others, so, except for the auto_* tables, it would be best to store any special information in another directory, for example, `local_dir.corp.bigco.com`.

It would be best to install the Solaris 2.3 release on NIS+ servers. Several significant improvements were made to the OS and to NIS+ in this later release.

The steps necessary to build an NIS+ master and an NIS+ replica are summarized below. They are fully documented in the following publications.

- *Administering NIS+ and DNS* — found in AnswerBook and as part of the full documentation set from Sun.

- *SunOS 2.3 NIS+ Quick Start* — a guide that lays out administrative steps but omits details; also can be found in System Administrator's AnswerBook for the Solaris 2.3 release.

   Note: This guide should only be used by System Administrators who are already familiar with the NIS+ product.

- *All About Administering NIS+, Second Edition*—a SunSoft Press publication, 1994.

The steps to establish a root-level domain and to fully populate a name space from scratch are beyond the scope of this book, but the following steps provide an overview of the process to set up a nonroot-level domain.

For these examples, a master and a replica for the domain corp.bigco.com. will be created. The instructions assume that the new servers are already clients of the domain bigco.com. The master for bigco.com. is named master-bigco, and the master and replica for the new domain are called corp-master and corp-replica.

> **Note –** All NIS+ servers should be clients of the domain above the namespace that they will support. Thus, a system supporting corp.bigco.com would need to be a client of the domain bigco.com. The exceptions to this rule are the root domain servers.

Since these systems must first be clients, the first procedure describes how to turn a system into an NIS+ client. This procedure must be followed on each client.

▼ Initializing an NIS+ client

1. Check for credentials.

Check for credentials for the host. This must be done on a system already running NIS+.

```
# nismatch corp-master.bigco.com. cred.org_dir.bigco.com.
```

If there is a match, then proceed to the next step. If not, log in to the master and run the following command to add a credential for the host:

```
# /usr/lib/nis/nisclient -c -l nisplus -d bigco.com. corp-master
```

2. Initialize the host client.

The nisclient script run in step 1 conveniently prints out the options to run to initialize the client. To initialize a client, run the following command on the client system as root:

```
# /usr/lib/nis/nisclient -i -h bigco-master -a 129.9.200.13 -d bigco.com.
```

After the script completes, the system must be rebooted. During the process, you are asked to type in the "secure-RPC password." The password is nisplus, unless you selected a different default password when creating the credential. Then the "real" root password for the system must be entered. Reboot the system so that all processes use the NIS+ namespace.

Warning – Each system must have a root password for this script to complete.

---

3. Enable DNS.

If DNS is used, make these changes.

a. Create a /etc/resolv.conf file.

The /etc/resolv.conf file, which is site-specific, must exist on all Solaris clients using DNS. See Chapter 19 of *SunOS 5.3 Administering NIS+ and DNS* for complete instructions.

b. Edit /etc/nsswitch.conf.

Uncomment the host line that includes DNS and comment out the other one, as follows:

```
#hosts: nisplus [NOTFOUND=return] files
hosts:  nisplus dns [NOTFOUND=return] files
```

4. Initialize an NIS+ user client.
The `nisclient` script can also be run as the user to reset the credentials for that user.

`% /usr/lib/nis/nisclient -u`

Again, the default password will be asked for, and the user must provide the real password.

▼   Creating an NIS+ Master Server

1. Log in to the master for bigco.com.
To create an NIS+ server on a client system, it is necessary to start the process on the master server for that client.

`# rlogin bigco-master`

2. Log in to the new master server and start `rpc.nisd`.
The command /usr/sbin/rpc.nisd must be running on the new server to allow the directory structure to be created in the next step. This process can be started with the flags –YB to allow the server to answer NIS requests and DNS forwarding requests from NIS clients. To run in this mode permanently, edit /etc/init.d/rpc on the server, uncomment the line starting with EMUL, and add the B to the options.

`# rlogin corp-master`

`# /usr/sbin/rpc.nisd -YB`

3. Create the domain from bigco-master.
There are now two ways to complete this step, the quick way and the long way. The long way is documented in *Administering NIS+ and DNS*; use the long method if the local environment needs a great amount of customization.

a. the quick way
The following command creates an empty namespace on the server corp-master for the domain or directory called corp.bigco.com. Run the command from bigco-master.

`# /usr/lib/nis/nisserver -M -d corp.bigco.com. -h corp-master`

The `nisserver` script allows the system administrator to reset values for the domainname of the new domain, the name of the new administrative group, and whether to run in NIS compatibility mode. It sets up the domain, using security level two, which uses DES credentials. If a different security level is required, it can be reset after the namespace has been created.

b. the long way

With the `nisserver` script, the following steps are not required for most installations. Under most circumstances it is simpler to modify the namespace that is created with the command in step 3a than to create things by hand.

i. Create the domain directory.

The following command creates a directory and several files on corp-master in `/var/nis`, including corp-master (which for now is an empty directory).

```
# nismkdir -D group=admin.corp.bigco.com. -m corp-master corp.bigco.com.
```

ii. Create the domain subdirectories and tables.

The following command creates the `org_dir` and `groups_dir` directories on corp-master and populates the `org_dir` directory with empty tables for hosts, passwd, and so forth. The `-Y` option is used only if the server answers NIS requests. After this command has completed, a listing of `/var/nis/corp-master` will list many files.

```
# /usr/lib/nis/nissetup -Y corp.bigco.com.
```

iii. Create an admin group for the new domain.

Each domain should have its own administrative group. This group will include all of the principals who can make changes to that domain's namespace.

```
# nisgrpadm -c admins.corp.bigco.com.
```

iv. Give group access to the directory.

Once the group has been created, give it access to the domain namespace; the namespace, by default, is not created with these permissions.

```
# nischmod g+rmcd corp.bigco.com.
```

4. Populate the tables.

This step can be completed in several ways, depending on the type of namespace that was set up previously. If a completely new namespace is being created, it is easier to populate from ASCII files, but if an NIS domain exists with current information, this data can be used. It is often easier to populate from an existing NIS domain because the data is already in the proper format. Both of these options should be run on the new NIS+ server, corp-master.

a. To populate from files

Create copies of the ASCII files in a special directory. These files must be formatted properly, and any information that should not be shared should be removed. For example, the root entry in the passwd file is generally not included in the namespace, as it is often uniquely set per system, and, in most environments, having one root password for all systems is a great security risk.

```
# nispopulate -F -p /tmp/nisfiles -d corp.bigco.com.
```

This command loads the files found in /tmp/nisfiles into the new directory namespace.

b. To populate from NIS maps

For established NIS sites, this is probably the best way to load data into the new directory. The command uses the NIS maps for the domain Bigco.COM found on the hostname harlie to populate the namespace. Note that the IP address for harlie is included. The name and address for a ypslave could be used here, but for the most up-to-date information, it is best to use the master.

```
# nispopulate -Y -d corp.bigco.com.-h harlie -a 192.9.200.1 -y Bigco.COM
```

The command displays the appropriate information about the NIS+ domainname, the NIS domain name, and the name of the ypmaster. These values can be reset if they are not correct.

Helpful Hint – The output from this command is quite long. Be sure to pay attention to all of it.

Note – This command creates credentials for all host and password entries using a default password of "nisplus." This saves the effort of completing this task manually.

5. Add credentials for administrators.

This step must be done if the namespace was not created from NIS maps. The procedure that loads data in from the maps also creates credentials automatically. The manual process for this is—

```
# /usr/lib/nis/nisclient -c -l nisplus -d corp.bigco.com. hostname username
```

—where nisplus is the default credential password, -d indicates the directory, and hostname and/or username is a list of hostnames and/or usernames that need to have credentials created. The script checks for proper permissions and also checks the hostname or username to make sure that no collisions occur in the credential table. A warning message is displayed if a name is found in both hosts and password, and the credential is not added. Also, if a credential exists already, it is not written over.

6. Add principals to the new administration group.

In this step, the principals that should be able to change the new directory are added. It is best to use the full principal name when specifying a host or user. This step can be done at any time after the namespace has been populated.

```
# nisgrpadm -a admin.corp.bigco.com. corp-replica.bigco.com.\
tim.corp.bigco.com.
```

In this example, the root account on corp-replica and the user tim in corp.bigco.com. are added to the admin.corp.bigco.com. group, which in the earlier steps was given permissions to make changes in the corp.bigco.com. directory. Note that the principal name for the replica is bigco.com., not corp.bigco.com., because corp-replica is a client of the bigco.com namespace. Most of your clients should not be in the top-level domain.

7. Change permissions for NIS clients.

In order for NIS clients to look up data in the namespace, all tables must be readable by the user "nobody." All NIS clients are unable to use credentials, so they will not be able to fully use the namespace. The following command is for only one table.

```
# nischmod n+r hosts.org_dir
```

For the password and group table, check the permissions within the table, as follows:

```
# niscat -o passwd.org_dir.corp.bigco.com
```

Or, you can use group in place of the passwd to look at the group table. In these tables, set up permissions so that everyone (including the user nobody) can read all columns except the passwd column (in both tables) and the shadow column (passwd table only). The passwd column should be restricted to "modify by owner"; the shadow column should be restricted to "no permissions."

NIS+ Replica Server

Once the master server is established, starting up a replica is simple.

▼ Creating an NIS+ Replica Server

1. Start `rpc.nisd` on the replica.

The command /usr/sbin/rpc.nisd must be running on the new server to allow the directory structure to be created in the next step. This process can be started with the flags -YB to allow the server to answer NIS requests and DNS forwarding requests from NIS clients. To run in this mode permanently, edit /etc/init.d/rpc on the server, uncomment the line starting with EMUL, and add B to the options. The options that `rpc.nisd` is started with on the replicas should be the same as those on the master for that domain.

```
# rlogin corp-replica
```

```
# /usr/sbin/rpc.nisd -YB
```

2. **Create the directories on the replica.**
   As with setting up the master, there are two paths to complete this step. Use the longer path on masters running the Solaris 2.2 release or earlier releases. The longer process is also good for debugging problems with the namespace. This command must be run on the master for the domain that the replica will support. In this example, the command is run on corp-master.

   a. **the quick way**
      The script creates `corp.bigco.com.`, `org_dir.corp.bigco.com.`, and `groups_dir.corp.bigco.com` on the new replica.

      ```
      # nisserver -R -d corp.bigco.com. -h corp-replica
      ```

   b. **the long way**
      This method also makes all three directories on the replica and should be run on the domain master.

      ```
      # nismkdir -s corp-replica.eng.sun.com.  corp.bigco.com.
      ```

      ```
      # nismkdir -s corp-replica.eng.sun.com.  groups_dir.corp.bigco.com.
      ```

      ```
      # nismkdir -s corp-replica.eng.sun.com.  org_dir.corp.bigco.com.
      ```

3. **Use `nisping` to populate the directories.**
   Since updating is automatic, you may not need to do this step manually, but if the replica is not updated, use `nisping` to force the transfer.

   ```
   # nisping corp.bigco.com.
   ```

   ```
   # nisping groups_dir.corp.bigco.com.
   ```

   ```
   # nisping org_dir.corp.bigco.com.
   ```

The `nisping` command used with the -u option shows the update times for all of the servers supporting that directory. Create the corp.bigco.com directory first, since it provides the structure for the next two directories. It does not usually matter if you create `groups_dir` before or after `org_dir`, but in a large domain, `org_dir` can take a long time to transfer, so create it last.

Several of these commands are scripts, so a special version of the `nisclient` script could be moved to a directory that can be mounted on all systems. This special version could automatically do the steps to enable DNS during the host initialization step. Or, other changes could be made to make working with the namespace easier.

NIS

The Network Information Service server programs run on Solaris 1.x systems. The files and programs necessary to create an NIS master server are best obtained by installing Solaris 1.x release on the system. During the installation, select the NIS Master option in the `suninstall` "hosts" form. Also configure a larger than normal `/var` partition so that there is sufficient space for the NIS maps. After the system is installed, follow the instructions below.

▼ Creating an NIS Master

1. Boot the master system into single-user mode.
This step is accomplished by supplying a `-s` option to the `boot` command. Without the `-s` option, this system, upon first boot, will attempt to locate a nonexistent domain and will continue looking until you halt the machine.

```
ok boot -s
```

2. Set the domain name.
When the shell prompt is displayed, set the NIS domain on the master server, which can be found by checking the contents of the `/etc/defaultdomain` file. The domain name is usually set automatically in the `/etc/rc.local` file, which has yet to be executed on a system running in single-user mode.

```
# domainname `cat /etc/defaultdomain`
```

3. Check the `/var` partition.
If you created a separate `/var` partition during the Solaris 1.x install process, you must manually mount that partition; the only partitions mounted in single-user mode are `/` and `/usr`. If `/var` is not a separate disk partition, then make sure there is sufficient room in the root filesystem before you proceed.

4. Run `ypinit -m`.
The `/usr/etc/yp/ypinit` file is not normally in the search path, so specify the full path. This procedure actually goes about making the `/var/yp/`*domainname* directory in addition to massaging ASCII files into name service maps, as detailed in the `/var/yp/Makefile`.

```
# /usr/etc/yp/ypinit -m
```

5. Finish booting.

After `ypinit` completes, the system can continue the boot process because the NIS database in the `/var/yp/``domainname` directory is functional. The system must also be able to contact other systems on the network to fully complete the task of populating the rest of the NIS data files.

6. Populate the ASCII data files and rebuild maps.

When the system is finished booting, the console login prompt is displayed. Log in as the superuser, root, and begin to populate the NIS data files with local network information. The best place to begin is the `hosts` data file. The ASCII `/etc/hosts` file on `harlie` is where all known hosts and IP addresses are kept. In the bigco.COM, the master `hosts` files would be similar to the following:

```
#
# BigCO Host Database
# If the NIS is running, this file is only consulted when booting
#
127.0.0.1      localhost
#
# The Backbone network
192.9.200.0  bigco-bb
192.9.200.1  harlie loghost timehost nismaster
192.9.200.2  minerva
192.9.200.3  dora
192.9.200.4  nomad
192.9.200.5  hal
192.9.200.6  red-bb
    .
192.9.200.12 harpo-bb
#
# Corporate Network
192.9.201.0  bigco_corp
192.9.201.1  red
192.9.201.2  blue
    .
192.9.201.10 black
#
# Engineering Network
192.9.202.0  bigco_eng
192.9.202.1  weddell
192.9.202.2  north
    .
192.9.202.10 irish
```

```
#
# The Operations Network
129.9.203.0  bigco_ops
192.9.203.1  moe
192.9.203.2  harpo
.
192.9.203.10 laugh
```

After populating the ASCII hosts file, update the maps by using the make command while situated in the /var/yp directory. This procedure converts the ASCII data into one or many database files, depending on the map. The hosts data file is changed into two separate databases, hosts.byaddr and hosts.byname. The first, hosts.byaddr, uses the IP address as the key, and hosts.byname uses the hostname.

Before the NIS domain can be fully functional, several other NIS data files must be edited and rebuilt.

The Passwd Maps

The password maps store user account information in the form of a login entry, an encrypted password, a unique user identification number (UID), a group identification number (GID), a description field, the home directory path, and the login shell. The NIS passwd data file, the file from which the maps are created, is nothing more than a copy of the system's /etc/passwd file. The exact same format is used. Many NIS master servers use their local /etc/passwd file as the ASCII data file for the whole domain. This practice can prove dangerous from a security standpoint.

When the ASCII data files are rebuilt under NIS, two separate maps are created in which different keys are used. The first, called passwd.name, keys on the first field of the password file, also called the user name. The other NIS database keys on the user ID number.

The Group Maps

The group maps contain UNIX group information on a network-wide basis.

The Netgroups Map

Hosts, users, and networks can be divided by a name service database, called *netgroups*, and implemented network-wide. Netgroups can be used to grant or deny mount access to NFS-shared directories. Additionally, netgroups can be used to direct NFS mount paths for workgroups using similar applications.

Other Maps

For things to run properly, you may have to populate other maps, including maps unique to the local installation or more generic maps like the auto_* maps. These maps may not be necessary for NIS installation, but if they are not created soon after the installation, problems can arise.

NIS Slave

Under NIS, slave server database files are stored under /var/yp/<*domainname*>. A large network, over 500 nodes, typically consumes 20 or 30 megabytes of space. For creation of an NIS slave server, the system must be running some version of the Solaris 1 operating environment or have the NIS Kit added on a Solaris 2.2 or later system. Be sure there is free space under /var/yp and that the system is bound to a valid NIS server, preferably the NIS master server.

▼ Creating an NIS slave server

As root, follow the steps below.

1. **Bring over the NIS maps with ypinit -s <*master_server*>.**
   For systems on the subnet to obtain NIS information, the maps must be placed on the slave server. A utility called ypxfr is especially designed for this purpose. A corresponding daemon, called ypxfrd, should be running on the master server before ypxfr is attempted. Check the NIS master's /etc/rc.local file and uncomment the line that pertains to ypxfrd, or start the daemon from the command line. The ypinit command calls ypxfr.

   ```
   # /usr/etc/yp/ypinit -s harlie
   ```

2. **Reboot or start the ypserv process manually.**
   Both NIS master and slave server run a process known as ypserv, to which NIS client systems connect. The ypserv process is started on systems that have a directory called /var/yp/`domainname`. This directory is created as a result of running ypinit. The process can be started by rebooting the machine or by entering ypserv from the command line as root.

DNS

The Domain Naming Service, DNS, is a naming convention designed for grouping networks on the Internet. There are a few major types of Internet domain names. When applying for an Internet number from the NIC, you are asked to provide some information about the type of activity on the requested IP address. Networks in the commercial realm are given the .COM suffix. Universities and other educational networks use the .EDU domain, and governmental institutions use the .GOV suffix. Another common domain is .ORG, which may be given to requestors with a single or low number of Internet addresses. The example network used throughout this chapter is for a corporation called Bigco and is part of the commercial Internet domain called bigco.COM.

Bigco is a corporation that develops both hardware and software products. The company is divided into three main domains: engineering, corporate, and operations. Bigco connects to the Internet on a machine whose name is "bigco." By virtue of the fact that this system connects to the Internet, its name is bigco.COM. All traffic to and from the Internet goes through this machine. Figure 6-5 illustrates the network.

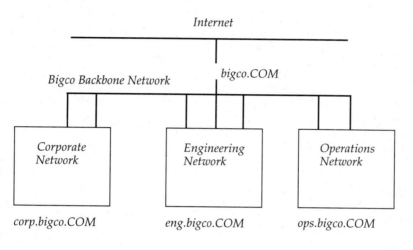

Figure 6-5   DNS Structure of Bigco

The manner in which you implement the naming of your network affects many things, including how electronic mail is sent and received both inside and outside the network, the NIS or NIS+ domain names, and how the organization of the company network is maintained.

Mail Server

The mail server directs electronic mail throughout the bigco domain, in addition to routing mail to and from the outside world. This function is accomplished though mail *aliases*, which may also be in the form of maps in the name service databases. The mail server system must be able to resolve email that does not contain a target host, but instead may be addressed to *username@bigco.COM*.

Router Systems

To create a router or gateway machine, either version of the Solaris operating system will suffice, as the procedures in both versions are identical. Begin by installing the system as a standalone machine, selecting a minimal amount of software. Initialize the second network interface by creating a `/etc/hostname.IFN` file, where IFN is the network interface name and relative number.

Most SPARC systems have an on-board network interface named *le0*, after the Lance Ethernet device that is built into the CPU board. Hence, these systems include a file called `/etc/hostname.le0`, which contains the nodename or hostname of the machine. Other SPARC systems have an on-board device called *ie0* and similarly use a `/etc/hostname.ie0` file. The hostname for the second or any other network interface cannot have the same name or IP address as the base nodename of the machine.

Note – The Solaris 2.x install process allows only one interface to be configured during installation. The procedures below must be performed after installation completes and the system is rebooted.

▼ Creating a Router

1. **Create /etc/hostname.*xxx* file.**
   First determine the name and number of the Ethernet interface. The network interface on-board the CPU is always called *le0* or *ie0*; check `ifconfig(8c)`. On SPARC systems using S-bus option cards, additional interface numbers are determined by the priority of the slot assignment. The first instance is called *le1*, the second *le2*, and so on. Solaris 2.x systems adhere to this numbering scheme but are rather touchy when devices are moved from their original slot after the devices and links have been made.

Helpful Hint – Try not to move cards around after the system has been installed or be prepared for some patchwork in the `/devices` tree.

The second interface on the machine red is called red-bb. The command below places the name of the interface into the appropriate file.

```
# echo red-bb >> /etc/hostname.le1
```

2. **Edit /etc/hosts.**
   Create an entry for the second interface in the `/etc/hosts` file. The entry must be in the local `hosts` file because all network interfaces are turned on before any name services are started. In this case, the two hostnames red and red-bb are included in the `/etc/hosts` file.

```
#
# Sun Host Database
#
# If the NIS is running, this file is only consulted when booting
#
127.0.0.1    localhost
192.9.201.1 red
192.9.200.8 red-bb
#
```

3. Reboot the system.

Reboot router systems after setting up the files for additional interfaces. Rebooting is necessary because the streams plumbing for network interfaces occurs very early on in the boot sequence, and there is no way to start interfaces that have not been plumbed.

4. Check the status of network interfaces.

After the system reboots, check the status of the additional networks by using the ifconfig command, as shown below. All network interfaces are reported.

```
# ifconfig -a
le0: flags=63<UP,BROADCAST,NOTRAILERS,RUNNING>
    inet 192.9.201.1 netmask ffffff00 broadcast 192.9.201.0
le1: flags=63<UP,BROADCAST,NOTRAILERS,RUNNING>
    inet 192.9.200.8 netmask ffffff00 broadcast 192.9.200.0
lo0: flags=49<UP,LOOPBACK,RUNNING>
    inet 127.0.0.1 netmask ff000000
```

You can also use the netstat(8c) command to obtain the status of network interfaces. The -ia option shows information on interfaces that were autoconfigured at boot time.

```
# netstat -ia
Name Mtu  Net/Dest   Address    Ipkts  Ierrs Opkts Oerrs Collis Queue
lo0  8232 loopback   localhost  20300  0     20300 0     0      0
le0  1500 bico_corp  red        31244  0     32322 0     10     0
le1  1500 bigco_bb   red-bb     3211   0     3222  0     3      0
```

Use the -r argument to netstat to monitor network route information, as shown below.

```
# netstat -r
Routing Table:
Destination    Gateway    Flags  Ref  Use  Interface
-----------------------------------------------------------
localhost      localhost  UH     0    35   lo0
bigco_corp     red        U      2    321  le0
bigco_bb       red-bb     U      2    123  le1
244.0.0.0      red        U      3    0    le0
```

As the number of networks grows, the routing table must also grow. Among the ways to implement routing procedures, one way is to allow the software to handle them without intervention.

Internet Router

The Internet router has one connection on the backbone network and one connection to the Internet via a high-speed data link. A number of products, both hardware and software, accomplish these connections. To obtain the Internet connection, correspondence with SRI and with some transport provider is necessary. After sending a request, SRI supplies the IP addresses and network class. The transport provider can be one of the many communication companies that offer open data lines to Internet hubs.

The Internet router system is functional with either version of Solaris software, but the Solaris 2.x release includes additional routing and security features not available in the earlier releases. Some of the routing services are designed for nonrouter systems, such as the router discovery daemon, in.rdisc, which dynamically searches for systems that broadcast routing tables on the local network segment. in.rdisc then adds default routes to the routing table so that constant polling is unnecessary. Systems running the Solaris 1.x release handle routing a bit differently, pulling in the entire routing tables at boot time, thereby occupying more system resources.

The Internet Router system is sometimes called a firewall because it protects the local network from the outside world. Security on the firewall machine should be as tight as possible to prevent intruders from gaining access to confidential company information or from interjecting computer virus activity inside the domain.

The procedures to set up tightened security are discussed in Chapter 7, "Security," which includes a section on how to start the Automated Security Enhancement Tool, ASET. In its basic form, the Internet router is similar to any other router machine in that it is the link between one or many networks.

Application Server

The NFS system is the key element in providing application resources to many systems concurrently. When set up properly, the application resource server can be a way to ensure access to an agreed-on set of identical applications throughout the entire corporation.

Common applications can be grouped into a single distribution volume and replicated throughout the organization, based on number of client machines that are using the resource. The rules concerning NFS clients vary, depending on whether the resource is used in read-only or read-write mode. Generally, more clients can use a resource that is read-only, because NFS read operations are less expensive. Read-write resources cost more in network bandwidth.

Another consideration in implementing an application server is the architecture type of the clients it serves. Administration is simpler when all clients share the same executables, so that only one occurrence of each application needs to be maintained.

A group of engineering professionals requires a different set of applications than do accountants or department administrators. However, some applications are common to all, such as word processing, spreadsheet, graphic presentation packages, or company-wide utilities such as a phone directory or a distributed on-line library.

In order to implement such applications, players from all support organizations should decide on a selected set of application software necessary for their particular groups. Common applications can be grouped into a single distribution volume and replicated throughout the organization, based on number of client machines that are using the resource.

At some specified period, usually at night, copies of the master server's NFS resources are distributed to a selected list of servers, each of which supports a local work group.

▼ Building a Simple Application Server

1. Install the machine.
   To build an application server, install the system as a standalone machine, selecting the End User or Developers install cluster. The entire release is not necessary because this system only needs to boot and share NFS resources.

2. Create the application area.
   You can create the application area during the Solaris installation process when you edit the Disks/File Systems forms. Or, you can create the application partition after installation completes. Select a disk partition with adequate space to house the shared applications and attach it to a local mount point, such as /export/apps. Use the format utility to change the partitioning of existing or add-on disks. Be sure you don't change the partitioning of a disk that is currently in use.

3. Install the applications.
   Install the application software into the newly created /export/apps directory. Use pkgadd or the software manager's related tools, swm and swmtool. Often, unbundled packages contain their own set of installation scripts and tend to place the bulk of their product into default directory names. You can circumvent this practice by determining the directory in which the application will be placed, then inserting a symlink that points to the preferred area.

4. Share the NFS resource.

The server in this example shares two applications on the corporate network: FrameMaker® and Lotus 1-2-3®. It is assumed that these applications have already been installed and placed under the /export/apps directory.

NFS resources are shared by placing the share command for that resource in the /etc/dfs/dfstab file, as follows:

```
# echo "share -F nfs -o ro /export/apps" >> /etc/dfs/dfstab
```

You can also use a file editor to edit the /etc/dfs/dfstab file.

5. Start the NFS services.

NFS server processes are not started on systems that are installed as standalone machines. NFS services must be started before remote mounting can occur; they can be started by rebooting the system or by executing the following command:

```
# /etc/init.d/nfs.server start
```

The script above executes the /etc/dfs/dfstab file and starts the appropriate daemons. Any previously shared NFS directories that are not included in the /etc/dfs/dfstab file will be unshared.

The Home Directory Server

A home directory server stores user files for its clients. Usually, servers of this type are powerful systems with large amounts of disk space, distributed over different controllers and disk partitions. For performance and ease of backup, several home directory partitions should be shared, as opposed to one single large partition. Home directory servers are also suited for NFS accelerator and writebuffering products, such as NVSIMM and the NFS Prestoserv module. Both of these products buffer NFS write operations so that network operations need not wait until the write has completed.

Size limits for individual user home directories can vary greatly. Users of graphics packages will undoubtedly require more space than those who write reports in FrameMaker or run spreadsheet programs. Home directories of software developers can require limitless disk space for source environments and binaries.

A good starting point is to allow 40 megabytes per user or workstation. For every 10 workstations, create a 400-megabyte partition on the home directory server. In this example, the home directory server, pink, has one such partition mounted on /export/home1. For the next 10 workstations, another 400 megabyte partition is created and mounted on /export/home2. As more home directory space is needed, more space can be allotted by adding hardware and local mount points.

After creating and adding the partitions to the /etc/vfstab file for permanent mounting, create the user accounts. The eight user accounts in this example are called user01 – user08. Each account needs an entry in the name service password map or the local password file. The password entries for these eight users are as follows:

```
user01:x:5000:10:User1 :/home/user1:/bin/csh
user02:x:5001:10:User2 :/home/user2:/bin/csh
user03:x:5002:10:User3 :/home/user3:/bin/csh
user04:x:5003:10:User4 :/home/user4:/bin/csh
user05:x:5004:10:User5 :/home/user5:/bin/csh
user06:x:5005:10:User6 :/home/user6:/bin/csh
user07:x:5006:10:User7 :/home/user7:/bin/csh
user08:x:5007:10:User8 :/home/user8:/bin/csh
```

Notice that each user's home directory entry is under /home/*username*, even though the actual locations are divided between pink:/export/home1 and pink:/export/home2. The reason for this will be explained shortly.

Once the account entries are defined and propagated, create the home directories, copy the prototype environment files, and apply proper permissions to each directory and its contents. The for-loop shown below accomplishes these tasks.

```
pink# for i in 01 02 03 04
>do
>mkdir /export/home1/user$i
>cp /etc/skel/local.cshrc /export/home1/user$i/.cshrc
>cp /etc/skel/local.login /export/home1/user$i/.login
>chown -R user$i /export/home1/user$i
>done
```

Sharing the Home Directories

Make the home directories available to client systems by editing the /etc/dfs/dfstab file and including the share commands for the appropriate place-name. For the home directory server known as pink, a Solaris 2.x system, the two partitions mentioned above can be shared by adding the following lines to the /etc/dfs/dfstab file:

```
# place share(1M) commands here for automatic execution
# on entering init state 3.
#
# share [-F fstype] [ -o options] [-d "<text>"] <pathname> [resource]
# .e.g,
# share -F nfs -o rw=engineering -d "home dirs" /export/home2

share -F nfs -o rw=corp1 -d "Pink Home 1" /export/home1
share -F nfs -o rw=corp2 -d "Pink Home 2" /export/home2
```

From left to right, the share command translates as follows: Share the NFS resource with the read/write option allowed to the corp1 netgroup on the /export/home1 path. Allow the same options to the corp2 netgroup on the /export/home2 path. Specific read-write options are much more secure than allowing full access.

It is also a good idea to increase the number of nfsd processes on servers that have many client systems. A default number of nfsd processes are started on NFS server systems as hard-coded into the /etc/init.d/nfs.server startup script. Open the file and search around line 35 for the following statement:

```
[ -f /etc/dfs/dfstab ] && /usr/sbin/shareall -F nfs

    if grep -s nfs /etc/dfs/sharetab >/dev/null ; then
        /usr/lib/nfs/nfsd -a 16
        /usr/lib/nfs/mountd
    fi
```

The shell statement above first checks for the existence of an /etc/dfs/dfstab file, then executes the shareall command, attempting to share all NFS-type resources. Output from the shareall command is written to the /etc/dfs/sharetab file. If any of the entries in /etc/dfs/sharetab contains the keyword nfs, then start 16 instances of /usr/lib/nfs/nfsd on all transport providers and start one instance of /usr/lib/nfs/mountd. You may wish to increase the number of nfsd processes, but remember that this increase can cause problems if the server does not have enough memory.

Modifying the Automounter Maps

After the directories are created and shared, create the automounter maps. To provide the highest security, each user account will be used as the key. Observe the following auto_home file:

```
user01  pink:/export/home1/user01
user02  pink:/export/home1/user02
user03  pink:/export/home1/user03
user04  pink:/export/home1/user04
user05  pink:/export/home2/user05
user06  pink:/export/home2/user06
user07  pink:/export/home2/user07
user08  pink:/export/home2/user08
```

Since auto_home controls the directories under /home, any reference to /home/user01 automatically mounts the directory pink:/export/home1/user01 under /home/user01.

Solaris 1.x Applications on Solaris 2.x Systems

Many sites that are currently using SPARC workstations and servers include systems running either version of the Solaris environment, often because the application software used on machines running the Solaris 1.x release may not run on Solaris 2.x systems. Several procedures can be implemented to ensure proper cohabitation. One such procedure uses the remote display capabilities of X11.

This procedure, which employs the NFS automounter, an application wrapper, and a remote display machine, launches the application from the Solaris 1.x machines and displays it on the Solaris 2.x workstation. When the wrapper is invoked, it tests the version of the operating system. If the application cannot run in that environment, the wrapper connects via `rsh` to a designated remote host (for example, a compute server) and `xhosts` the application back to the originating system. This method usually requires that the user's home directory be accessible to the remote hosting system.

6

Security   7 ≡

Protecting data from unauthorized access increasingly concerns many organizations. Networked systems are intended to make vast amounts of information available while maintaining an adequate level of security. The basic security features that are included in Solaris 2.x are not unlike most UNIX-based systems, but Solaris provides an even greater level of security than generic versions of UNIX. Even higher levels are available as add-on products, capable of bringing the Solaris 2.x environment to security levels found in the "Orange Book," published by the United States Department of Defense. Discussions on security levels of this type are beyond the scope of this book. This chapter explores the security tools and programs that are bundled in the base Solaris environment.

Solaris 2.x contains the following security enhancements, not bundled in Solaris 1.x:

- Account Resource Management (ARM)
- Automated Security Enhancement Tool (ASET)
- ONC+ Federated Security

The Account Resource Management is a tool to maintain one or many user accounts on a single machine. The Automated Security Enhancement Tool is a way to monitor and set certain system resources to one of three desired security levels. ONC+ Federated Security can be defined as a set of security tools, chosen from adopted standards, such as Kerberos and other Data Encryption Standards (DES).

Each of these tools can help protect systems from unauthorized entry and are discussed in some detail. However, security begins at far higher levels than a suite of tools and programs. Each user has a certain amount of responsibility while participating in a networked environment such as Solaris.

Security Theory

Security consists of verifying the identity of a user requesting a service and then permitting only specific access. These processes are called *authentication* and *authorization*. When the computer world consisted of a single mainframe computer, verifying identification by a password was considered enough. It has since been proven that passwords are shared, accounts for terminated users are not cleaned up in a timely manner, passwords can be cracked, and most network actions are sent as clear text available to anyone who has the ability to snoop the network. Therefore authentication and authorization procedures have been enhanced on Solaris 2.x to provide more security.

Authentication

The authentication process across networks can be improved by using encryption techniques for network transactions, requesting secondary passwords, changing passwords frequently, and setting minimum standards for what a good password should be. One additional authentication for modem lines is to institute a dial-back setup. By agreeing that the user will only use this account from a specified number, authentication can be done by connecting only to specific sites.

Authorization

Once users have been authenticated, they should be given access only to the services that they need to do their job. Granting blanket access is asking for trouble. For a standard user, access to most of the user-level utilities, their own personal files, and all files for their department or workgroup should be sufficient.

Careless use of supervisor permissions is a significant cause of security breaches, intended or not. Superuser functions can be off-loaded to utilities such as `automount`, `vold` (volume management), and `admintool` when used as a member of the *sysadmin* group.

Suid programs, (programs that can have a different effective id -- usually root), have been severely limited in Solaris 2.x. Refer to the section at the end of this chapter on suid notes.

Data Encryption

With local, physical network access, such as the use of `snoop` in promiscuous mode, a persistent person can listen to all the chatter on the network. He can see passwords and read data. Without the network, most of the UNIX functionality is limited. Since Solaris 2.x is so heavily network based, this limitation would be extreme. To improve the situation, the data that is placed on the network can be encrypted. Several methods are available currently.

crypt

crypt is the original encryption tool found on a UNIX system. It works by simply taking a key that the user defines and encrypting the data with that key. The problem with this scheme is that, like a password, the key must be remembered to again gain access to the data. Also, the more often the key is used, the more likely it is that knowledge of the key spreads to other users.

DES

Data Encryption Standard (DES) is a method that creates two keys, a public and private key. Using DES for network traffic can be complex.

The public and private keys are actually related to each other. Usually, there are two sides to a DES-encrypted conversation, and both sides of a DES conversation have their own DES keys. Consider this *very simplified* example.

Key	Decoder (Destination)	User (sender) (Source)
Private	23	17
Public	28	22

A user's private key is 17. The public key relates to the private key by adding 5 to the private key: 22. Assume that the private/public key combination of 17/22 is the source DES key combination. Assume further that the destination has 23/28 as its private/public key combination. Now, transactions occur between the decoding system's private key and the sending system's public key; in this case, that would be 23 and 22, or a total of 45. The sending system encrypted its private key (17) and the destination public key (28) respectively, for a total of 45.

Case 1: DS private (23) + SS public (22)   = 45
Case 2: DS public (28) + SS encrypted private (17) = 45

It must be emphasized that the actual algorithm is far more complex than this simple addition.

Initially, users set up knowledge of the DES key when they log in. The keylogin program uses the login password to obtain its private DES key from the DES key server. If users have a DES key that is based upon something other than their password, they must reexecute the keylogin program and use the appropriate password to obtain the DES key. The DES key is stored in a buffer for the duration of the user's session.

When a user wishes to access a remote DES-maintained service, a dialog is started between the two sides, and they exchange public keys. The destination system verifies that this is actually a valid user for its services and sends an acknowledgment back to the source system.

Each request for service is now encrypted with a combination of the source private and destination public keys, time of encryption, and *some other value*. This *some other value* is usually some constant defined for this DES service. Since DES is used by NIS+, `admintool`, Secure NFS, and SunNet Manager™ currently, each service uses a unique *some other value*. Since a time value is part of the encryption scheme, timing is important. Invalid transmissions can happen because of time differences. However, this means that a program similar to `crack` cannot be used to decrypt the answer and forge a reply of its own in the time frame required here.

Kerberos

Kerberos uses a different encryption algorithm, but it effectively works the same. Solaris offers the Kerberos client-side use, but the Kerberos key server must be obtained from other sources.

PGP

Pretty Good Privacy (PGP) is a method, similar to `crypt`, for encrypting data. Both ends of a conversation must share a key. This key is primarily used for sending data across the Internet or other network where common encryption configurations such as DES or Kerberos are not available. This method does require that the user manually maintain the encryption key. This is a shareware product and is not included with Solaris 2.x.

Login Security

Logging in is the primary place where user authentication is done. Controlling the entry point is a big step toward controlling security of the entire network.

User Logins

The most critical components of security lie at the user level. A single user can be the weak link in the security chain of your network. Many problems can be avoided if users are properly educated and the rules regarding account usage are posted and enforced.

Individual users must not compromise the environment by allowing unauthorized persons to use their login and password, thereby gaining access to the network. This problem is most commonly found over modem connections but can also occur via the Internet. While you cannot keep people from passing out their login and passwords to friends, you can make them accountable for situations that occur during a login session. UNIX has a very good accounting mechanism. Most actions can be traced back to a single point by using the normal system accounting data files and utilities.

There will always be persons interested in gaining access to machines on which they do not belong. Certain steps that can be taken to make unauthorized entry more difficult than normal are discussed below.

User Accounts

Login names are somewhat easy to guess in many environments, usually consisting of some combination of first and last names. A higher level of security would be to use a combination of upper and lower case characters or special characters, not easily chosen by "cracking" programs. Since login names can be easily obtained from virtually any electronic mail message, the password and shadow files must protect entry into the next level.

User accounts that use a local /etc/passwd file are the most secure, since each password has a similar entry in the local /etc/shadow file. The NIS+ naming service offers a similar level of security when it is used at level 2. This is not the case if NIS compatibility is used in NIS+. The shadow file is readable only by the superuser, which stalls most attempts at system cracking. This password scheme is new to veteran SunOS users who are used to the BSD 4.2 semantics of placing all user account information in one file. Unfortunately, the NIS naming service used by Solaris is built under this scheme.

In a naming service such as NIS, the master password database contains not only the login name but also the encrypted password. This situation offers an easy target for folks interested in checking on their co-worker's files and email. Company policies to prohibit such action should be enforced. Most naming services contain massive security holes. You must balance the risk with the benefit of having network-wide password maps.

Superuser Login

You must also decide upon some form of superuser implementation. Do you want the superuser password for individual workstations to lie with the normal user of that machine? If you create a network "root" account, you double the risk of superuser access to your network. Each form of network-wide superuser implementation entails some risk. You need to weigh the risk with the benefit to determine how the superuser accounts are managed.

Much of the superuser access problem has been resolved since the introduction of the Administration Tool. Most administrative functions that require root access can be accomplished through admintool. You can also use admintool to change a remote system's /etc/passwd file, modifying or installing a superuser account therein.

But superuser access is still necessary to solve special problems, such as printer or queuing jams and filesystem-full messages, to name a few. A network-wide superuser account works well in these situations, since you can let individual users control their own superuser password, while still maintaining a "back door."

Another way to implement superuser accounts throughout the network is by using AutoInstall. After each system installation, a superuser password must be entered during the subsequent boot phase. When encountered by the individual user, the root password screen is thought to be meaningless, often skipped by pressing the RETURN key a few times. This leaves the system wide open, with no root password.

If installations are automated by means of AutoInstall, a known password can be placed on the machine during the postinstall phase. This is one way to ensure that a superuser password is installed and that root access is enabled.

Administrators familiar with BSD 4.3 will notice that, as a default, root logins are disabled from everywhere but the console. Disabling is accomplished in the /etc/default/login file. Users must first log in to a valid account and execute the su command to obtain root privileges. Because logs are maintained, this method provides better tracking of who can become the superuser on any machine. To override this default, simply comment out the line that begins with CONSOLE.

Special Logins

In addition to user who log in locally or across the net, there can be special users, such as ftp users or uucp users.

Recording Logins

You can use the /etc/default/su file to track who becomes a superuser on a system. Also, the messages about logins, such as *x* number of login failures, can be recorded and forwarded from syslog.

Password Security

Passwords are the next level of security for systems on the network. Once a password is known, access to the network is generally granted unless certain flags are set, disallowing such action. There are many ways to discourage hackers from gaining access to passwords.

One way is to implement rules that require users to combine upper and lower case in passwords or that require a numeric character. Inform users not to use passwords that are easily guessed, such as a combination of names, license, or social security number, names of automobiles, or almost any dictionary entry. Also, the system administrator can force users to change their passwords regularly. Enforcement of these rules is accomplished through the Account Resource Manager.

Account Resource Management

Account Resource Management (ARM) provides account protection at the user level by setting certain flags in the `/etc/shadow` file and files in the `/etc/default` directory, controlling such things as password aging, account expiration, automatic logout, password qualification, and disabling logins after repeated invalid attempts or at specified time periods. Other ARM features include enabling an automatic lock screen, which closes window access on inactive workstations, and prompting for an additional password on dial-in connections.

Much of the account resource management is handled through the User Account Manager portion of the GUI-based `admintool`, as shown in Figure 7-1.

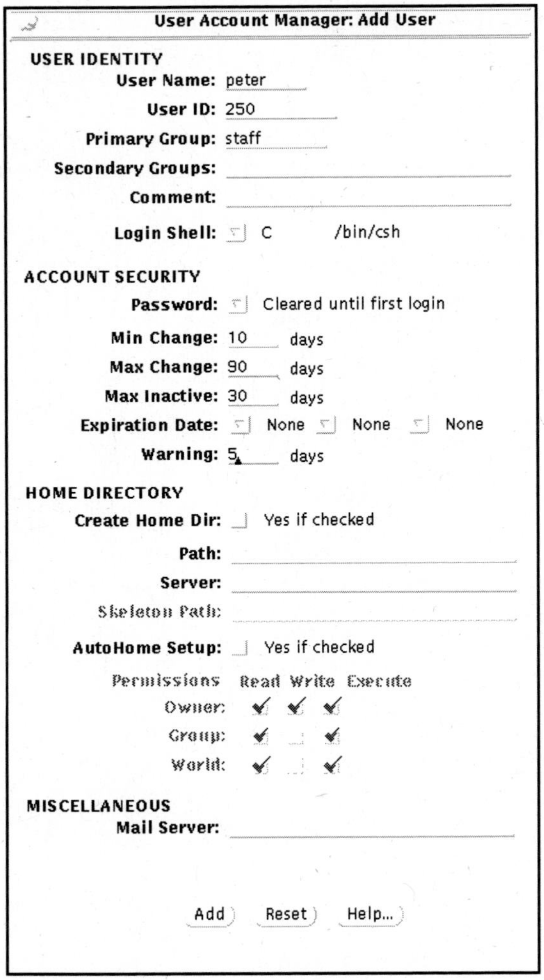

Figure 7-1   Account Security in the User Account Manager

Password Aging

The Account Security section provides space to enable or disable accounts, enforce a minimum and maximum number of days that a password can be used, turn an account off after a specified number of inactive days, and set up an account expiration date. Warnings can be sent to the user in the form of email messages as each of these dates approaches.

In Figure 7-1, notice that the Password field is set to "Cleared until first login," which means that when the account is first used, entry of a password will be required. The password entered at that time will be the password of record until either the value of Max Change is reached, in this case 90 days, or until the password is manually changed.

The password cannot be changed sooner than Min Change, in this case ten days. Attempts to change the password before ten days will be disallowed.

The password characteristics are as follows:

- Set the minimum password length by changing the PASSLENGTH parameter in the `/etc/default/passwd` file. Default length is six characters. Remember, only the first eight characters of a password are significant. For example, *eightbits* and *eightbit* are equivalent passwords.

- Set the Min Change value to the minimum time between password changes for this user. The default value here is 0. To change this default and institute system-wide minimum time frame, change the MINWEEKS parameter in the `/etc/default/passwd` file. This change can also be made from the command line.

```
# passwd -n 30 {username}
```

Note – If the Min Change value is 0, users can change their password when forced to, and then immediately change it back to the original value, defeating the purpose.

- Set the Max Change value to the longest allowable time before a password change. The default here is blank, meaning that a user is not forced to change a password. As with the minimum value, a system-wide default can be defined with the MAXWEEKS parameter in the `/etc/default/passwd` file. This change can be made from the command line.

```
# passwd -x 90 {username}
```

- The Max Inactive field instructs the system to lock the account after 13 days of inactivity. The command line equivalent is:

```
# usermod -f 30 {username}
```

- An account can be specified to end or expire on a certain date. This specification is useful when the system administrator is notified that a person is leaving the company. The command line equivalent is:

```
# usermod -e {date} {username}
# usermod -d 10/30/94 johnd
```

- The warning field specifies the number of days notice the user receives to change his/her password before the account is locked. The command line equivalent is:

```
# passwd -w 10 {username}
```

Secondary Passwords

A secondary password can be set up for a modem line. This password is specific to the connection shell, instead of being specific to a user. To add this secondary password authentication, you must create two files.

The first file, /etc/dialups, is a list of the device names that will be receiving logins and requiring a second password. This file should be owned by user and group root. It should have 600 for permissions. The following is an example:

```
/dev/term/a
/dev/term/b
```

The second file, /etc/d_passwd, contains the shell types that require a password and the encrypted passwd entry with colons as delimiters. This file should also have permissions of 600 and should be owned by user and group root. The following is a sample entry:

```
/usr/bin/csh:v18FysV1I9V9c:
```

Helpful Hint – You should also maintain checks on files that grant network access without passwords, such as the .rhosts and /etc/hosts.equiv files. Avoid creating a .rhosts file in the root directory, since its existence and proper contents may enable root logins from any machine, a huge security hole.

Maintaining System Integrity with ASET

ASET performs tasks that monitor and change the level of security on a particular machine. ASET can be configured to observe security-sensitive files for changes in contents or permissions and to report areas of risk, as well as changing those files to bring the system into conformance.

Running ASET

ASET runs on a local machine, not network wide, and is included in the SUNWast package. A good candidate for running ASET is a system with connections to the outside world, such as a modem server, a firewall that connects to the Internet, or a timeshare machine.

ASET Security Levels

ASET security can be set to one of three levels: low, medium, or high. Each level increases a system's security from just monitoring without limiting access, to modifying files that are considered to be a medium-to-serious security risk.

At the lowest level, ASET checks security levels that are expected on a newly installed system. No files are changed, only observations are reported. At the medium level, the security is tightened, but the system is still accessible. At the highest level, ASET is very restrictive and may be too secure to accomplish many tasks in a networked environment. Without any arguments, ASET runs at the lowest security level and executes all seven tasks, informing you where the reports are being stored. See the output below for the task list.

Executing ASET

To run ASET interactively, change the working directory to /usr/aset and execute the command in the example run.

```
harlie# /usr/aset/aset
======= ASET Execution Log =======

ASET running at security level low

Machine = harlie; Current time = 0718_18:18

aset: Using /usr/aset as working directory

Executing task list ...
 firewall
 env
 sysconf
 usrgrp
 tune
 cklist
 eeprom

All tasks executed. Some background tasks may still be running.
```

```
Run /usr/aset/util/taskstat to check their status:
 /usr/aset/util/taskstat [aset_dir]
```

where aset_dir is ASET's operating directory, currently=/usr/aset.

```
When the tasks complete, the reports can be found in:
 /usr/aset/reports/latest/*.rpt
You can view them by:
 more /usr/aset/reports/latest/*.rpt
```

Each time ASET runs, a new report directory is created and named with the date and time. A pointer to the latest reports directory is also maintained through the use of a symlink called latest, always pointing to the youngest directory.

Many ASET tasks run in the background, as indicated in the output above. Status on tasks that have not completed can be obtained by means of the /usr/aset/util/taskstat utility. Output from taskstat may be similar to the following:

/usr/aset/util/taskstat

```
Checking ASET tasks status ...
Task firewall is done.
Task env is done.
Task sysconf is done.
Task usrgrp is done.

The following tasks are done:
 firewall
 env
 sysconf
 usrgrp

The following tasks are not done:
 tune
 cklist
 eeprom
```

As each task completes, a report is placed in the reports directory. Standard output from the overall aset run is placed in execution.log file, also in the latest directory.

ASET Tasks and Reports

ASET tasks can be run from the command line or configured into the `crontab` file to execute as often as necessary. Each ASET task produces a report, placed in the `/usr/aset/reports` directory, unless specified differently in the `/usr/aset/asetenv` file.

Helpful Hint – Take care when selecting the reports directory. You don't want to make these reports available to the world. You should also be concerned with disk space, since reports that execute via a cron job are often forgotten until they fill up a filesystem.

If you are running ASET on a number of systems, you may want to create an NFS-mounted reports directory where all systems store their reports. Be sure to include the system name in the path, so that results from other systems are not overwritten.

The first time you run `aset`, files are created from which comparisons are made. Many of the reports from the initial `aset` run will contain messages about the tasks that were performed. The reports for each ASET task are outlined in the table below.

Table 7-1 ASET Tasks and Report Names

ASET Task	Report Name
Set system file permissions	tune.rpt
User/group check	usrgrp.rpt
System files checklist	cklist.rpt
eeprom check	eeprom.rpt
System configuration files checklist	sysconf.rpt
Firewall	firewall.rpt

Set System File Permissions

At the lowest level, ASET checks system files for the default permissions at installation time. At the medium level, permissions are modified to provide an adequate level of security for most environments. At its highest level, permissions are tightened even further.

A typical `tune.rpt` shows the following messages when executed on a newly installed system.

```
# more tune.rpt

*** Begin Tune Task ***

... setting attributes on the system objects defined in
 /usr/aset/masters/tune.low
chmod: WARNING: can't change /home
chmod: WARNING: can't change /home
chown: /home: Operation not applicable
chgrp: /home: Operation not applicable
chgrp: /home: Operation not applicable


*** End Tune Task ***
```

You'll notice the warning messages concerning the /home directory because this system employs the automounter as a way to attach NFS-mounted home directories. The permissions for root access over NFS mounts must be explicit. The task at hand attempted to not only search the /home path as root, but also attempted to modify its attributes, as indicated by the chmod and chown warnings.

To disable checking this or any other NFS mount, edit the /usr/aset/masters/tune.* file, depending on your security level. Simply comment out the entry for /home by preceding it with the "#" sign, a common method of disabling services.

Conversely, you can add files or directories to this file so that permissions and access are checked each time this aset task is executed. You may like to add custom or site-specific path names to this list, directories not found on a vanilla system.

User / Group Checks

ASET scans the local /etc/passwd and /etc/shadow files for user accounts without passwords and checks for users that share the same UID. The User/Group check also checks for anomalies in the /etc/group file and reports its findings in the usrgrp.rpt in the ASET report directory.

A good candidate for this check is the name service master, since this is where network-wide, user account information is usually stored. If you are using the NIS name service, you cannot run this task since ASET is bundled on Solaris 2.x. As of this writing, NIS domains can only be mastered by systems running Solaris 1.x.

The User/Group report is similar to the screen output below.

```
harlie# cat usergrp.rpt

*** Begin User And Group Checking ***

Checking /etc/passwd ...

Checking /etc/shadow ...

Warning! Shadow file, line 1, no password:
 root::6445::::::

Warning! Shadow file, line 16, no password:
 usr1::8355::::::

... end user check.

Checking /etc/group ...

... end group check.

*** End User And Group Checking ***
```

To allow more than one user to share the same UID, you can create an alias in the /usr/aset/masters/uid_aliases file. Simply follow the syntax shown in the commented section of this file. Notice that two entries were found to contain no user passwords. At the lowest level, this situation is only reported. When ASET is executed in the highest level, flags in the /etc/shadow file are changed to prompt for a password at the next login.

System-level Security

ASET also performs tasks on system-level, security-related files, those that enable setuid or remote access form network peers. As with most ASET tasks, snapshots are created upon the initial execution and compared with current attributes of the files and directories contained in the snapshot.

System Files Checklist

The System Files Checklist task scans the files and directories listed in the
/usr/aset/masters/cklist.* file, placing its findings in the cklist.rpt. Many of
the files included in this checklist are located in the /etc directory. Each file and expected
attributes are listed in a syntax that is easy to follow, so that custom files can be entered
and included in the scan. The report produced is similar to the following:

```
harlie# more cklist.rpt

*** Begin Checklist Task ***

... Checklist snapshot is being created. Wait ...
... Checklist snapshot created.

No differences in the checklist.

*** End Checklist Task ***
```

Notice that there were no differences in this report—which should emphasize a point.
Make sure that you have the proper permissions set before you start ASET. There is no
use in comparing system files if the masters have left the system wide open. The report
file merely states that no differences were found.

EEPROM Check

The eeprom check looks at current settings in the system's EEPROM or Non-Volatile
RAM, specifically, the password setting that prevents access to a machine by halting and
booting single user. When an EEPROM password is enabled, a machine cannot be
rebooted without the password being provided.

At the lowest level, the eeprom task only reports its findings in the eeprom.rpt file. At
the highest level, EEPROM passwords are enabled.

Network-level Security

ASET also performs security checks on files that affect systems at the network level.
Permissions of NFS shared directories are checked for network mount access; in addition,
files in the /etc/default directory are checked.

System Configuration Files Check

Reports for this task are placed in the sysconf.rpt file. At the lowest level,
discrepancies are only reported. At the highest level, changes are made to files deemed to
be of greatest security risk, and the changes are logged in the appropriate report. One of

these files is /etc/default/login, which enables direct root logins from machines over the network, as discussed above. Authentication checks are done in the /etc/inetd.conf file for services that started by inetd. Any services that are deemed to be insecure are modified or removed.

NFS-shared directories that are open or accessible by everyone are included in the report, but are not changed, since NFS has a somewhat natural level of security, disallowing root privileges unless specifically granted. A typical sysconf.rpt file, run at the highest security level, is similar to the following:

```
harlie# more sysconf.rpt

*** Begin System Scripts Check ***
Warning! Root login allowed at any terminal.
Changing /etc/default/login to allow root login only at the console terminal.

Warning! finger has poor authentication mechanism
not recommended on a secure system. (/etc/inetd.conf)

Entry fixed. finger entry is commented out.

Warning! rusersd has poor authentication mechanism
not recommended on a secure system. (/etc/inetd.conf)

Entry fixed. rusersd entry is commented out.

Warning! Shared resources file (/etc/dfs/dfstab) , line 8, file system
exported with no restrictions:
 share -F nfs /export/tools

Warning! Shared resources file (/etc/dfs/dfstab) , line 9, file system
exported with no restrictions:
 share -F nfs /export/funstuff

Warning! /etc/ftpusers should contain root at high security level.

Root entry has been appended in /etc/ftpusers.

*** End System Scripts Check ***
```

Notice the actions taken as a result of this task. The /etc/default/login file was updated, since root logins were enabled on devices other than the system console. ASET also found poor authentication of the finger and ruserd services in the /etc/inetd.conf file and changed them to more secure levels. Another action taken as a result of running the System Configuration Files task at the highest security level was to create and place the root keyword in the /etc/ftpusers file. This action disables file transfers using the ftp protocol while running as the superuser from remote machines.

Firewall

The firewall task is not intended for normal machines, but rather for those systems that relay information between networks both in and out of a site. At the lowest and medium levels, the firewall task takes no action. At the highest level, the forwarding of Internet Protocol packets is disabled, hiding routing information from the external network. You can omit the firewall task by editing the /usr/aset/asetenv file.

Restoring the System

Restoring the system to values found prior to the execution of ASET can be accomplished by means of the /usr/aset/aset.restore command. You may have found that ASET tightens the system too much, negating some desired behavior within the network. You may have just been experimenting and wish to disable ASET. Whatever the reason, it is always good to have a utility that returns the system to the previous state.

Files that were modified by ASET are reported during the restore cycle, as shown below:

```
# /usr/aset/aset.restore
tune.restore completed.

Executing /usr/aset/tasks/usrgrp.restore

Beginning usrgrp.restore...

Restoring /etc/passwd. Saved existing file in /etc/passwd.asetbak.

Restoring /etc/group. Saved existing file in /etc/group.asetbak.

Restoring /etc/shadow. Saved existing file in /etc/shadow.asetback.

usrgrp.restore completed.

Resetting security level from high to null.

aset.restore: restoration completed.
```

Controlling Access

Once users have been authenticated as being valid, they are granted access. This access should be based on need; in most cases users should have the run of the system at user level. However, some users should be restricted. One example of this would be granting accounts to people outside the company, such as vendors who require information transfers. Some systems should be locked down even further. An example of this would be a database system where the only access other than that for the database administrators should be to a select group of users authorized to run a single program. In this case, a captured account is the preferred method of controlling access.

Root privileges should not be given out. However, there are times when someone needs to have a remote disk or CD-ROM mounted on the system. For these occurrences, a utility was created to execute this one root function. In this case, the utilities are `automount` and `vold`. For users who share in the administration of their own system, `admintool` can be run by any user who is a member of a special *sysadmin* group, thus removing another need for root.

Restricted Accounts

Solaris 2.x includes an SVR4 feature that enables restricted shells. A user can be situated in a directory that has limited functionality, disabling certain elements of normal shells such as:

- Changing the working directory, `cd`
- Setting or changing the $PATH variable
- Using absolute path names or commands containing "/"

A restricted shell is invoked in one of four ways:

- Setting the login shell in the `/etc/passwd` file to `/usr/lib/rsh`
- Setting the SHELL variable to `rsh` in `.profile`
- Using `rsh` as the first argument to `sh`
- Using the `/bin/sh -r` command

The creator of the `.profile` file is ultimately responsible for the level of restrictions allowed. Usually, administrators create restricted commands directories, such as `/usr/rbin` or `/usr/rlib`, and place in those directories only the commands that are approved for restricted users. This technique saves you from placing the usual `/usr/bin` or `/usr/sbin` directories into a restricted shell's PATH variable, while still providing access to the necessary executables.

Captured Accounts

In the case where access is needed to only one program, a captured account can be created. To make this type of account:

1. Create a home directory for a user. Do not create `.cshrc` or `.login` files.

2. Make a one-line file that executes the program.

3. Change permissions for this file to 555.

4. Make a `/etc/passwd` entry that calls the one-line `exec` file in place of a shell.

Permissions on Home Directories

Home directories that are NFS-mounted can also be deemed insecure unless proper mount path names are used and a *netgroups* map maintained. Automounter maps or NFS mount points should attach to a user's home directory rather than its parent, since the parent usually contains the home directories of many other accounts. Often this is unavoidable unless explicit `share` options are maintained along with the `auto_home` database.

Proper owner and group flags are of utmost importance in shared environments. User accounts should be owned by the user, and permissions should be set according to the rules of your particular environment. Many times it is acceptable for users to access other accounts, since this is one of the main reasons for networking. Try to keep account sharing confined to the work group instead of leaving user accounts wide open.

Data Protection Through Encryption

Much of the underlying network activity relies on Remote Procedure Calls, specifically from NIS and NFS operations. Generally, these calls are not authenticated, allowing any system to use RPC services at defined port numbers. When the secure RPC protocols are implemented, secret keys are passed between machines to validate users and machines, thus regulating access to network data.

Secure RPC is based on an enhanced authentication scheme known as the Data Encryption Standard (DES), available only in the United States and Canada. The DES operates on an algorithm for basic data encryption with a public key. Both NIS and NFS operations can use secure RPC to control access to confidential information.

NFS Encryption — DES

Using DES encryption on Solaris usually means using NIS+, because NIS+ has built-in hooks for using DES. The `publickey` table is where DES keys are kept for each entity. This data can be maintained on individual systems in the `/etc/publickey` file. However, since the `publickey` is usually based upon the user's (or root's) password, all systems must be updated immediately after the password is changed in order to access the data. If NIS is used, the `publickey` map must be updated and then pushed—the same problem that the `passwd` map encounters when passwords are changed.

To use DES from NIS+, both of the systems that will be communicating need to have an entry placed in the publickey table. This entry is accomplished by adding credentials for the system. (In NIS+, root is not a unique user across all systems. Therefore, root on each system is associated with the system itself.)

1. Verify that a `publickey` entry exists for the system.

   # **nismatch {system} publickey.org_dir**

2. If an entry does not exist, create one.

   # **nisclient -c {system}**

Once the entries exist for both systems, add the `-o secure` option to the `share` and `mount` commands.

1. Edit `/etc/dfs/dfstab` on a server and add a share line with the `-o secure` option

   share -F nfs -o rw,secure -d "Private Project" /export/project

2. Mount the filesystem on the client with the `-o secure` option.

   # **mount -F nfs -o secure black:/export/project /project**

NFS Encryption — Kerberos

Kerberos is an encryption facility similar to DES. The server side of Kerberos is not included on Solaris 2.x systems. A public domain version of a Kerberos server can be obtained from several sites on the Internet. Once Kerberos is in place and functioning, the process is virtually the same. Instead of `-o secure`, use `-o kerberos`.

Note on suid under Solaris

Suid is the process by which a program can change from one effective uid to another, usually root. Solaris 2.x has adopted POSIX standards for suid. This means that virtually all suid scripts are disabled. It does not affect programs that are compiled and installed as suid, just scripts that have the suid bit set. The only way to circumvent this disabling is to include the -b option as the only option in a csh script. Doing so allows the script to change its effective uid to that of superuser.

Software Management   8 ☰

Package Management

In the SunOS system, `suninstall` offered to install sets of files for uucp, versetec, or security, among other things. SVR4 takes the idea of a group of files one step further with packages, that is, a set of related files. The Solaris environment now provides a set of utility programs to install, remove, identify, and verify these packages. Information about what is installed is maintained on the system in the `/var/sadm` directory.

Packages can be managed by utilities invoked from the command line or by a GUI tool called `swmtool`. The process is the same for both methods; only the appearance is different. In addition, package installation and removal can be automated with shell scripts.

What's in a Package?

Packages have standard names and structures. All packages are installed in a directory named after the package. The pieces of each package are the same, so that a standard installation utility can be used for everything.

Package Structure

Each package has a `pkgmap` file, a `pkginfo` file, and a `reloc` directory. A package can contain other items, but these are the foundation.

- The `pgkmap` file is a list of all the files (including special files, such as directories and links) that are in the package. The file also lists the permissions that should be set for each file, the size of the file, and a checksum value.

- The `pkginfo` file contains a list of variables used during the installation process.

- The `reloc` directory contains the package items themselves.

Naming Convention for Packages

Sun uses a naming convention for its packages, based on the Sun stock symbol (SUNW), the product abbreviation (e.g., "lp" for "Line Printer Package"), and the filesystem on which the package is to be installed (e.g., "r" for / — root).

Definition of Terms

- Source device

  The `-d` option to `pkgadd` identifies the source of the packages to be installed, listed, or otherwise operated on. Some common sources are:

  `-d /dev/dsk/c0t6d0s2` — Obtain package from CD-ROM

  `-d ‘pwd‘` — Obtain package from the current working directory

  `-d <path>` — Obtain package from *path*

- Destination — root directory

  Each package has a designated place where it will be installed by default. For example, *SUNWowrqd* is installed into `/usr/openwin`. If this were to be installed in `/share/openwin`, the root directory would be designated as `/share`. The option `-R` designates this. To find the default root directory for a package, execute `pkginfo -r` *<pkgname>*.

- Packages

  All the man pages use the word *pkginst* to mean the package instance. The instance can be a single package or a list of packages. Wildcards are not expanded, so `SUNWlp*` is not a valid name. In the case of `pkgadd` and `pkgrm`, not specifying a pkginst causes the program to list all possible values and to prompt for the package(s) to operate on.

Adding Packages

Adding a package can be done interactively or via a script or other batch method.

Interactive Package Addition

A package installation looks like the following output.

pkgadd -d `pwd`

```
The following packages are available:


  1        SUNWabe        Solaris 2.3 User AnswerBook
                          (sparc) 8.12.9
  2        SUNWaccr       System Accounting, (Root)
                          (sparc) 11.5.0,REV=2.0.13
  3        SUNWaccu       System Accounting, (Usr)
                          (sparc) 11.5.0,REV=2.0.13
  4        SUNWadmap      System & Network Administration
                          Applications
                          (sparc) 6.0.9
  5        SUNWadmfw      System & Network Administration Framework
                          (sparc) 6.0.8
  6        SUNWadmr       System & Network Administration Root
                          (sparc) 6.0,REV=2.0
  7        SUNWapppr      PPP/IP Asynchronous PPP daemon
                          configuration files
                          (sparc) 11.5.0,REV=2.0.13
  8        SUNWapppu      PPP/IP Asynchronous PPP daemon and PPP login
                          service
                          (sparc) 11.5.0,REV=2.0.13
  9        SUNWarc        Archive Libraries
                          (sparc) 11.5.0,REV=2.0.13
 10        SUNWast        Automated Security Enhancement Tools
                          (sparc) 11.5.0,REV=2.0.13


... 125 more menu choices to follow;
<RETURN> for more choices, <CTRL-D> to stop display

Select package(s) you wish to process (or 'all' to process
all packages). (default: all) [?,??,q]: 1
```

At this point, select the desired package(s). The installation lists all copyright and trademark information about a package before doing the install, as shown in Code Examples 8-1 to 8-3.

Code Example 8-1

```
Processing package instance <SUNWabe> from </net/thyme/export/s10-
93/latest/Solaris_2.3>

Solaris 2.3 User AnswerBook
(sparc) 8.12.9

 Copyright 1993 Sun Microsystems, Inc. All Rights Reserved.
 Printed in the United States of America.
2550 Garcia Avenue, Mountain View, California, 94043-1100 U.S.A.
```

(Additional copyrights deleted)

Code Example 8-2

```
RESTRICTED RIGHTS LEGEND: Use, duplication, or disclosure by the
government is subject to restrictions as set forth in subparagraph
(c)(1)(ii) of the Rights in Technical Data and Computer Software clause at
DFARS 252.227-7013 and FAR 52.227-19.

Sun, Sun Microsystems, the Sun Logo, Solaris, SunOS, ONC, NFS,
OpenWindows, DeskSet, AnswerBook, SunLink, SunView, SunDiag, NeWS,
OpenBoot, OpenFonts, SunInstall, SunNet, ToolTalk, X11/NeWS, Sunsoft,
the SunSoft Logo and XView are trademarks or registered trademarks of
Sun Microsystems, Inc. UNIX and OPEN LOOK are registered trademarks of
UNIX System Laboratories, Inc. PostScript is a registered trademark of
Adobe Systems, Inc. All other product names mentioned herein are the
trademarks of their respective owners.
```

(Additional trademark notices deleted)

Code Example 8-3

```
This product incorporates technology used under license from Fulcrum
Technologies, Inc.
Using </opt> as the package base directory.
## Processing package information.
## Processing system information.
## Verifying package dependencies.
## Verifying disk space requirements.
## Checking for conflicts with packages already installed.
## Checking for setuid/setgid programs.
```

At this point, the install program is checking for several standard verifications. The person doing the installation will be prompted if the installation encounters any potential problems or areas that require a decision.

Code Example 8-4

```
This package contains scripts which will be executed with super-user
permission during the process of installing this package.

Do you want to continue with the installation of this package [y,n,?] y

Installing Solaris 2.3 User AnswerBook as <SUNWabe>

## Installing part 1 of 1.
/opt/SUNWabe/ps
/opt/SUNWabe/ps/ADVOSUG
/opt/SUNWabe/ps/ADVOSUG/01.Logging_In_to_SunOS__and_Starting_Ope
/opt/SUNWabe <implied directory>
/opt/SUNWabe/ps <implied directory>
/opt/SUNWabe/ps/ADVOSUG <implied directory>
/opt/SUNWabe/ps/ADVOSUG/02.Basic_SunOS_Commands
/opt/SUNWabe/ps/ADVOSUG/03.Working_with_Files_and_Directories
/opt/SUNWabe/toc/SUNWab_8_12.rec
```

(Files deleted for conciseness)

Code Example 8-5

```
[ verifying class <PostScript> ]
## Executing postinstall script.

Installation of <SUNWabe> was successful.
```

Batch Package Installation

"Interactive" in this case means that a human response is needed somewhere in the installation process. An installation may require a response for three different reasons: a package name may be required, responses to the standard verifications may be specified as *ask* by a configuration file, or the package to be added may have a postinstall script that requires interaction.

- Package Names

  When a package name is required, it can be entered from the command line or in the batch file. For example, the following command installs the SUNWabe package.

  ```
  # pkgadd -d `pwd` -n SUNWabe
  ```

- Configuration File Automation

  Several standard verifications are made when any package is installed, including disk space verification and disposition of suid programs. All these decisions are made by default by the `/var/sadm/install/admin/default` file. For most options, the default answer is to *ask* during the installation, making the installation interactive. Code Example 8-6 illustrates the point.

Code Example 8-6

```
#ident"@(#)default1.492/12/23 SMI"/* SVr4.0 1.5.2.1*/
mail=
instance=unique
partial=ask
runlevel=ask
idepend=ask
rdepend=ask
space=ask
setuid=ask
conflict=ask
action=ask
basedir=default
```

To make a session noninteractive, copy the `default` file to a second file and modify it. Code Example 8-7 is a sample of a `default` file modified for batch processing.

Code Example 8-7

```
#ident"@(#)default1.492/12/23 SMI"/* SVr4.0 1.5.2.1*/
mail=
instance=unique
partial=nocheck
runlevel=quit
idepend=nocheck
rdepend=ask
space=quit
setuid=nocheck
conflict=quit
action=nocheck
basedir=default
```

This configuration responds to the suid verification by not checking for suid, resulting in a security hole. However, most package additions are done by responding *yes* to allowing suid. All of the options that each variable can be set to can be found in `admin(4)`.

The *conflict* variable should be customized for each package addition.

Note – The *rdepend* variable is used for `pkgrm` not `pkgadd`.

This alternative default file is specified with the **-a** option during `pkgadd` execution.

```
# pkgadd -d `pwd` -n -a /tmp/default.batch SUNWabe
```

• Postinstallation Answer Automation

In the case of a postinstallation script requiring interaction, create a response file by running an install with `pkgask` instead of `pkgadd`. This section is purely theoretical currently, since there aren't any postinstall scripts that require additional responses as yet.

```
# pkgask -d `pwd` -r /tmp/pkginst1 SUNWsomething1
```

```
# pkgadd -d `pwd` -n -r /tmp/pkginst1 SUNWsomething1
```

To run several packages sequentially, name the response files `pkginst[1...]` and place them all in the same directory.

```
# pkgask -d `pwd` -r /tmp/pkginst1 SUNWsomething1
```

```
# pkgask -d `pwd` -r /tmp/pkginst2 SUNWsomething2
```

```
# pkgadd -d `pwd` -n -r /tmp SUNWsomething1 SUNWsomething2
```

Putting all of this together, the following command is a sample of how a noninteractive package installation looks.

```
# pkgadd -d `pwd` -n -a /tmp/default.batch -r /tmp/pkginst1 SUNWsomething1
```

The output of this package installation shows only the copyright and trademark messages and the final completion status message:

```
Installation of <SUNWabe> was successful.
```

Removing Packages

Removing a package is similar to adding a package. The one thing to remember here is that to remove a package, a record of its installation must exist in the `/var/sadm` directory.

Removing Packages Interactively

A typical package removal looks like the following output:

```
# pkgrm SUNWabe


## Removing installed package instance <SUNWabe>
## Verifying package dependencies.
## Processing package information.
## Removing pathnames in class <ContentsDB>
/opt/SUNWabe/toc/SUNWab_8_12.rec
/opt/SUNWabe/toc/SUNWab_8_12.lock
/opt/SUNWabe/toc/SUNWab_8_12.ind
## Removing pathnames in class <none>
/opt/SUNWabe/ab_cardcatalog
/opt/SUNWabe
```

(Filenames deleted)

```
## Updating system information.

Removal of <SUNWabe> was successful.
```

Batch Package Removal

Package removal can be automated by using specific names on the command line and specifying an alternate defaults file that has the *rdepend* variable set to *nocheck* or *quit*. Removing packages automatically also requires the -n option. Here is an example of a command line for package removal.

```
# pkgrm -n -a /tmp/default.batch SUNWabe
```

The only output that will be received from this command is:

```
Removal of <SUNWabe> was successful.
```

Verifying Packages

Things may go wrong during a package installation, for example, files may be corrupted. A user may have changed permission to 777 from / on down. Murphy lives. The command `pkgchk` verifies a package installation and fixes changed file attributes. Table 8-1 summarizes some of the common uses of `pkgchk`.

Table 8-1   Verification of Package Installation

Command	Use when:
`pkgchk -n`	The system just seems to be missing something here and there, and you are not sure where to start looking.
`pkgchk -a -f -n`	A user changed permission on most of the system to 777.
`pkgchk -n -c` <*pkg*>	Software *pkg* appears to be corrupt.

See `pkgchk`(1M) for a complete list of options.

Obtaining Package Information

Quite a bit of information can be obtained about each package. Use the `pkginfo` command to obtain this information. Table 8-2 lists some common uses of `pkginfo`:

Table 8-2   `pkginfo` Options for Obtaining Information about a Package

Option	Description
`pkginfo`	List the packages installed on a system.
`pkginfo -p`	List any packages only partially installed.
`pkginfo -r` <*pkg*>	List the root directory for a package.
`pkginfo -l` <*pkg*>	List all known package information. (This listing includes a line called Hotline — someday a single place will tell where to find support for every product.)
`pkginfo -d 'pwd'`	List package abbreviations and full names for all packages in a certain directory. Useful for finding all the PPP packages to install.

See `pkginfo`(1) for a complete list of options.

Package Management by swmtool

Solaris offers `swmtool` as the GUI alternative to the package management utilities that are invoked from the command line.

Startup and Introduction

To start the `swmtool` utility, enter

```
# swmtool &
Checking sizes of installed software. This may take moment... done.
```

Packages are grouped in what are called clusters. When the path area displays a full distribution of the OS, four clusters are displayed: Core System Support, Developer, End User, and Entire Distribution. No command-line options enable viewing of clusters and their contents.

Note – The product looks first at the CD-ROM device. If nothing is found, change the Source Media from the Properties menu. To save the values permanently, select File->Save.

Figure 8-1 illustrates a display of the OS clusters.

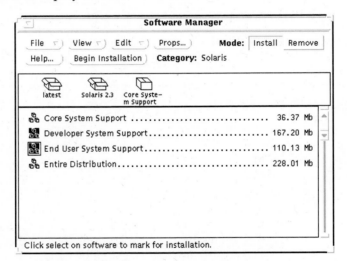

Figure 8-1   Software Manager Display of Package Clusters

Move down to the next level by double-clicking on the Core Support cluster to view more clusters below this one. If there is more than one package for a specific product, such as OpenWindows or Line Printing, all associated packages are grouped into a cluster. At this level there are some actual packages in addition to the clusters here.

Figure 8-2 shows an example of the display of both packages and clusters.

Software Manager				
File ▽ View ▽ Edit ▽ Props...			**Mode:**	Install Remove
Help... Begin Installation			**Category:** Solaris	

latest   Solaris 2.3   Core System Support

Core Architecture, (Kvm)...................................	2.68 Mb
Core Architecture, (Root)................................	8.94 Mb
Core SPARC	19.58 Mb
Dumb Frame Buffer Device Drivers........................	0.41 Mb
Extended System Utilities	1.20 Mb
GX (cg6) Device Driver	0.23 Mb
Network Information System (NIS)	0.89 Mb
OpenWindows kernel modules	0.04 Mb
OpenWindows Window Drivers	0.18 Mb
System & Network Administration Root....................	0.28 Mb
Terminal Information	1.59 Mb
Volume Management	0.37 Mb

Click select on software to mark for installation.

Figure 8-2   Example of Packages and Clusters of the Core Support Cluster

Property Configuration

`swmtool` can use a Properties configuration to reduce the need for retyping setup information.

Adding Packages

Select either clusters or packages or a mixture of both. Verify that the Mode is set to Install and click on the Begin Installation button. The actual package installation or removal is still done via command-line utilities, but a window opens to allow you to monitor the progress and respond to prompts.

Figure 8-3 shows a typical command window.

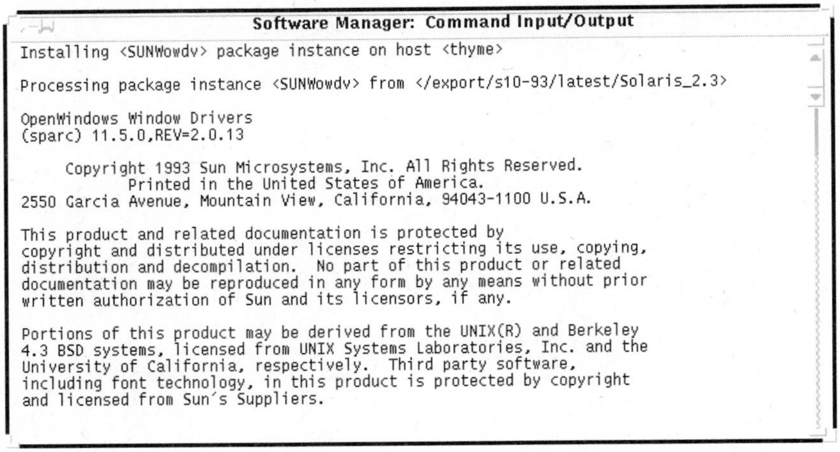

```
┌─────────────────────────────────────────────────────────────────────┐
│  ─│▄│          Software Manager: Command Input/Output                 │
│ ┌─────────────────────────────────────────────────────────────────┐ │
│ │ Installing <SUNWowdv> package instance on host <thyme>         ▲ │ │
│ │                                                                 █ │ │
│ │ Processing package instance <SUNWowdv> from </export/s10-93/latest/Solaris_2.3> ▼ │ │
│ │                                                                   │ │
│ │ OpenWindows Window Drivers                                        │ │
│ │ (sparc) 11.5.0,REV=2.0.13                                         │ │
│ │                                                                   │ │
│ │     Copyright 1993 Sun Microsystems, Inc. All Rights Reserved.    │ │
│ │          Printed in the United States of America.                 │ │
│ │ 2550 Garcia Avenue, Mountain View, California, 94043-1100 U.S.A.   │ │
│ │                                                                   │ │
│ │ This product and related documentation is protected by            │ │
│ │ copyright and distributed under licenses restricting its use, copying, │ │
│ │ distribution and decompilation.  No part of this product or related │ │
│ │ documentation may be reproduced in any form by any means without prior │ │
│ │ written authorization of Sun and its licensors, if any.           │ │
│ │                                                                   │ │
│ │ Portions of this product may be derived from the UNIX(R) and Berkeley │ │
│ │ 4.3 BSD systems, licensed from UNIX Systems Laboratories, Inc. and the │ │
│ │ University of California, respectively.  Third party software,    │ │
│ │ including font technology, in this product is protected by copyright │ │
│ │ and licensed from Sun's Suppliers.                                │ │
│ └─────────────────────────────────────────────────────────────────┘ │
└─────────────────────────────────────────────────────────────────────┘
```

Figure 8-3   Software Manager Command Window

Removing Packages

Change the Mode to Remove to display the current installed contents of the system. Select a package, cluster, or both and click on the Begin Removal button to start the removal process.

Obtaining Package and Space Information

Double-clicking on a cluster always reveals the packages that comprise the cluster. Double-clicking on a package displays information about the package. The package information for swmtool is more complete than for the pkginfo version. This version displays how much space in each partition the package will use. The disk space used in /var is only for the package information stored in /var/sadm.

Figure 8-4 shows a typical package information screen.

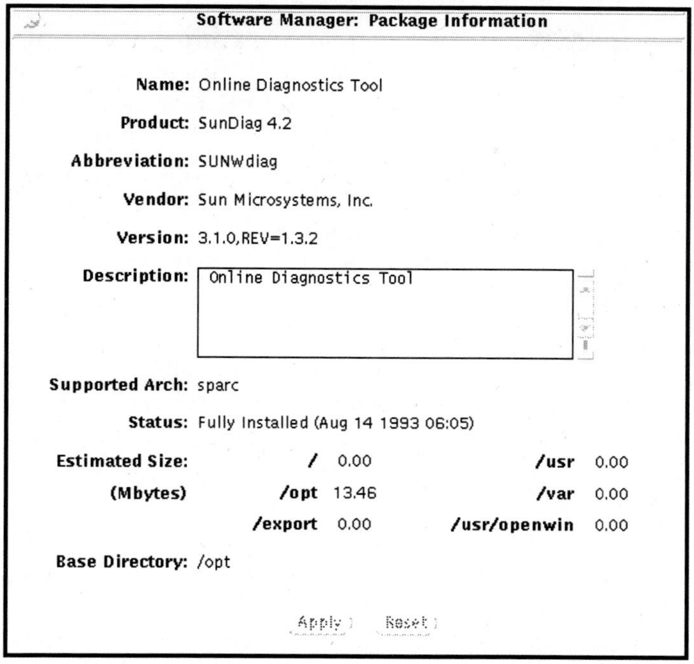

Software Manager: Package Information

Name: Online Diagnostics Tool

Product: SunDiag 4.2

Abbreviation: SUNWdiag

Vendor: Sun Microsystems, Inc.

Version: 3.1.0,REV=1.3.2

Description: Online Diagnostics Tool

Supported Arch: sparc

Status: Fully Installed (Aug 14 1993 06:05)

Estimated Size:	**/**	0.00	**/usr**	0.00
(Mbytes)	**/opt**	13.46	**/var**	0.00
	/export	0.00	**/usr/openwin**	0.00

Base Directory: /opt

Apply   Reset

Figure 8-4   Software Manager Package Information Screen

swmtool can display the amount of free and used disk space on a system, as shown in Figure 8-5.

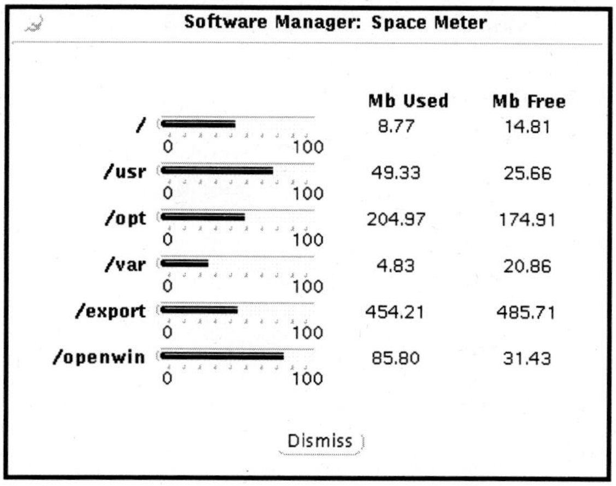

Software Manager: Space Meter

	Mb Used	Mb Free
/	8.77	14.81
/usr	49.33	25.66
/opt	204.97	174.91
/var	4.83	20.86
/export	454.21	485.71
/openwin	85.80	31.43

Dismiss

Figure 8-5   Example of Software Manager Display of System Disk Space

Patches

Patches are a fact of life. In Solaris 2.x, patches have a structure similar to that of packages. A patch is a directory with the name of the patch number. In the directory are the scripts, called `installpatch` and `backoutpatch`, that invoke installation and removal. A README.*<patch number>* explaining what the patch fixes is always included; the last section of the README lists the caveats for each patch. It is a good idea to skip to the bottom of a README file before installing the patch. Finally, there will be one or more minipackages containing the actual files that replace the current files. Replacement is done package-by-package, so that the only part of the patch that is installed is for packages that are already installed on the system.

Note – Since the patch management keeps a copy of the old files that the patch replaces, the `/var` filesystem can become full. It is a good idea to check the size of the patch and the available space in `/var` before starting.

Adding Patches

Install patches by invoking the `installpatch` script with the path to the patch as the parameter. The patch installation script does the following:

- Verifies that it has files to install

```
thyme# cd ../101307-01
/export/s10-93/latest/Patches/101307-01
thyme# ./installpatch /export/s10-93/latest/Patches/101307-01
@(#) installpatch 3.7 93/08/11
generating list of files to be patched
```

- Moves the old versions of the files to `/var/sadm/`*<patch name>*

```
Save old versions of files to be patched
/var/sadm/patch/101307-01/save/usr/openwin
/var/sadm/patch/101307-01/save/usr/openwin/bin
/var/sadm/patch/101307-01/save/usr/openwin/bin/X
/var/sadm/patch/101307-01/save/usr/openwin/bin/Xsun
/var/sadm/patch/101307-01/save/usr/openwin/server
/var/sadm/patch/101307-01/save/usr/openwin/server/lib
/var/sadm/patch/101307-01/save/usr/openwin/server/lib/libfont.so
/var/sadm/patch/101307-01/save/usr/openwin/server/lib/libfont.so.1
5705 blocks
```

- Uses `pkgadd` to add the minipackages found in the patch

```
Installing patch packages
Doing pkgadd of SUNWowrqd package:
5712 blocks

Installation of <SUNWowrqd.2> was successful.
Patch installation finished
```

Removing Patches

Removing a patch is the opposite of installing one. Use the `backoutpatch` script with the patch number as the parameter. The script does the following:

- Verifies that it has the old files to restore; if the files exist, no message is displayed

- Uses `pkgrm` to remove the patch files

```
thyme# ./backoutpatch 101307-01
@(#) backoutpatch 3.5 93/08/11
Doing pkgrm of SUNWowrqd.2 package:

Removal of <SUNWowrqd.2> was successful.
```

- Restores the previous version of the files

```
Restoring previous version of files
.
/usr
/usr/openwin
/usr/openwin/bin
/usr/openwin/bin/X
/usr/openwin/bin/Xsun
/usr/openwin/server
usr/openwin/server/lib
/usr/openwin/server/lib/libfont.so
/usr/openwin/server/lib/libfont.so.1
5705 blocks
```

- Updates its database to reflect that the patch no longer exists on that system

```
Making the package database consistent with restored files:
backoutpatch finished.
```

■ *8*

Solaris Implementation: A Guide for System Administrators

Disk Utilities 9 ≡

This chapter contains information on disk utilities found in the Solaris 2.x environment. Many of these utilities are generic UNIX commands, others are SunOS specific. Some utilities, such as `format`, deal directly with the disk itself as a means to set up and partition the disk to a specific arrangement. Other utilities, such as `mkfs` and `newfs`, create filesystems within the partitions as defined by `format`. Still others, such as `tunefs`, operate on existing filesystems, making them more efficient to maximize performance.

Disk Hardware

When you have worked with UNIX systems for some time, you often realize that there is seldom enough free disk space available for what needs to be accomplished. To combat this problem, it is often easiest to look at NFS to fulfill the local disk space deficit, but even a network mount is a local disk somewhere. There is never enough money to spend on disks until they get full. Then, you have to move or compress files on the existing disks or purchase more disks drives.

Adding a disk to an existing system is a simple and straightforward procedure. Partitioning the disk to a particular specification is also painless when you know how to use the tools. The base Solaris environment contains all the tools to accomplish this feat.

When purchasing new disk drives for your Solaris 2.x system, keep in mind a few things:

- The Sun Microsystems, Inc. (SMI) hardware company, Sun Microsystems Computer Corporation (SMCC), works diligently with disk drive vendors to resolve firmware and environmental issues before blessing a particular device. Some software drivers may be written specifically for a disk model number to utilize certain features of that device. You can usually buy the same disk directly from the disk drive manufacturer or from a computer wholesale house, but without the firmware changes. It might seem less expensive at first, but may end up costing much more in the long run.

- If purchasing disks from other vendors, know your device and its characteristics, such as cylinder, head, and sector counts. Understand special features such as SCSI tag queuing and how to enable or disable those features, if not in the software driver, then on the disk itself.

SCSI

Solaris 2.x for SPARC supports a number of different disk and controller types. The most widely used are those that adhere to the Small Computer Systems Interface (SCSI) of which there are also different levels. Most, if not all, SPARC systems contain an on-board SCSI controller. (On-board means that the controller is built into the main CPU unit). There are also many add-on boards available for SBus- or VME-based systems that use SCSI disks or other peripherals.

There are a few different SCSI connector types among SPARC machines: the large 50-pin D connector, used on the VME SCSI boards and older SPARC systems; a mini 50-pin connector on the SPARCstation through SPARCserver 1000 and 2000; and the still mini, but wider, Differential SCSI connector, only available on the SBus, Differential SCSI Bus Ethernet (DSBE) card.

IPI

Other SPARC disk peripherals include the Sun-developed Intelligent Peripheral Interface or IPI, which is available as a VME option to deskside and server systems. IPI disks are expensive in space utilization for their capacity compared to their SCSI counterparts but, nevertheless, are still a supported option on the 4/300, 4/400, and 4/600 product lines through the 2.3 release.

SMD

Support for two more disk controller types are included in Solaris 2.3 release: the Xylogics 7053 and 451 SMD controllers, known only to ancient SPARC systems. These disks are lovingly referred to as xd and xy, respectively, and are the only disk types to omit the target# field in the /dev/rdsk and /dev/dsk device entries.

Disk Software

A number of utilities manipulate disks within the Solaris environment. The lowest-level user interface to a disk is an interactive program called `format`, which is used to format, partition, and name disk volumes. In addition to these low-level disk utilities, `format` can be used for testing the integrity of the media. `format` is most beneficial when a new disk is added to an existing system. Once a disk is formatted, it can be partitioned or grouped into logical sections and named according to the volume naming convention.

Many administrators choose to format the disks on new systems before they are placed in production, which may or may not be necessary. Each disk that is included in a system has undergone thorough testing in that system. You can use `format` to partition disks prior to installation, but the preferred method of configuring and partitioning disks is while running the Solaris install system.

Before a new disk can be recognized by the system, it must have the device nodes and links present in the `/devices` and `/dev` directories. This can be accomplished by attaching the device to the systems, while the power is off, and rebooting with the reconfigure option, `boot -r`. Or, before shutting down the system to add a new disk, create a file called `/reconfigure`, which flags the boot process, forcing a reconfigure.

probe-scsi

Ensure that the new device ID or target number does not conflict with any other devices on the bus. For instance, most desktop systems have internal disks with predefined target numbers set on the drive itself. The internal target number of most desktop systems is c0t3, or target three. When adding a new SCSI device to this particular system, configure the disk as something other than target 3, for example, as target 0.

On most of the newer systems (those that use the "ok" prompt), you can obtain SCSI information, target numbers, and drive identification strings while the system is waiting at the boot-PROM level. The `probe-scsi` boot-level command returns this information. Some of the newer systems can probe multiple SBus SCSI controllers and devices by using an extended version of the `probe-scsi` command, called `probe-scsi-all`. Both commands are shown below.

```
<#0> ok probe-scsi
Target 0
 Unit 0 Disk CONNER CP30545  SUN0535A8A89242J021PW
Target 1
 Unit 0 Disk CONNER CP30545  SUN0535A8A89242J010CS
Target 2
 Unit 0 Disk CONNER CP30545  SUN0535A8A89242J0108H
```

```
Target 3
 Unit 0 Disk CONNER CP30545 SUN0535A8A89242J0105M
Target 5
 Unit 0 Removable Tape ARCHIVE Python 28454-XXX4.44
Target 6
 Unit 0 Removable Read Only device SONY CD-ROM CDU-8012 3.1e
<#0> ok



<#0> ok probe-scsi-all
/io-unit@f,e1200000/sbi@0,0/dma@0,81000/esp@0,80000

/io-unit@f,e0200000/sbi@0,0/dma@0,81000/esp@0,80000
Target 0
 Unit 0 Disk CONNER CP30545 SUN0535A8A89242J021PW
Target 1
 Unit 0 Disk CONNER CP30545 SUN0535A8A89242J010CS
Target 2
 Unit 0 Disk CONNER CP30545 SUN0535A8A89242J0108H
Target 3
 Unit 0 Disk CONNER CP30545 SUN0535A8A89242J0105M
Target 5
 Unit 0 Removable Tape ARCHIVE Python 28454-XXX4.44
 Unit 1 Tape
 Unit 2 Tape
 Unit 3 Tape
 Unit 4 Tape
 Unit 5 Tape
 Unit 6 Tape
 Unit 7 Tape
Target 6
 Unit 0 Removable Read Only device SONY CD-ROM CDU-8012 3.1e

<#0> ok
```

Figure 9-1   Using the `probe-scsi` *Commands*

Remember that the `probe-scsi` boot-PROM command reads the device only at the PROM level. A disk may seem to be functional at this level, but unable to come to full ready state, usually caused by some kind of spin-up problem.

To change a target number on a SCSI device, consult the specific device instructions. On many desktop add-on devices, a rotary switch on the back of the unit sets the ID number of the entire device. Some disks have shunt jumpers directly on the drive itself and use an octal numbering scheme between a three jumper set. Know how to set these IDs before you install the device.

On older systems, such as those from the Sun-4™ family, the only way to see what is on the bus is to boot the system with the −rv option, observing the devices found. Setting disk drive IDs on these devices can sometimes be much more difficult than setting SCSI target numbers, except for the IPI disks, which can be changed via the disk drive front panel.

Helpful Hint – The most important rule is that no two devices should have the same ID numbers, unless on different controllers.

Reconfiguring the Software

Once the new disk is connected to the system and all address contentions are worked out, issue the boot −r command and see that the new devices are created. The device name given to the new disk will be different, depending on where the device is placed. If you have multiple controllers on the system and you have not used all of the device slots within each controller, be prepared for a wacky device name.

If you have configured the system and its peripherals in physical and logical sequence, then there should be no surprises. Systems with large numbers of disks and controllers often leave "device holes" on a controller chain. When new devices are added to that chain, the links created are not always the same as for other devices on that controller.

Helpful Hint – Remember that you can always change the device names in /dev/dsk/ and /dev/rdsk directories to something more logical. After the new disk has been physically connected and the system knows about its address, you can begin running the format utility.

The format Utility

As the superuser, invoke format from the UNIX shell while the Solaris software is up and running in some form. You have the most flexibility if you run format when running Solaris from a local CD-ROM or while booting over the network.

```
# format
Searching for disks...done

AVAILABLE DISK SELECTIONS:
  0. c0t0d0 <SUN0669 cyl 1614 alt 2 hd 15 sec 54>
   /sbus@1,f8000000/esp@0,800000/sd@0,0
  1. c0t3d0 <SUN0207 cyl 1254 alt 2 hd 9 sec 36>
   /sbus@1,f8000000/esp@0,800000/sd@3,0
Specify disk (enter its number):
```

Figure 9-2 Entering the format Utility

Upon invocation, `format` searches for local disks that are attached to a system that have entries in the `/dev/rdsk` and `/dev/dsk` directories. Disks that are attached but do not have links or device nodes are ignored. To run `format` on these disks, you need to reboot using the reconfigure option explained above.

After the disks are probed, they are displayed for selection, as shown in Figure 9-2. Each disk is identified by two lines. The first line shows the controller, target, and disk number followed by the type, number of cylinders, alternate cylinders, heads, and sectors per track. This is the SVR4 standard disk name located in the `/dev/rdsk` and `/dev/dsk` directories. Immediately following this line is the path to the actual device node, relative to the `/devices` directory.

In Figure 9-2, selection 0 is known as `c0t0d0`, that is, controller zero, target zero, disk zero. The disk type is known as a SUN0669 with 1614 cylinders, two alternate cylinders, 15 heads and 54 sectors per track. Its device node file resides in the `/sbus@1,f8000000/esp@0,800000` directory and is called `sd@0,0`, a somewhat logical name for SCSI disk at target zero, disk zero. A symbolic link that points to this node is placed in the `/dev/dsk` and `/dev/rdsk` directories.

To operate on a particular disk, select the device by its menu selection. The submenu shown in Figure 9-3 is displayed. From this menu, all the operations are done to a selected disk. The most frequently used utilities within this menu are the format, analyze, search, partition, and repair commands.

```
selecting c0t3d0
[disk formatted]


FORMAT MENU:
 disk - select a disk
 type - select (define) a disk type
 partition - select (define) a partition table
 current - describe the current disk
 format - format and analyze the disk
 repair - repair a defective sector
 label - write label to the disk
 analyze - surface analysis
 defect - defect list management
 backup - search for backup labels
 verify - read and display labels
 save - save new disk/partition definitions
 inquiry - show vendor, product and revision
 volname - set 8-character volume name
 quit
format>
```

Figure 9-3   The `format` *Main Menu*

While in `format`, you can select a disk that has partitions currently mounted. You are informed of this when the `format` main menu is displayed. Built-in safeguards disallow destructive action to mounted partitions. You can execute read tests on a mounted disk to isolate a problem area, but you cannot format or perform write tests to a disk that is currently mounted.

Adding New Format Types for Disks

When you are adding a new disk to a system, you may see a message such as "drive type unknown" upon entering `format`. If this happens, try to locate that disk type in the `/etc/format.dat` file, a data file that contains certain specifics about each disk type supported. There are two sections to `/etc/format.dat`: the first section contains a list of entries for each disk type, and the second section is a list of predefined partition arrangements for disks listed in the above section.

You may want to add disks to your systems that are not in the `format.dat` file. You can create your own entries, provided you know all the pertinent information, such as the number of cylinders, heads, alternate cylinders, rotation speed, number of blocks per sector and track. Most of this information can be obtained from the data sheet that is provided when new disks are purchased. You may not get such a sheet if you purchase add-on disks from a Sun dealer; disks that you purchase from a Sun dealer are already formatted and labeled with the proper drive type and are known to the `/etc/format.dat` file.

Extracting Known Disk Defects

Before you format a disk, first extract any known defects from the defect list. Invoke the defect menu and use the original option to extract the primary defect list.

Formatting the Disk

After you extract the defect list, exit the Defect menu; from the `format` main menu, type `format`. The system displays an approximate time of completion and a few confirmation messages before actual formatting takes place.

Some disks take much longer to format than others, especially disks without servo media, a dedicated platter for read-write head positioning. Disks that have a larger total capacity take much longer than do smaller capacity disks because of the increased number of sectors that must be written and verified.

After the actual formatting procedure is complete, the entire disk is analyzed twice sequentially, using patterns to write and read every sector. Sectors that mismatch compared to what was written during the analysis are added to the defect list. Such sectors will not be used when their address is selected. Instead, alternate sectors are reserved for such purposes.

You can change the parameters in the Analyze menu to run more or fewer passes, depending on your need. You might want to run an extended analysis on a new disk before you put it into production.

Partitioning the Disk

After a successful format, a label is written to the first and last cylinders of the formatted disk. The default label sometimes falls short of being useful in its present form. Therefore, it is necessary to change the partitioning on most disks after they have been formatted. If you are going to run the install program using the newly formatted disk as a target, then you can skip partitioning at this point because the install program places its own label on the disk unless modified manually.

If you are adding an additional disk to an already installed Solaris 2.x system, then some sort of partitioning is necessary. You should have some idea as to how the new disk partitions will be laid out. Some systems need to use an entire disk as one filesystem; others may use several different partitions.

The Partition Menu

The Partition menu allows you to change the partition arrangement of a disk. Eight slices are available for editing on any given disk. The choices to partition the disk are select, modify, name, print, and label selections. To select a predefined partition table as defined in the /etc/format.dat file, use the select option. All known partition tables for the currently defined drive type are offered as choices. To modify the current table or to create a new partition table in batch mode rather than individually, use the modify option. This option is an enhancement to the Solaris 2.x version of format; it has proven to be quite helpful, especially when you have predetermined the partition sizes or cylinder counts for the current disk.

```
PARTITION MENU:
 0 - change '0' partition
 1 - change '1' partition
 2 - change '2' partition
 3 - change '3' partition
 4 - change '4' partition
 5 - change '5' partition
 6 - change '6' partition
 7 - change '7' partition
 select - select a predefined table
 modify - modify a predefined partition table
 name - name the current table
 print - display the current table
 label - write partition map and label to the disk
 quit
partition>
```

Figure 9-4   The Partition Menu

The modify option requires that you specify a free-hog partition to account for all unused disk space. This is a good way to prevent the overlapping of slices or blocks of unused disk space. You cannot directly edit the specified free-hog partition. To change it, adjust the size of other partitions; making them smaller increases the free-hog, making them larger takes disk space away from the free-hog. If you try to take more space than is available in the free-hog, an error message is returned, disallowing such action. You then have to decrease the size of another partition to free up space.

Figure 9-5 shows a session with the modify option. The partitioning base menu offers two choices; the current partition table or all free-hog. To modify the current table, select 0. To start with a clean disk and define a new table, select All Free Hog. All current partition information will be removed. In either case, you are then required to specify the free-hog partition before you can modify the table.

When defining a partition that will be used as a UNIX filesystem (UFS), think in terms of cylinder groups. When a filesystem is created by mkfs or newfs, one of the default parameters divides the partition into groups of 16 cylinders, called a cylinder group. Filesystems will function properly with fewer than 16 cylinders per group but tend to become more fragmented, possibly costing data access time.

You can use one of three different units of measure to set partition sizes: number of bytes, number of cylinders, or number of megabytes. You cannot define a partition size that is less than one cylinder. If you try, a message informs you of the problem, and no action is taken.

Once you have completed defining the new partition table, it is displayed for your inspection. Upon confirmation, you are prompted to name the table you have just created. The named table can be used on other disks of the same geometry to make identical partition arrangements while this session of format is active, but is lost when you exit format and return to the shell, unless you saved the table to a file.

Calculating Partition Size

There are many methods to calculate the partition sizes needed for a particular disk. Most systems need a certain amount of space for a given partition rather than a randomly selected size. One method for achieving the desired partition size while maintaining a multiple of 16 cylinder group size is detailed next.

In the example, a 207-megabyte disk is added to an existing system. The current requirement calls for the disk to be divided into three different partitions of roughly 60, 70, and 70 megabytes. The idea is to make the partitions as close to the needed size while still maintaining the number of cylinders to a factor of 16.

```
partition> modify <RETURN>
Select partitioning base:
 0. Current partition table (df)
 1. All Free Hog
Choose base (enter number) [0]? 1 <RETURN>

Part Tag Flag Cylinders Size Blocks
 0 root wm 0 0 (0/0/0)
 1 swap wu 0 0 (0/0/0)
 2 backup wu 0 - 1253 198.39MB (1254/0/0)
 3 unassigned wm 0 0 (0/0/0)
 4 unassigned wm 0 0 (0/0/0)
 5 unassigned wm 0 0 (0/0/0)
 6 usr wm 0 0 (0/0/0)
 7 unassigned wm 0 0 (0/0/0)

Do you wish to continue creating a new partition
table based on above table[yes]? <RETURN>
Free Hog partition[6]? <RETURN>
Enter size of partition '0' [0b, 0c, 0.00mb]: <RETURN>
Enter size of partition '1' [0b, 0c, 0.00mb]: <RETURN>
Enter size of partition '3' [0b, 0c, 0.00mb]: <RETURN>
Enter size of partition '4' [0b, 0c, 0.00mb]: 60mb <RETURN>
Enter size of partition '5' [0b, 0c, 0.00mb]: 70mb <RETURN>
Enter size of partition '7' [0b, 0c, 0.00mb]: 70mb <RETURN>
`70.00mb' is out of range
Enter size of partition '7' [0b, 0c, 0.00mb]: 68mb <RETURN>
```

```
Part Tag         Flag   Cylinders      Size      Blocks
  0 root          wm     0              0         (0/0/0)
  1 swap          wu     0              0         (0/0/0)
  2 backup        wu     0  -  1253     198.39MB(1254/0/0)
  3 unassigned    wm     0              0         (0/0/0)
  4 unassigned    wm     0  -  379      60.12MB (380/0/0)
  5 unassigned    wm     380 -  822     70.08MB (443/0/0)
  6 usr           wm     823 -  823     0.16MB  (1/0/0)
  7 unassigned    wm     824 -  1253    68.03MB (430/0/0)
```

```
Okay to make this the current partition table[yes]? <RETURN>
```

Figure 9-5   Using the Modify Option

Calculate the partition sizes by using the modify option. Select the all free-hog choice and designate a free-hog partition. Enter the sizes, in megabytes, of the partitions of your choice. In Figure 9-5, partitions 4 and 5 were allocated 60 Mbytes and 70 Mbytes. Partition 7 was also allocated 70 Mbytes, but the free-hog did not have that much space to give away, as indicated by the message: "'70.00mb' is out of range." In order to continue, its size was reduced to 68 megabytes.

The partition map then displayed the new disk layout. The prompt at the bottom asks for confirmation to use the current table. At this point, observe the Blocks column of partition number four in Figure 9-5. This field indicates that 380 cylinders are allocated to this particular slice. Check to see if the number of cylinders is equally divisible by 16. In this case, 380 is not evenly divisible by 16. The closest cylinder that is a factor of 16 is cylinder number 384. Repeat the procedure for partition number five. The Block column shows that 70 megabytes use 443 cylinders. The nearest cylinder that is a factor of 16 is cylinder 448.

Now that you know the optimum cylinder sizes for these two partitions, use the modify option again to enter the partition sizes, this time using cylinders instead of megabytes. Invoke the modify option and again select the All Free Hog option, designating the free-hog partition of your choice. Figure 9-6 shows the modify session setting partitions four and five to even multiples of 16. The free-hog partition, number six, takes up the remaining disk space, not evenly divisible by sixteen, but two out of three is better than none.

```
partition> modify <RETURN>
Select partitioning base:
 0. Current partition table (original sd3)
 1. All Free Hog
Choose base (enter number) [0]? 1 <RETURN>
```

```
Part Tag Flag Cylinders Size Blocks
 0 root wm 0 0 (0/0/0)
 1 swap wu 0 0 (0/0/0)
 2 backup wu 0 - 1253 198.39MB (1254/0/0)
 3 unassigned wm 0 0 (0/0/0)
 4 unassigned wm 0 0 (0/0/0)
 5 unassigned wm 0 0 (0/0/0)
 6 usr wm 0 0 (0/0/0)
 7 unassigned wm 0 0 (0/0/0)
```

Do you wish to continue creating a new partition
table based on above table[yes]? **<RETURN>**
Free Hog partition[6]?
Enter size of partition '0' [0b, 0c, 0.00mb]: **<RETURN>**
Enter size of partition '1' [0b, 0c, 0.00mb]: **<RETURN>**
Enter size of partition '3' [0b, 0c, 0.00mb]: **<RETURN>**
Enter size of partition '4' [0b, 0c, 0.00mb]: **384c**
Enter size of partition '5' [0b, 0c, 0.00mb]: **448c**
Enter size of partition '7' [0b, 0c, 0.00mb]: **<RETURN>**

```
Part Tag Flag Cylinders Size Blocks
 0 root wm 0 0 (0/0/0)
 1 swap wu 0 0 (0/0/0)
 2 backup wu 0 - 1253 198.39MB (1254/0/0)
 3 unassigned wm 0 0 (0/0/0)
 4 unassigned wm 0 - 383 60.75MB (384/0/0)
 5 unassigned wm 384 - 831 70.88MB (448/0/0)
 6 usr wm 832 - 1253 66.76MB (422/0/0)
 7 unassigned wm 0 0 (0/0/0)
```

Okay to make this the current partition table[yes]? **<RETURN>**

Figure 9-6   Reentering the Modify Option

Other Partition Menu Options

The name option allows you to name the current partition table and save it to a file. This option can be of great assistance if you plan on defining more than one system with the same partition arrangement. The actual saving of file names is done in the topmost format menu, not under the partition submenu.

The print option displays the current table, complete with cylinder ranges and sizes, as well as a few new fields associated with each partition that were not in BSD-based versions of format. One new field is the partition tag or name, which can be any of the customary mount points to which partitions are attached, such as root, swap, boot, backup, usr, and home. The tag is used by the install program and the `prtvtoc` utility, which reads the volume table of contents, `vtoc`. The other new field included in the table display is the partition permission flag, which may be one of the following:

```
wm - read-write, mountable
wu - read-write, unmountable
rm - read-only, mountable
ru - read-only, unmountable
```

You can effectively make a partition unmountable or read-only by setting the proper flag. You could use these flags to denote a certain slice as an unmountable read-write partition, a type of partition often required by database applications. You could also configure a partition as a read-only slice for static data. Most partition flags on UFS filesystems should be defined as read-write, mountable.

The label option writes out the current table to two areas of the disk. The primary label is placed on the outermost track of the disk, usually cylinder zero. A backup label is placed on one of the innermost cylinders, in case the primary label becomes corrupt. The primary label becomes corrupt only in rare circumstances, such as a hardware or power failure or an attempt to attach or remove devices on a live bus. Recovery from a bad primary disk label may be as simple as restoring from the backup. The problem is reaching a point from which you can run `format` if the corrupt label happens to be your boot disk. If this is the case, boot from a CD-ROM or become an install client to fix the system disk.

Making Filesystems with the newfs Command

After the disk label has been written, filesystems can be built inside the partitions specified. Two commands build filesystems: `newfs` and `mkfs`. `newfs` calls `mkfs` with certain arguments, found by polling the disk label of the device to find out partition size, the cylinder counts, and other information.

Run `newfs` by selecting the partition in which the filesystem will reside; use the raw partition name as an argument.

```
# newfs /dev/rdsk/c0t1d0s1
newfs: construct a new file system /dev/rdsk/c0t1d0s1: (y/n)? y
/dev/rdsk/c0t1d0s1: 262640 sectors in 469 cylinders of 7 tracks, 80 sectors
 128.2MB in 30 cyl groups (16 c/g, 4.38MB/g, 2112 i/g)
super-block backups (for fsck -F ufs -o b=#) at:
 32, 9072, 18112, 27152, 36192, 45232, 54272,
 63312, 71712, 80752, 89792, 98832, 107872, 116912,
 125952, 134992, 143392, 152432, 161472, 170512, 179552,
 188592, 197632, 206672, 215072, 224112, 233152, 242192,
 251232, 260272,
```

After `newfs` completes, a filesystem exists in the partition and can be added to the `/etc/vfstab` file for automatic mounting at subsequent reboots. The following line accomplishes this task.

```
/dev/dsk/c0t1d0s1 /dev/rdsk/c0t1d0s1 /spare1 ufs 2 yes - -
```

Using mkfs Options with newfs

The command-line arguments to `mkfs` are much more cumbersome than those for `newfs`. But, as with other UNIX commands, more cumbersome also means more flexible. The `newfs` command has a number of built-in defaults that work in most situations, but the arguments to `mkfs` can change nearly every parameter of a filesystem during its creation. Some of the more interesting arguments to note are:

- `bsize` — The logical block size of the filesystem. Can be either 4096 Kbytes or 8192 Kbytes (the default). Smaller block sizes can be more efficient on filesystems with a large number of small files as opposed to filesystems with fewer large files.

- `cgsize` — The cylinder group size. Each cylinder group is assigned its own backup superblock. The default is 16.

- `nbpi` — The number of blocks per inode. Again, this argument is useful on filesystems with a large number of small files. The default is 2048. Decrease the number to create more inodes.

- `minfree` — The minimum percentage of free space to keep unwriteable by normal users. The default of 10 percent often seems to be too much. When a filesystem becomes 90 percent full, "filesystem full" messages are displayed on the console. To make more of the filesystem usable, set `minfree` lower. For example, for a 2.1-Gbyte disk, accepting the defaults wastes 200 Mbytes of disk space; a 2 or 3 percent free space limit would suffice. This free space can be changed later by means of `tunefs`.

To use `mkfs` options while running `newfs`, simply place those options on the `newfs` command line, as shown below. See also `newfs(1M)`.

```
# newfs -i 4096 /dev/rdsk/c0t1d0s1
```

Using tunefs

Use `tunefs` to dynamically change filesystem parameters. Some of the parameters discussed above can be changed without using `newfs` or `mkfs`, particularly:

- m — Change the amount of reserved space on the partition.

- o — Change the optimization characteristics of a filesystem. Generally, you should optimize for time unless the filesystem is over 90 percent full. At this point, you can change the optimization to space.

You must unmount a filesystem before you can execute `tunefs` on it. Changes you make take effect after the filesystem is remounted.

Swap Space

The Solaris 2.x configuration no longer needs two times memory for swap space. In fact, a system can boot without any swap space if it has 32 Mbytes of memory. However, this does not mean that Solaris and the applications that run on it do not use swap space. The Solaris 2.x environment actually tends to use a little more swap per application than the SunOS 4.x applications did.

Checking Swap Usage

In Solaris 2.x, the `pstat` command has been replaced with the `sar` utilities. However, the `sar` utilities are not one of the packages included in an end-user installation. Moreover, they require that their associated cron jobs be run regularly, and they usually do not give a snapshot of what the system is like at the moment that you need it most. For real-time swap monitoring, use the `swap` command.

To list the amount of swap space used and available:

```
# swap -s
total: 35884k bytes allocated + 8508k reserved = 44392k used, 106476k
available
```

To list the swap devices currently active:

```
# swap -l
swapfile              dev swaplo    blocks  free
/dev/dsk/c0t3d0s1 32,25   8        262432  196800
/usr/swap             -      8        20472   20472
```

Adding Swap Space

As applications grow in their need for resources, more swap space may need to be added to a functioning system. If you have a spare partition to use for this purpose, follow steps 2 and 3, below. If you need to use some space on a partition that is a regular filesystem, then start with step 1.

1. If you are using a regular filesystem, create a contiguous file with the `mkfile` command.

   ```
   # mkfile 32m /usr/swap
   ```

2. In all cases, add the swap space to the `/etc/vfstab` file.

   ```
   #device              device          mount   FS    fsck  mount    mount
   #to mount            to fsck         point   type  pass  at boot  options
   #
   #/dev/dsk/c1d0s2 /dev/rdsk/c1d0s2 /usr
   /dev/dsk/c0t3d0s1       -             -      swap   -      no       -
   /usr/swap               -             -      swap   -      no       -
   ```

3. Reboot the system or issue the swap command to add the swap space.

   ```
   # swap -a /usr/swap
   ```

Backing Up the Disks

Disasters happen. They can be great problems like an earthquake or flood, or they can be simple like a user deleting too many files. Backups are the most tangible preventive maintenance a system administrator does. System problems and human error make it necessary to have a copy of most files stored off-line. UNIX provides several ways to copy data from disk to a tape of some kind. This section discusses the new tape device names that come with Solaris 2.x and then describes the utilities provided for backups.

Device Naming

For compatibility, the Solaris 2.x environment retains the SunOS naming conventions. Thus, `/dev/rst0` or `/dev/rst1` can still refer to the low density 60M QIC (Quarter-Inch-Cartridge) or 2.3G 8mm tape drive. Also, `/dev/rst8` or `/dev/rst9` will refer to the high density 150M QIC or 5.0G 8mm tape drives. However, here as everywhere, it is a good idea to think in Solaris terms.

Solaris separates all the removable magnetic tape devices into a directory called `/dev/rmt`. Each device has several names, depending on features or options of the device that you want to use. A device name itself can be from one to five characters long. Chapter 1 describes the new device names in detail; see Chapter 1, "Device Name Changes."

Copy and Archive Programs

Copy usually refers to a program that copies specific files to another disk or tape; cp and dd fall in this category. Archive programs make a copy of the data in a specialized format. Despite its name, cpio is actually an archive program like ufsdump and tar. The cp program is not covered here; see the cp(1) man page for information.

There are good reasons for using each of the above named commands. Some copy special files; some are limited to regular files. Some handle incremental backups internally, others can be used with find to provide incremental backups, and some have no incremental capabilities at all. It is important to know how to back up the data, how to find out what is on the tape, and how to recover the data. Check the man page for each command for additional options, such as maintaining permissions or setting the blocking factor.

The dd Command

dd is a file-copying program. It does not have an incremental function and cannot be combined with find to make one. It can copy UNIX special files from one disk to another and is particularly useful for copying partitions to another disk because it copies the boot sector.

To back up a disk, use one of the following:

```
dd if=/dev/dsk/c0t0d0s0 of=/dev/rmt/0bn
```
or
```
dd if=/dev/rdsk/c0t0d0s0 of=/dev/rmt/0bn bs=126
```

if specifies the device being read from and of specifies the output device name. To use the character device name (i.e., the device found in /dev/rdsk), specify the block size that you want to use, as in the second example.

To restore a disk, use one of the following:

```
dd if=/dev/rmt/0bn of=/dev/dsk/c0t0d0s0
```
or
```
dd if=/dev/rmt/0bn 0f=/dev/rdsk/c0t0d0s0 bs=126
```

if and of specify the input and output device names. If you are restoring a root partition, run fsck before attempting a boot.

Note that dd does not put identification labels or headers on the tape with information about what it backed up. A catalog type listing is not available with this program. When copying a raw device, dd notes each bad sector and transfers that information to the new disk. In most cases, dd is not useful for backups but is very good for manipulating data.

The cpio Command

cpio is an archiving program. It can copy special files when used by the superuser. Used with find, it can do an incremental backup. In fact, it actually needs a list of files to work from, so find is usually the logical choice as its partner. cpio will copy special files and symbolic links.

To back up a disk, use one of the following:

```
# cd /usr; find . -print | cpio -oBv >> /dev/rmt0bn
```
or
```
# cd /usr; find . -xdev -print | cpio -oBv >> /dev/rmt/0bn
```

cpio creates its own format, and the -o option indicates that the output of this command will be in cpio format. The second example here finds only the files on the specified partition. If you are endeavoring to dump only the root partition, this is an effective method.

To restore a disk:

```
# cd <restore place>; cpio -iBvd < /dev/rmt/0bn
```

The i option indicates that the cpio-formatted data is part of the input stream instead of the output stream. The d option creates directories if they do not currently exist.

To list the tape contents:

```
# cpio -itBv < /dev/rmt/0bn
```

The t option instructs cpio to generate a table of contents instead of extracting the data from the cpio format.

The tar Command

tar is a useful backup command. It can copy a single file, a list of files, or a directory tree, and it can copy symbolic links. It cannot copy special files.

To back up a disk:

```
# tar cvf /dev/rmt/0bn .
```

The c option creates a new tar file, v stands for verbose, and f indicates that the value following it will be the file or device where the data will be placed. The . (period) indicates that the backup should start with the current directory.

To restore a disk:

```
# cd <destination>; tar xvf /dev/rmt/0bn
```

The x option means to extract from the `tar` file, v stands for verbose, but here f indicates the source of the `tar` file. f always indicates the `tar` file, so whether it points to the source or the destination depends on whether you are putting something into or taking something out of a `tar` file.

To list the tape contents:

```
# tar tvf /dev/rmt/0bn
```

t lists a table of contents of the `tar` file specified by f.

Use the `mt` command to skip over the tape files if there are multiple tape files on one physical tape. This command is discussed on page 239.

A shortcut for `tar` is available on System V systems. The `/etc/default/tar` file holds eight device definitions. Figure 9-7 shows a sample file.

```
#ident "@(#)tar.dfl 1.5 92/07/14 SMI" /* SVr4.0 1.1
#The block size and the number of blocks are put for completion
# purpose. The tape size is infinite and is defined at usage time
# directly from tape. Tape size should be non-zero for non-tape devices
# (e.g., floppy).
# device block size
archive0=/dev/rmt/0 20 0
archive1=/dev/rmt/0n 20 0
archive2=/dev/rmt/1 20 0
archive3=/dev/rmt/1n 20 0
archive4=/dev/rmt/0 126 0
archive5=/dev/rmt/0n 126 0
archive6=/dev/rmt/1 126 0
archive7=/dev/rmt/1n 126 0
```

Figure 9-7   Alternate Devices for `tar`

Use one of the archive numbers above in place of the f option of `tar`. For example,

```
tar cv6 .
```

means to back up the current directory and below to `/dev/rmt/1`, using a block size of 126 and no specified limit on the size of the tape.

Remember to use relative addressing when specifying directories and files with `tar`. Relative addressing means starting the path definition without a /. Absolute addressing is the opposite, always starting with a /, which means to start at the root and work down. If you back up a path with absolute addressing, the only place that it can be restored is the same path.

For example, if you back up /etc with tar like this:

```
tar cv6 /etc
```

then the only place that this data can be restored to is /etc.

The ufsdump Command

ufsdump is the Solaris version of the BSD favorite, dump. The only thing that changed is the name; functionality is still the same. ufsdump backs up partitions by copying the data and referencing which inodes the data are in.

Full backups are usually done anywhere from once a week to once a month. In between these full backups, incremental backups are done. Incremental means different things to different people. To some it means all the things that have changed since the last backup *of any kind*. This method is usually referred to as a true incremental. To others it means all of the things that have changed since the last *full* backup. This method is called a comprehensive incremental. Using the first method means that fewer files are backed up, fewer tapes are used, and, usually, less time is spent maintaining the backups. Using the second method means that data recovery is quicker, as it requires only the data from two backups to restore a filesystem, instead of the full and *x* number of incremental backups.

The creators of the UNIX dump command took both philosophies to heart and designed a multilevel backup system in which 0 means a full dump, 9 means a true incremental, and 1 through 8 are graduated stages in between. ufsdump uses this multilevel approach. Schemes for implementing this can become quite complex. For the details of the Towers of Hanoi, one of the more elegant approaches to determining what dump levels to use, refer to *UNIX System Administration Made Difficult Handbook* from Prentice Hall.

Note: The multilevel dump schemes work only if you specify the u option during dumps to update the dump record.

To back up a disk:

```
# ufsdump 0dsf 54000 6000 /dev/rmt/0 /usr
```
or
```
# ufsdump 5f /dev/rmt/1bmn /opt
```

The number at the start of the options indicates the level of the dump. The remainder of the options can be specified in any order. The partition to dump is specified last. If an option has a value, that value must be in the same order as the option itself.

In the first example, the options d, s, and f all have values. The value for the d option is specified first, the s value is next, and the f value is last. The d and s options refer to defining characteristics of the tape drive. In the second example, the information that would be normally indicated by d and s is determined by the system's knowledge of the device. This shortcut can usually only be used by 8 mm and 4 mm systems.

To put multiple files on a tape, use the no-rewind option of the tape device to position the tape at the end.

To restore a disk:

cd *<mountpoint>*; **ufsrestore vf /dev/rmt/0bn** — (restores the whole partition)

cd *<mountpoint>*; **ufsrestore ivf /dev/rmt/0bn** — (restores files, directories interactively)

cd *<mountpoint>*; **ufsrestore ivfs /dev/rmt/0bn x** — (restores interactively from file X on the tape)

f specifies the device on which the dump is found, and v means verbose. The i option loads a virtual copy of the filesystem dumped and starts an interactive session in which you can change directories and select specific files. See ufsrestore(1M) for a full list of available options.

<mountpoint> refers to the mountpoint of the partition that you are restoring to. You can restore to a place other than that you originally dumped from. In this case, a full directory tree is built. For example, to restore /export/home/terimaul/marym/testfiles to the /tmp directory, the actual file will be found in /tmp/export/home/terimaul/marym/testfiles.

The last example shows how to restore from a file other than the first file on a tape.

Tape Handling with mt

The magnetic tape handling program, mt, retensions tapes, erases them, obtains status and device information, and positions a tape.

To retension a tape (i.e., running it from beginning to end and back to the beginning—useful for new tapes):

mt -f /dev/rmt/0 retension

To erase a tape (usually a security function):

mt -f /dev/rmt/0 erase

To obtain the status of a specific drive:

mt -f /dev/rmt/0 status

Status can tell you:

- whether the drive does not have a tape loaded, for example,

  ```
  /dev/rmt/0: no tape loaded or drive offline
  ```

- if another process has the drive, for example,

  ```
  /dev/rmt/1: device busy
  ```

- the type of tape drive, for example,

  ```
  Exabyte EXB-8200 8mm tape drive
     sense key (0x0) = No Additional Sense residual = 0 retries= 0
     file no= 0 block no=0
  ```

Most of the functionality of mt lies in its ability to position a tape to different files.

- To position a tape to the beginning of the tape

  ```
  # mt -f /dev/rmt/0 rewind
  ```

- To position a tape to the end of the last tape file:

  ```
  # mt -f /dev/rmt/0n eom
  ```

- To eject a tape:

  ```
  # mt -f /dev/rmt/0 offline
  ```
  or
  ```
  # mt -f /dev/rmt/0 rewoffl
  ```

- To position a tape to the second file on the tape, start at the beginning of the tape and forward space file by one file. Another way of doing this is to use the absolute space file option where a rewind is assumed.

  ```
  # mt -f /dev/rmt/0 rewind
  # mt -f /dev/rmt/0n fsf 1
  ```
  or
  ```
  # mt -f /dev/rmt/0n asf
  ```

Online: DiskSuite

The Online: DiskSuite™ tools operate on disks and disk devices. This unbundled Sun product creates filesystems that can spread over multiple disks, also known as concatenation. To gain the most performance over multiple disks, you can use a feature call "striping" to interlace tracks between devices. You may also want to mirror a disk with critical information so that if one disk goes bad, the information therein will still be accessible.

Another feature, known as "hot-spares," allows you to keep devices on reserve so that if a disk dies it will be immediately replaced by one of the spare disks. The contents of the bad disk will be copied to the hot-spare transparently.

≡ *9*

Solaris Implementation: A Guide for System Administrators

Solaris 2.x Products 10 ☰

This chapter describes two products in the Solaris 2.x environment—Online: Backup and Wabi.

Online: Backup

Backing up a single system is easy—just set up a cron entry and let it run after you leave for the day. Backing up multiple systems was not so simple—putting a tape drive on every local system, supplying tapes for those drives, and paying someone to change those tapes on those drives is hardly cost effective. However, the advent of tape drives capable of holding the data from several systems has made a server-oriented paradigm for backups the optimal method. Coordinating client systems, remembering when to run full or incremental backups, and the general logistics of handling tape drive access for all clients make a dump management system a good idea.

Note – Online: Backup is based upon `ufsdump`. The actual command is called `hsmdump`. Since dump and backup are virtually synonymous and dump is no longer a command itself, backup and dump are used interchangeably.

Sun's offering in this area was called Online: Backup Copilot™ on Solaris 1.x systems. The name was changed to Online: Backup for Solaris 2.x releases. Online: Backup also collects information on what was dumped, when it was dumped, and which tape it was dumped to. This information is stored in a database so that the system administrator does not need to guess what tape the data is on and check file after file to find it. Third-party vendors are adding value to this product by offering tape changers for even more automation.

Planning is a very important stage of the Online: Backup installation. By strategically placing each component, you can maximize the use of your resources. After designing the layout, you should determine how your configuration files should be set up. The next section, "Architecting the Design," covers the design issues in depth.

Architecting the Design

When designing the backup strategy, you need an understanding of the key components of the architecture and configuration files. First we discuss the layout of the hardware components, then the important concepts of the configuration files, and finally, a real-world example.

Component Systems

There are five key components to the Online: Backup architecture:

- configuration master server
- tapehost
- database host
- client
- opermon host

With Sun's distributed approach, each function can be distributed to a different system or the functions can be combined.

Configuration Master Server

The configuration master server, or configmaster, is the system that holds all the configuration files. These files list the clients, the schedule of the clients' dumps, what tapehost(s) the clients will use, who the dump operator is, who is notified by email, and how long to retain the information in the database about each tape.

Note – One important consideration in choosing your configmaster system is that an Online: Backup (Solaris 2.x systems) server can dump Online: Backup Copilot (Solaris 1.x) clients, but an Online: Backup Copilot configmaster system cannot dump Online: Backup clients. Therefore, if you have Solaris 2.x clients, you must have a Solaris 2.x/Online: Backup configmaster.

Tapehost

The tapehost is the system that contains the tape drive(s) that the data will be written to. You can use more than one tape drive, and they can be connected to different systems. The tape drives are used sequentially, that is, when one tape becomes full, the dump switches to the next tape drive defined. All drives in a specific configuration must be the same type and density. There are no OS requirements for tapehost systems.

Database Host

The database host is the system that holds the database and its daemon, rpc.dumpdbd. This system requires considerable disk space. Plan on using at least 7 percent of the disk space that you dump to retain a reasonable size database. It is not mandatory to use a Solaris 2.x system here, but we strongly recommend the Online: Backup version of the database.

The 7 percent quoted above is a rough estimate. Use the formula below for a more accurate estimate of the disk space needed for the database.

space used = ((220 + (56 * number of dumps)) * number of inodes) + 10,000

1. **Determine how many backups you will retain.**

2. **Multiply this number by 56.**

3. **Add 220.**
   There are 56 bytes of activity information for each dump and 220 bytes of structural information stored in the database for each inode.

4. **Use the BSD version of df to obtain the number of inodes. There isn't any Solaris 2.x equivalent of df -i.**

5. **Multiply the number of inodes by the result in the step above.**

6. **Add 10,000.**
   There are 10,000 bytes of general information stored for each filesystem that is dumped.

Example 10-1   A User's System

```
terimaul# /usr/ucb/df -i
Filesystem              iused    ifree    %iused   Mounted on
/dev/dsk/c0t2d0s0       1962     18518      10%    /
Filesystem              iused    ifree    %iused   Mounted on
/dev/dsk/c0t2d0s6       11651    85629      12%    /usr
Filesystem              iused    ifree    %iused   Mounted on
/dev/dsk/c0t2d0s3        155     25445       1%    /opt
```

Example 10-1   A User's System (Continued)

```
Filesystem                iused   ifree   %iused  Mounted on
/dev/dsk/c0t2d0s7         1142    439178    0%    /export/home
terimaul#
```

There are 14,910 inodes in use on this system. The /usr partition rarely changes, so it will not be backed up daily. This leaves 3,259 inodes. Backups are done Monday through Friday and are retained for two weeks or 10 backups. That gives the following:

$$2,552,020 = (220 +56 *10) * 3259 + 10,000$$

This client requires about 3 Mbytes of disk space in the database.

Example 10-2   A Server

```
# /usr/ucb/df -i
Filesystem                iused   ifree   %iused  Mounted on
/dev/dsk/c0t3d0s0        2198    19306    10%    /
Filesystem                iused   ifree   %iused  Mounted on
/dev/dsk/c0t3d0s6        8431    64145    12%    /usr
Filesystem                iused   ifree   %iused  Mounted on
/dev/dsk/c0t3d0s3          75    16053     0%    /opt
Filesystem                iused   ifree   %iused  Mounted on
/dev/dsk/c0t3d0s7          10    40310     0%    /tmp
Filesystem                iused   ifree   %iused  Mounted on
/dev/dsk/c0t0d0s6       24429   605331     4%    /export/home/agent99a
Filesystem                iused   ifree   %iused  Mounted on
/dev/dsk/c0t1d0s6       41864   587896     7%    /export/home/agent99b
Filesystem                iused   ifree   %iused  Mounted on
/dev/dsk/c0t2d0s6       30757   599003     5%    /export/home/agent99c
Filesystem                iused   ifree   %iused  Mounted on
/dev/dsk/c1t1d0s6        3474   479854     1%    /export/home/agent99d
Filesystem                iused   ifree   %iused  Mounted on
/dev/dsk/c1t2d0s6       16137   467191     3%    /export/home/agent99e
Filesystem                iused   ifree   %iused  Mounted on
/dev/dsk/c1t3d0s6       48097   435231    10%    /export/home/agent99f
Filesystem                iused   ifree   %iused  Mounted on
/dev/dsk/c2t3d0s6        3327   480001     1%    /export/home/agent99g
```

There are 178,789 inodes in use on this system. Backups are done Monday through Friday and are retained for six weeks or 30 backups. That gives the following:

$$339,709,100 = (220 +56 *30) * 178,789 + 10,000$$

This client requires about 340 Mbytes of disk space in the database.

Client

The client is the system that is being dumped. The only constraint here is that the disks must reside locally on the system that is being dumped. Neither Online: Backup nor Online: Backup Copilot can dump an NFS- or RFS-mounted filesystem.

Opermon Host

The opermon host is the system that communicates with the dumps. The `rpc.operd` process, which allows these communications, runs on this system. Online: Backup does not have a terminal session established to communicate information and problems, because it is started from a cron job. An operations monitor process, or `opermon`, was developed to communicate with the dumps. Most of the messages that pass through this process are information for the system administrator to monitor the progress of a dump configuration. There will be times when you will need to insert an additional tape or deal with a tape drive that did not respond properly. For this reason, `opermon` is a two-way communications package. You can reply to requests from a backup as well as watch its progress.

Database Planning

You can use the Online: DiskSuite product to join two or more disks for a large contiguous database. Split up your databases when the size of the database becomes larger than a single tape, or when the reclaim time becomes unmanageable, or when the database's disk partition is more than 70–80 percent full.

Configuration File Concepts

Configuration files control the dump cycles for each client, the retention time of the tapes, the definition of specific users or aliases for the dumps themselves, and the notification procedure. Once you know who the clients are and where the other components are in the layout, you can start grouping clients into configuration files.

Dump Cycle

Because Online: Backup uses a derivative of `ufsdump`, it can use ten different dump levels in varying combinations. Determine the dump levels you need (i.e., how often you need to have full dumps done and what levels of dumps you want in between). Refer to the section on `ufsdump` in Chapter 9 for a description of dump levels. When you reach the point where your dumps start recycling the tapes, you have a complete dump cycle.

Example 1: You do a level 0 dump on Monday. Then on Tuesday, Wednesday, and Thursday you do a level 9 dump, which backs up only the data that changed that day. On Friday, you might do a level 5 dump, which picks up all changes that have happened since Monday. Writing this process out as a set of dump levels would look like this:

```
M T W T F
0 9 9 9 5
```

Example 2: If you want to do a level 0 dump only once a month, you can do a level 9 dump every Monday, Tuesday, Wednesday, and Thursday for the rest of the month. Then you have two options for Friday. You can do a level 5 dump each Friday, which will back up any changes since the previous Friday (level 5), or you can use increasing dump level numbers to pick up all of the changes since the last level 0. These two dump schemes would look like this:

	M T W T F S S	M T W T F S S	M T W T F S S	M T W T F S S
First method	0 9 9 9 5 – –	9 9 9 9 5 – –	9 9 9 9 5 – –	9 9 9 9 5 – –
Second method	0 9 9 9 5 – –	9 9 9 9 4 – –	9 9 9 9 3 – –	9 9 9 9 2 – –

Staggering Dumps

Online: Backup is designed to stagger dumps, that is, to start the dump cycle on different days for each partition. If you were to stagger Example 1 for a server with five disks, it would look like this:

```
/                0 9 9 9 5
/usr             5 0 9 9 9
/opt             9 5 0 9 9
/export/home     9 9 5 0 9
/export/home1    9 9 9 5 0
```

One of the advantages of dumping like this is that you do not need to have enough tape space to do a full dump on every filesystem at the same time. In general, a single 5 Gbyte tape drive can dump about 10–15 Gbytes of disk space. This strategy would mean that you would be intermixing your full and incremental dumps on the same tape. It may seem heretical, but it is a good idea, really. Restores are transparent to you, so you do not need to organize your dumps for simplicity of restores. Using a staggered method allows you to cut down on the number of tape devices that are needed for dumps.

Online: Backup also lets you configure the tape eject cycle. You can configure so that the tapes eject only on any specific day or whatever you want. If you choose, you can use a new tape every day of the week. However, if you leave the tape in the drive until it is full, you will also cut down on tape usage.

Tape Retention

The next decision is how long to keep your tapes. If you chose to use staggering, remember that all of your dumps will be kept for the same amount of time. You can only retain level 0s for three months and level 9s for a week if they are on separate tapes.

Your tape retention decision should be based upon how often you send tapes off-site for long term storage and how old the data is that your users request to be restored. Usually, 90 percent of all restores are done from data that is less than one week old, and 99 percent of all restores are from data that is a month or less old. Please remember that these figures are an average—your mileage may vary.

Dump Operator

Online: Backup uses a variation of `rsh` to execute its dumps, so it is a good idea to designate a dump operator other than root. There is no restriction on the UID of the dump operator. The GID of the dump operator must be 5 or `sys` (this would be 3 or `dev` on 4.1.x systems).

Putting the Pieces Together

The most important rule of thumb is to keep the clients and their tapehosts on the same subnet. If a dump has to pass through a router, it will take considerably longer than one that is kept to the local subnet. Also, if dumps are kept local to their own subnet, simultaneous dumps of several subnets can occur without conflicting with one another. As noted before, you can use more than one tape drive for a configuration. The tape drives are accessed sequentially, that is, when the first drive is full, the second drive will be used. The dump files can span tapes. It is not advisable to use more than three tape drives for a config file because it will take about 8–10 hours to complete a dump of that size.

It is not critical to keep the configmaster, database, and opermon functions on the same subnet. A single configmaster can service dump configurations on several subnets at the same time.

Consider the setup shown in Figure 10-1. The configmaster, candibarr, resides on the 167 subnet. In this case, the configmaster is also the opermon host and the database host. There are 80 clients and four servers on the four subnets 8, 19, 162, and 167. There are 10 tape drives shared by the tapehosts. Each config file has a pair of tape drives assigned to it, so that dumps need not wait for human intervention, and the dumps are not so large that they cannot finish in the night hours.

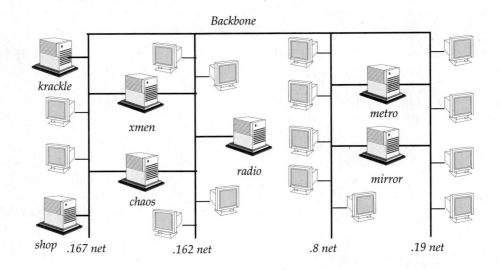

Figure 10-1   Sample Network

- The tapehost radio supports clients on the 162 subnet.

- The tapehosts krackle and shop support clients on the 167 subnet

- The tapehosts xmen and chaos support clients on both the 162 and 167 subnets.

- The tapehosts mirror and metro support clients on both the 8 and 19 subnets.

Note – Online: Backup will not be offered after November 1994. Support will continue for installed products through 1998 to 2000, depending on the level of support.

Helpful Hint – Since you will be recycling your level 0 dumps with the rest of the files on tape, you should probably do regular full dumps of your servers for offsite storage outside of the Online: Backup procedures.

Wabi

Wabi stands for Windows Application Binary Interface. It is a method of running Microsoft Windows 3.x applications on Solaris 2.2 and later systems. Wabi runs these applications by intercepting the Windows API calls and converting them to X-window calls. Currently, with Wabi 1.0, this process tends to make device interfaces a bit slow, but performance is usually increased by moving from x86 to SPARC systems.

Note – Wabi will be bundled in future releases. Those who purchased the Solaris 2.2 or 2.3 operating environment were provided a coupon to obtain Wabi when it was released.

This chapter discusses basic installation of Wabi, application installation, and Wabi server management issues.

Installation

Since Wabi is an interface between X-windows and Microsoft Windows applications, installing Wabi is just the beginning. Wabi does not require Microsoft Windows in order to run applications. However, Wabi does not have equivalents for the Microsoft Windows tools such as the calculator, clock, and text editor. To acquire these utilities, you must load Microsoft Windows.

Wabi Installation

Wabi installation is a simple pkgadd. However, for Solaris versions 2.2 and 2.3, associated patches enable Wabi to work with the OS. The most significant patch is the one for vold.

To install Wabi, mount the CD-ROM as follows:

 # mount /dev/dsk/c0t6d0s2 /mnt (for systems without volume manager running)

 # cd /vol/cdrom0 (for systems with volume manager running)

There will be two directories here: one for SPARC architecture and one for the x86 architecture (also known as i86pc). Run pkgadd on the appropriate architecture, for example:

 # pkgadd -d `pwd` SUNWwabi.sparc

Respond to the prompts. When this is complete, Wabi is installed.

Application Installation

Installing applications on Wabi is a straightforward process. Start the Wabi interface by typing **wabi**. (If this is the first time that Wabi is run, it may take up to 10 minutes for the fonts to be built.)

1. Pull down the File menu and select Run.

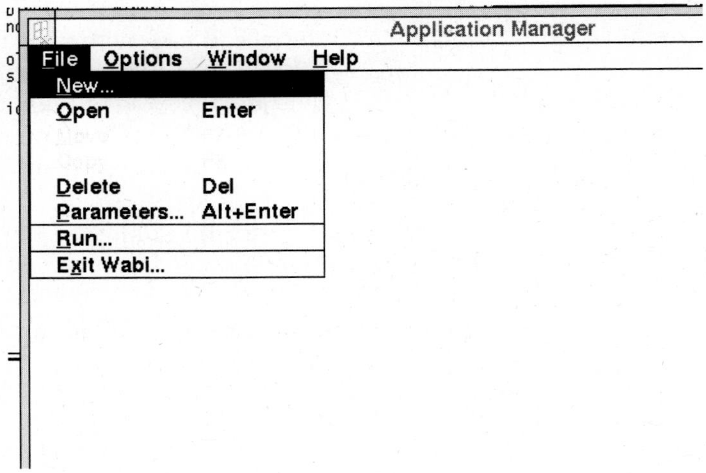

Figure 10-2   Application Manager File Menu

2. Select the Browse button and locate the installation file (usually called `setup.exe`) for the application.

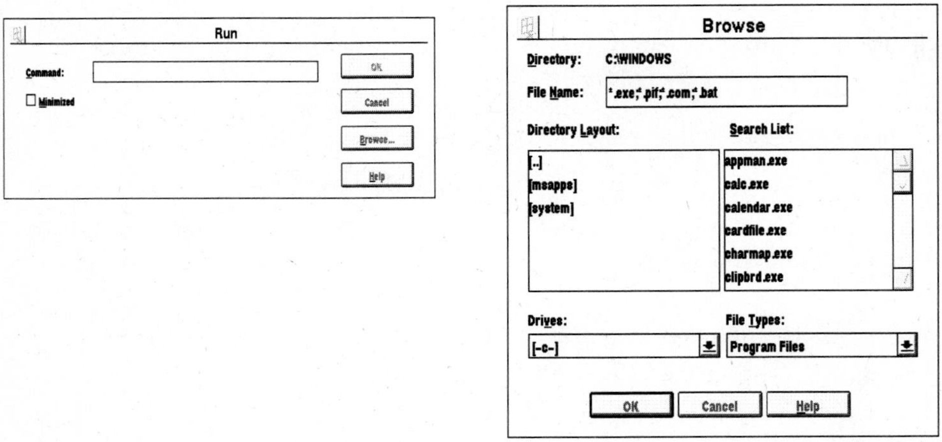

Figure 10-3   Browse and Run Dialog Boxes

3. Click on OK in both the Browse and Run dialog boxes. This starts the installation program.

Microsoft Windows Installation

Installation of Microsoft Windows is no more difficult than installing an application. However, Microsoft Windows is installed with a different method.

1. Open up the Tools icon.

2. Double-click on the Windows Install icon.

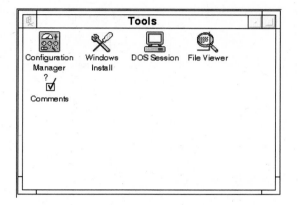

Figure 10-4   Microsoft Tools Window

3. Select the location of the installation media (usually A: i.e., the first floppy known to the system).

4. Click on OK to start the installation.

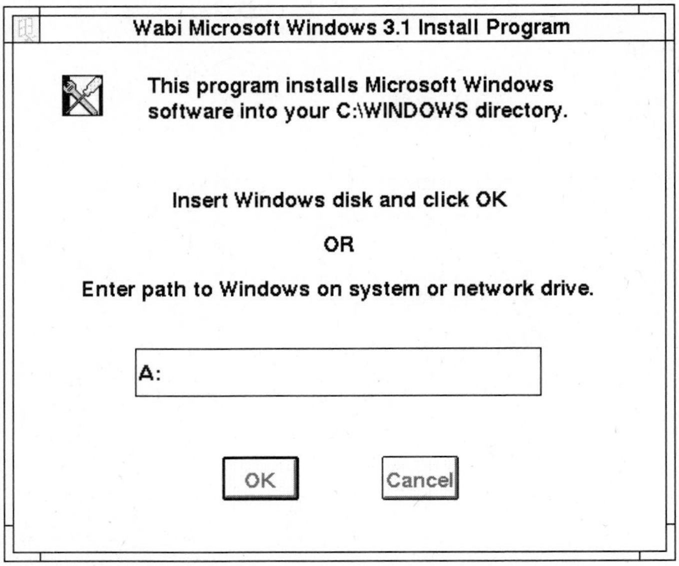

```
┌─────────────────────────────────────────────────────┐
│ ▦     Wabi Microsoft Windows 3.1 Install Program     │
├─────────────────────────────────────────────────────┤
│                                                       │
│   ✗    This program installs Microsoft Windows        │
│        software into your C:\WINDOWS directory.       │
│                                                       │
│                                                       │
│           Insert Windows disk and click OK            │
│                                                       │
│                          OR                           │
│                                                       │
│    Enter path to Windows on system or network drive.  │
│                                                       │
│    ┌─────────────────────────────────────────────┐   │
│    │A:                                            │   │
│    └─────────────────────────────────────────────┘   │
│                                                       │
│         ┌────────┐        ┌────────┐                  │
│         │   OK   │        │ Cancel │                  │
│         └────────┘        └────────┘                  │
│                                                       │
└─────────────────────────────────────────────────────┘
```

Figure 10-5   Windows Install

Wabi Configuration

Several items in Wabi can be configured, including the serial ports, printers, hard and floppy disk drives, and basic sounds.

1. **Open the Tools icon.**

2. **Double-click on the Configuration Manager icon.**
   This displays the window shown in Figure 10-6. Each icon in this window configures one part of the Wabi environment. Below are steps to set up each of the configurable items.

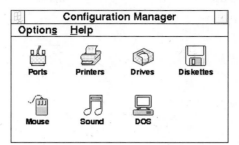

Figure 10-6   Wabi Configuration Manager Window

Configuring Serial Ports

1. Double-click on the Ports icon. The Port Settings window, shown in Figure 10-7, will be displayed.

2. Use the pull-down arrow on the right of the Port item to select the appropriate port. Ports COM1–4 are considered to be serial ports; ports LPT1–2 are considered to be parallel ports.

3. Select the appropriate information from the rest of the pull-down menus in the window and click on the Connect button when the information is complete. If the device was a COM1–4 device, the COM Port Connections window will be displayed. Here you associate the DOS type device with its UNIX equivalent.

4. Select the appropriate UNIX serial device to associate with the COM port and click on the OK button. The Port Settings window will be redisplayed.

5. When you are finished with all port definitions, click on the OK button.

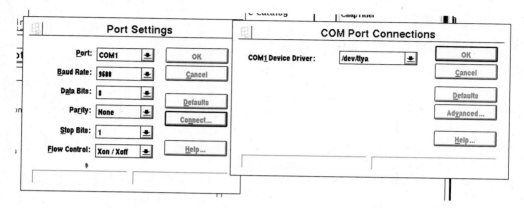

Figure 10-7   Wabi Port Configuration Windows

Defining Printers

1. Double-click on the Printers icon. The window shown in Figure 10-8 is displayed.
2. Select the printer that you want from the scrolling list at the bottom left side of the window.

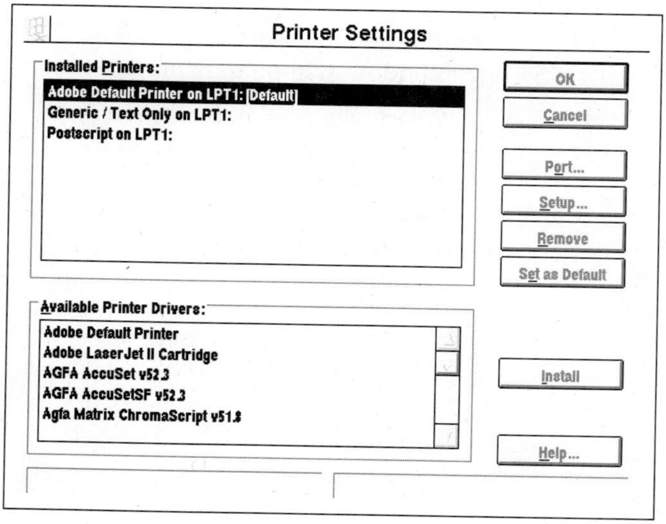

Figure 10-8   Wabi Printer Configuration Window

3. Click on the Port button to summon the Printer Port Selection window, shown in Figure 10-9.

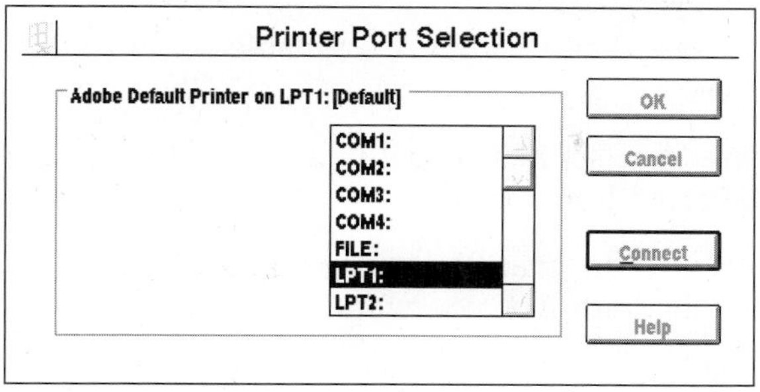

Figure 10-9 Wabi Printer Port Selection Window

4. Select the appropriate device, for example, COM1:

5. Click on the Connect button to summon the Printer Output Connections window, shown in Figure 10-10.

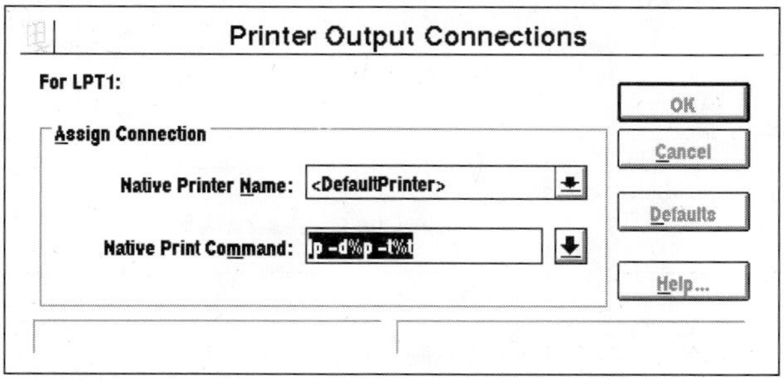

Figure 10-10 Wabi Printer Output Connections Window

6. Change any information that appears incorrect. Usually, this window does not need changes.

7. Click on the OK button. The Printer Port Selection window will be redisplayed.

8. Click the OK button here. The main Printer Settings window will be redisplayed.

9. Click the OK button.

Defining Disk Devices

1. Double-click on the Drives icon. The window shown in Figure 10-11 is displayed.

2. Select a drive from the left-hand menu. A scrollable list of available paths will appear in the right-hand menu.

3. Double click on a path to select it. This path name will be displayed in the box labeled Directory Path for Selected Drive x:

4. All available directories under that directory will be displayed. Continue selecting drives until you have the path that you want.

5. Click on the Connect button.

6. When you have finished configuring your drives, click on the OK button.

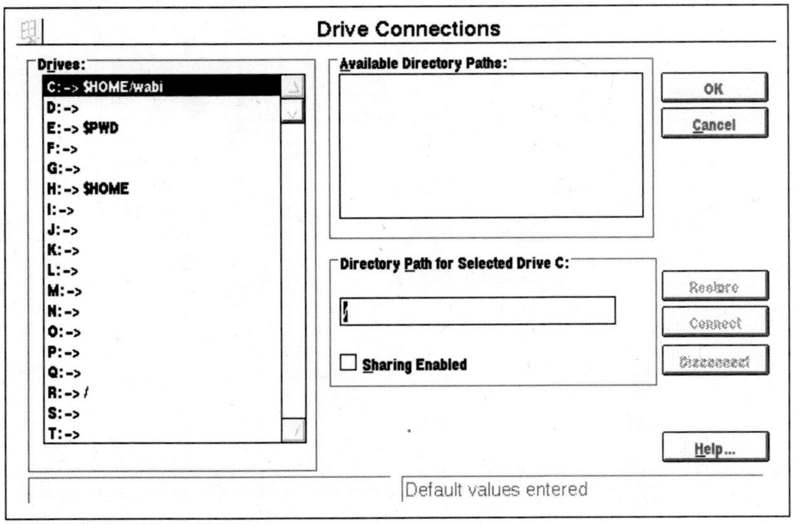

Figure 10-11 Wabi Drive Connections Window

Defining Floppy Drives

1. Double-click on the Diskettes icon. The window shown in Figure 10-12 is displayed.

2. Use the Arrow Button on the right side of each floppy to see a list of the available floppy devices.

Solaris Implementation: A Guide for System Administrators

3. Select a device. The pull-down box will be dismissed.

4. When you have finished configuring your drives, click on the OK button.

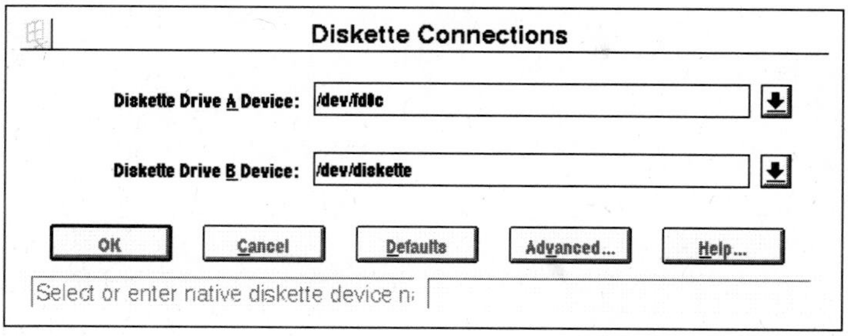

Figure 10-12 Wabi Diskette Connections Window

Wabi Server Management Issues

Microsoft Windows was originally developed as a single-user application. There are some networking environments that have pushed Microsoft towards application sharing. However, many of the technical and legal issues surrounding Microsoft Windows applications have not been resolved.

Providing /usr/local Equivalents for Microsoft Windows Applications

Wabi places the C: pointer to the user's home directory; most Microsoft Windows applications try to install into the C: drive. So, to use the software for several people, change the C: pointer to a writeable /usr/local type area and install there. Then change the C: drive for all other users to this location as well. Note this one caveat: Microsoft Windows applications create temporary files while the application is in use. If more than one person use the application at the same time, the temporary files can be corrupted. To circumvent this problem, use multiuser or designated networked applications, if they are available.

Licensing Issues

Most Microsoft Windows applications do not use licenses. However, this does not mean that you can run as many copies of the software as you like. It only means that there is no method of policing the use of the software. System administrators and their company are still required to purchase copies of the software for each copy used.

10

AutoInstall Samples

A ≡

Example AutoInstall Entries

The AutoInstall process consists of several components. There are `rules` files, which direct each installation to the appropriate *host_config* file and scripts. There are the *host_config* files themselves, and there are the scripts. Samples here are taken from the AutoInstall samples found on the Solaris 2.x CDs and from Sun's internal Solaris transition program. Explanations follow most of the samples.

Example Rules

The least complicated condition for comparisons is matching per hostname. The sample `rules` file uses the following example:

```
hostname sample_host - host_class set_root_pw
```

The first two fields compare the hostname of the AutoInstall client to the name in `sample_host`. When the comparison is satisfied, the remaining arguments on the line are executed in the following order. There is no begin script as indicated by the "-" in the third field. The *class* file named `host_class` is used to select disk partitioning sizes and software packages. The finish script, called `set_root_pw`, is executed after the `host_class` script has completed.

Another more complex comparison, shown on line 73 of the sample `rules` file, illustrates how powerful the AutoInstall process can be.

```
network 924.222.43.0 && \
     karch sun4c - net924_sun4c finish_924
```

This example states that any AutoInstall client of the sun4c kernel architecture that boots up on the network IP address of 924.222.43.0 satisfies the match. These clients use no begin script, an install class file called `net924_sun4c`, and when completed execute the finish script named `finish_924`. This type of entry works well on workgroups of systems that are connected to the same subnet—a common case in network topology.

The following comparison match checks the disk size of the AutoInstall client and makes decisions based on the current disk size.

```
disksize c0t3d0 400-600 && installed c0t3d0s0 solaris_2.1 - upgrade -
```

If the device at controller zero, target three, disk zero is greater than 400 megabytes but less than 600 megabytes, and currently has Solaris_2.1 installed, then use the install class file named `upgrade`, omitting both begin and finish scripts.

And finally, the last example in the sample `rules` file uses the wildcard keyword *any* to satisfy comparisons.

```
any - - any_machine -
```

This entry allows any AutoInstall client to be installed with the profile called `any_machine` and does not use a begin or a finish script, as indicated by the hyphens.

The `rules` file you maintain can have as many entries as you wish, provided they follow the proper format and can pass the `check` script without reporting errors. Make sure that you do not have more than one match opportunity for AutoInstall clients or things can get rather confusing.

Usually a `rules` file starts with specific entries such as hostnames. For example, in a building with around 100 systems, usually the servers and customized systems would be itemized by a hostname entry in the `rules` file. The next criteria would depend on such things as diskspace shortages, workgroups with special needs, and how the systems are organized on the network. For instance, if the Finance people need additional packages, and they will all have more than the minimum needed space, and they occupy the 129.148.27 subnet, then the next entry in a rules file would be a network address.

In practice, however, separate *install_config* directories are usually made for categories of users, because the directories tend to get cluttered and creating a `rules.ok` file requires that all associate files be in the same directory.

Sample Begin Scripts

The most common use of a begin script is to save the key files on a user's system before starting an install.

Basic Save of Key Files

```
#!/bin/sh
# ROOTPART == current root partition for system config files to be preserved
ROOTPART=c0t3d0s0
# non-interactive auto-install save script for solaris -> solaris installs
#
# - alvinc
#

mount /dev/dsk/$ROOTPART /a

#
# mount the rest of the partitions according to old (v)fstab
#

#
# Creating list of files to be saved
#

if [ -d /a/dev/dsk ]; then
cat > /tmp/root/save.tmp << END
./.cshrc
./.login
./.profile
./.rhosts
./etc/.rootkey
./etc/auto_*
./etc/auto.*
./etc/defaultdomain
./etc/dfs/dfstab
./etc/hosts
./etc/passwd
./etc/mail/aliases
./etc/group
./etc/vfstab-
./etc/shadow
./etc/lp/Systems
./etc/lp/classes
./etc/lp/default
./etc/lp/forms
./etc/lp/interfaces
./etc/lp/printers
./etc/licenses
./etc/nsswitch.conf
./etc/rmmount.conf
```

```
./etc/resolv.conf
./etc/uucp/Devices
./etc/uucp/Sys*
./var/spool/cron/crontabs/*
./var/spool/lp/system/pstatus
./var/spool/calendar/callog.*
./var/mail
./opt/SUNWhsm
./usr/dumpdb
./etc/opt
./var/opt
./usr/demo/sounds
./etc/vfstab
./etc/rc2.d/*
END
 else
cat > /tmp/root/save.tmp << END
./.cshrc
./.login
./.profile
./.rhosts
./etc/auto_*
./etc/auto.*
./etc/passwd-
./etc/aliases
./etc/group
./etc/fstab-
./etc/printcap
./etc/licenses
./etc/uucp/Devices
./etc/uucp/Sys*
./etc/hosts
./etc/exports
./etc/rc.local
./var/spool/cron/crontabs/*
./var/spool/calendar/callog.*
./var/spool/mail/*
END
 fi
```

```
#
# Backup /etc/vfstab or /etc/fstab, passwd, and crontabs
#

if [ -d /a/dev/dsk ]
then
 cp /a/etc/vfstab /a/etc/vfstab-
else
 cp /a/etc/fstab /a/etc/fstab-
 cp /a/etc/passwd /a/etc/passwd-
fi
cd /a/var/spool/cron/crontabs
for crons in `ls`
do
 mv ${crons} ${crons}-
done

cd /a
cp /dev/null /tmp/root/save.dat
for a in `cat /tmp/root/save.tmp`
do
 if [ -f $a ] || [ -d $a ]; then
 echo $a >>/tmp/root/save.dat
 fi
done

#
# Create save directory, cd /a (root) and tar
#

echo "Saving to /tmp/root/$SI_HOSTNAME.save_tar file"
cd /a

tar cpf /tmp/root/$SI_HOSTNAME.save_tar `cat /tmp/root/save.dat`

echo "Saving to /dev/rmt/1b"
cd /a

tar cpf /dev/rmt/1b `cat /tmp/root/save.dat`

echo ""
echo "Save is completed ..."

cd /
umount /a
```

Fancy Save Begin File

```
#!/bin/sh
#
cp /tmp/root/etc/mnttab /tmp/root/etc/mnttab.orig
mkdir /tmp/mountroot

POSS_ROOTDISKS=`echo /dev/dsk/c0t[012345]d0s0`
for disk in $POSS_ROOTDISKS
do
 echo "Checking $disk ... \c"
 mount -o rw -F ufs $disk /tmp/mountroot

# testing if we have found a Solaris 2.x root disk
# if so, backup some files

 if [ -d /tmp/mountroot/dev/dsk ]; then
 echo "got it ... Solaris 2.x root disk !"
 cd /tmp/mountroot/etc
 cp vfstab vfstab-
 cp nsswitch.conf nsswitch.conf-
 cd ../var/spool/cron/crontabs
 mkdir pre_upgrade
 cp * pre_upgrade
 elif [ -f /tmp/mountroot/vmunix ]; then
 echo "got it ... Solaris 1.x root disk !"
 cd /tmp/mountroot/etc
 cp fstab fstab-
 cp passwd passwd-
 cp group group-
 mkdir mail
 cp aliases mail
 cd ../var/spool/cron/crontabs
 mkdir pre_upgrade
 cp * pre_upgrade
 else
 echo "bummer ... this isn't a root disk"
 umount $disk
 fi
done
```

```
#
# Creating list of files to be saved
#

if [ -d /tmp/mountroot/dev/dsk ]; then
cat > /tmp/save.tmp << END
././cshrc
././login
././profile
././rhosts
./etc/.rootkey
./etc/auto_*
./etc/auto.*
./etc/defaultdomain
./etc/dfs/dfstab
./etc/hosts
./etc/passwd
./etc/mail/aliases
./etc/group
./etc/vfstab-
./etc/shadow
./etc/lp/Systems
./etc/lp/classes
./etc/lp/default
./etc/lp/forms
./etc/lp/interfaces
./etc/lp/printers
./etc/licenses
./etc/nsswitch.conf
./etc/resolv.conf
./etc/uucp/Devices
./etc/uucp/Sys*
./var/spool/cron/crontabs/pre_upgrade
./var/spool/lp/system/pstatus
./var/spool/calendar/callog.*
./var/mail
END
 else
cat > /tmp/save.tmp << END
././cshrc
././login
././profile
././rhosts
./etc/auto_*
./etc/auto.*
./etc/passwd-
```

```
./etc/aliases
./etc/group
./etc/fstab-
./etc/printcap
./etc/licenses
./etc/uucp/Devices
./etc/uucp/Sys*
./etc/hosts
./etc/exports
./etc/rc.local
./var/spool/cron/crontabs/pre_upgrade
./var/spool/calendar/callog.*
./var/spool/mail/*
END
fi


cd /tmp/mountroot
cp /dev/null /tmp/save.dat
for a in `cat /tmp/save.tmp`
do
 if [ -f $a ] || [ -d $a ]; then
 echo $a >>/tmp/save.dat
 fi
done


echo "Saving tarred files to /tmp/$SI_HOSTNAME.save_tar file"
cd /tmp/mountroot

tar cpf /tmp/$SI_HOSTNAME.save_tar `cat /tmp/save.dat`

echo ""
echo "Save is completed ..."

cd /
umount /tmp/mountroot
mv /tmp/root/etc/mnttab.orig /tmp/root/etc/mnttab
rmdir /tmp/mountroot
```

Sample Class Files

Three install class files exist in the sample directory: `any_machine`, `host_class`, and `net924_sun4c`. Each file provides examples of different AutoInstall installations. The contents of the `any_machine` class are targeted at standalone machines. The `host_class` file is similar to the `any_machine` file except for an NFS mount, placed in the system's `/etc/vfstab` file for automatic mounting.

The any_machine File

Three install class files are included that are not on the Solaris CD-ROM. These files are used to install a basic end-user configuration, an NFS server configuration, and a diskless client-server configuration.

The `any_machine` file contains the following information.

```
# cat any_machine
install_type initial_install
system_type standalone
partitioning default
cluster SUNWCuser
cluster SUNWCxgl delete
package SUNWaudmo add
filesys any 40 swap
filesys any 50 /opt
```

The entries have the following meaning.

The install_type entry can use the keywords *initial_install* or *upgrade*. The system_type entry can be *standalone*, *server*, or *dataless*. These system types are also found during a manual Solaris Install. The partitioning entry is defined as *default*, allowing the install program to select the partition sizes for the necessary disk slices. Other options for the partitioning entry are *explicit* or *existing*. If explicit partitioning is selected, then partition names, sizes, and mount point directories must be included.

The cluster entry defines SUNWCuser as the bundled software to be installed, which is known by the Solaris Install program as the End User System cluster. Alternatives to including entire clusters are to select individual packages, one per line, using the keyword *package* instead of *cluster*. The next cluster entry, SUNWxgl, a normal part of the End User cluster will be deleted, as indicated by the keyword delete. The package SUNWaudmo, the audio demo package, will be installed in addition to the end user cluster.

The last two lines in the `any_machine` class file set the swap slice to 40 megabytes and the `/opt` filesystem to 50 megabytes. Since these are greater than the defaults, the extra space for these slices is taken from partitions that have space to give, particularly `/export/home`.

In the manual standalone installation discussed earlier, the default partitioning left something to be desired, especially the size of root and `/usr` partitions. If the default partitioning is chosen during AutoInstall, be prepared to find free disk space in half-filled partitions such as `/usr`. Also, expect the minimum amount of root filesystem space to be configured.

The host_sample File

The second class file to be examined is the `host_sample` file, which includes many of the same definitions as the `any_machine` class file. The only notable difference is the addition of the last line in the file, which places an NFS type mount into the `/etc/vfstab` file. Other NFS mounts can be placed in the class file by the same technique.

```
# cat host_sample
install_type initial_install
system_type standalone
partitioning default
cluster SUNWCuser
cluster SUNWCown delete
cluster SUNWCtltk delete
cluster SUNWCxgl delete
cluster SUNWCxil delete
filesys srvr:/usr/openwin - /usr/openwin ro,intr
```

This class file is a good starting point for systems that use an NFS-mounted OpenWindows. The SUNWCuser meta-cluster contains a large part of OpenWindows. The clusters that are deleted effectively clean up the contents of the `/usr/openwin`, `/opt/SUNWxil`, and `/opt/SUNWxgl` directories. An alternative to adding the entire User cluster and then removing pieces of what was just installed is to explicitly select the packages that you want to install. If you use this example class file, be sure to change the name of the OpenWindows server.

The net924_sun4c Class File

The final class file to be examined is one that installs a server system of diskless clients. Kernel architecture and disk space requirements for those clients are configured with special key words.

```
# cat net924_sun4c
install_type initial_install
system_type server
partitioning default
cluster SUNWCall
num_clients 7
client_swap 32
client_arch sun4c
client_arch sun4m
filesys c0t3d0s0 20 /
filesys c0t3d0s1 40 swap
filesys c0t3d0s5 80 /opt
```

The major changes between this class file and the others are the following: the system_type is a *server* instead of *standalone*; the SUNWCall cluster is selected, which installs the entire Solaris release; three new sample entries deal with diskless systems— num_clients, client_swap, client_arch; and the filesys entries are different from those seen before.

The num_clients entry configures free disk space based on the number and the size of client_swap, in addition to approximately 13 megabytes for individual root directories. The client_arch entries select the kernel architecture of diskless client systems. In this example, only systems from the sun4c and sun4m kernel architectures will be able to boot from this machine. Other architectures may be added as desired.

The filesys entries define the size of root, swap, and /opt explicitly, leaving the remainder of the partition arrangement to the install program. Again, the default partitioning is good to use if you do not know the required mount points for servers or if you want to make sure that all of the disk is used. Experience says you would be better setting the partition sizes to known quantities, leaving no room for error.

Sample Upgrade Class File

An upgrade is one of the simplest class files. You cannot modify partitioning and still consider the class file to be an upgrade. You can change the packages, but usually an upgrade is for no reason other than to obtain the latest version of the software.

```
install_type upgrade
product Solaris_2.3
```

Sample of Class File for Minimal User Configuration

This file demostrates the *auto* and *free* variables. *auto* is used in place of a number to indicate that the indicated partition should use the size value that would be auto-configured for that package layout. The *free* variable indicates which partition should be used as the free-hog partition. Free hog is a term carried over from SunOS 4.x; it means that whatever space is left over after other partitioning should go here.

```
install_type initial_install
system_type standalone
partitioning explicit
filesys any 30 /
filesys any auto /opt
filesys any 110 /usr
filesys any free swap
```

Sample Server Class File

There is no specific cluster for an NFS server. This class file shows the packages that are normally added to give the End User cluster additional needed services.

```
install_type initial_install
system_type standalone
partitioning explicit
cluster SUNWCuser
package SUNWman add
package SUNWaccr add
package SUNWaccu add
package SUNWast add
package SUNWbnur add
package SUNWbnuu add
package SUNWdiag add
usedisk c0t3d0
filesys c0t3d0s0 30 /
filesys c0t3d0s1 128 swap
filesys c0t3d0s5 60 /opt
filesys c0t3d0s6 auto /usr
filesys c0t3d0s4 free /var
```

Diskless Client Server Class File Sample

The following class file is used for building a diskless/dataless client server. It includes the sun4, sun4c, sun4m, and sun4d client architectures with the *client_arch* definition. Included with this are the *num_clients* and *client_swap* definitions. These items would be mandatory if the partitioning was not explicit. However, in this case they are just optional values.

```
install_type initial_install
system_type server
partitioning explicit
usedisk c0t3d0
cluster SUNWCall
num_clients 5
client_swap 16
client_arch sun4
client_arch sun4c
client_arch sun4m
client_arch sun4d
filesys c0t3d0s0 25 /
filesys c0t3d0s1 256 swap
filesys c0t3d0s3 125 /export
filesys c0t3d0s4 150 /export/swap
filesys c0t3d0s5 152 /opt
filesys c0t3d0s6 222 /usr
filesys c0t3d0s7 70 /var
```

Sample Finish Scripts

Usually, the best method for maintaining finish scripts is to make small and modular scripts and then create a single master script that calls the ones that are needed for each purpose. The samples below comprise many of the common configuration items that need to be done for a new installation.

As noted previously, if both the begin and host_class fields are null (i.e., -) in the `rules` file, the finish script can be invoked alone, and patches or packages can be added to a system without performing an upgrade.

Finish Examples Found on the Solaris 2.x CD-ROM

The sample finish script, `set_root_pw`, installs a root password based on the contents of the PASSWD definition inside the script. You must change this entry to a known encrypted password entry from an installed system's `/etc/shadow` file. Otherwise, you may install an unknown root password on many systems.

```
#!/bin/sh
#
# This is an example bourne shell script to be run after installation.
# It sets the system's root password to the entry defined in PASSWD.
# The encrypted password is obtained from an existing root password entry
# in /etc/shadow from an installed machine.
```

```
echo "setting password for root"

# set the root password
PASSWD=dKO5IBkSF421w
mv /a/etc/shadow /a/etc/shadow.orig
sed -e "s/root::6445:/root:$PASSWD:6445:/" /a/etc/shadow.orig >
/a/etc/shadow

# set the flag so sysidroot won't prompt for the root password
sed -e 's/0 # root/1 # root/' ${SI_SYS_STATE} > /tmp/state.$$
mv /tmp/state.$$ ${SI_SYS_STATE}
```

Sample pkgadd script

A few products are not bundled with the OS, including Wabi, NeWSprint™, and the NIS-compatibility package. Below is a sample of a script that installs a package.

```
#!/bin/sh
# mount the unbundled directory
mkdir /a/Unb
mount unb_srv:/unbundled/newsprint /a/Unb

# create an admin file to specify no interactive questions
cat >/a/tmp/admin <<NEW_ADMIN
mail=root
instance=unique
partial=ask
runlevel=nocheck
idepend=nocheck
rdepend=ask
space=nocheck
setuid=nocheck
conflict=nocheck
action=nocheck
basedir=default
NEW_ADMIN

# pkgadd
chroot /a /usr/sbin/pkgadd -a /tmp/admin -d /Unb -n -r /Unb/resp SUNWsteNP
```

Sample Patch Install Script

Solaris comes with patches. It is easy to make a script to install the patches during installation. One variation here might be to leave the begin and host_class fields blank and just add the `install_patch` script as a finish script to install the patches on all systems without doing an installation. The following script installs all patches that are available. If only specific patches are to be installed, the `for` line could be changed. This script also specifies the IP number of the server to use. This is important in cases where no name service is available via broadcast, such as in the case of NIS+ that does not exist on the local subnet.

```
#!/bin/sh

mount -F nfs 129.148.22.152:/latest/Patches /a/mnt

cd /a/mnt
for patch in `ls`
do
#cd $patch
/usr/sbin/chroot /a /mnt/$patch/installpatch /mnt/$patch
#cd ..
done
```

Sample of Automounter Customization

In this case, the script is copying generic copies of key system files into place.

```
#
# Automounter Config
#

echo add Automounter Config

cp /tmp/install_config/auto_master /a/etc/auto_master
cp /tmp/install_config/auto_home /a/etc/auto_home
cp /tmp/install_config/auto_direct /a/etc/auto_direct
chmod 644 /a/etc/auto_master
chmod 644 /a/etc/auto_home
chmod 644 /a/etc/auto_direct
```

Sample Script to Mount Partitions

In cases where modular scripts are used, it is good to have a starting script that mounts all the needed local filesystems before anything else is done.

```
#
# Mount everything
#

mount /dev/dsk/c0t2d0s0 /a/
mount /dev/dsk/c0t2d0s3 /a/opt
mount /dev/dsk/c0t2d0s4 /a/usr
```

Sample sys-unconfig

There may be cases where a system cannot be built on-line. Another system could be used to build the disk, then a sys-unconfig command can be run to blank out the system name, IP number, and name service. When the disk is attached to its new system, it automatically requests new information for these values.

```
#
# run sys-unconfig when done, move disk to server, reboot w/out net,
# answer questions, GO!

#echo "y" > /tmp/resp
#/usr/sbin/chroot /a /usr/sbin/sys-unconfig < /tmp/resp
```

Sample of Changing EEPROM Entries

If you know that you will be placing the OS on a disk that is not the standard boot disk, you can change the boot device to the new disk with the following script.

```
#
# Reset Boot Device
#
eeprom boot-device=disk1
eeprom boot-file=
```

Sample Restore for the Save Begin Script

In the begin script samples, a `save` script backed up key files. The following script restores those files.

```
#!/bin/sh

# restore
# non-interactive auto-install restore script
#

#
# cd to /a (root) and tar (restore)
#

cd /a
# tar xvpf /tmp/root/$SI_HOSTNAME.save_tar
tar xvpf /dev/rmt/1b

mv /tmp/root/$SI_HOSTNAME.save_tar /a/var/sadm
echo "Restore completed ..."

#don't know why /a/$SI_HOSTNAME.save_tar isn't being removed ...
rm /tmp/root/$SI_HOSTNAME.save_tar

# set the flag so sysidroot won't prompt for the root password
sed -e 's/0 # root/1 # root/' ${SI_SYS_STATE} > /tmp/state.$$
mv /tmp/state.$$ ${SI_SYS_STATE}

#
# newaliases
#
/usr/bin/newaliases

#
# reset boot device
#
/usr/sbin/eeprom boot-device=disk
/usr/sbin/eeprom boot-file=
```

≣ *A*

Sample of Adding Workman to vold

This sequence adds a new line to a current configuration file.

```
if [ -f /a/etc/rmmount.conf ] && [ "`grep workman /a/etc/rmmount.conf`" = "" ]
then
 echo "Adding workman to volume managers configuration"
 echo "action cdrom action_workman.so /usr/dist/exe/workman" >>/a/etc/rmm
ount.conf
fi
```

Sample Disk Configurations   B

Because it is often useful to know what others use regularly, we include sample configurations for standard uses. These examples include *estimated* sizes for the Solaris 2.4 software layouts as well.

End User #1 Configuration

An End User Configuration with OpenWindows mounted from a server has the partitions shown in the tables below. For End User #1 configuration:

- Select the End User option from the Custom Install Software Selection menu.

- Choose Edit to modify the clusters.

- Zoom in on the OpenWindows version 3 cluster and deselect all options *except* OpenWindows window drivers and OpenWindows binary compatibility.

- Choose Done from that screen to return to the main Edit screen.

- Deselect the ToolTalk cluster. Deselect the XGL Runtime Libraries.

Solaris 2.3 layouts are slightly different. OpenWindows kernel modules are a new addition to the Solaris 2.3 release and cannot be deleted.

- Zoom in on the XIL software and deselect the XIL DeskSet Loadable Pipeline Libraries.

If these items are not deselected, 65 Mbytes of the OpenWindows software will be installed onto a place that will be hidden by mounting a remote OpenWindows over it.

Note – Choosing this set of options produces a warning message that says there are selected packages that rely on the OpenWindows required core package. Disregard the message.

Solaris 2.2 Release

Partition	Size	Notes
/	18 Mbytes	This includes /var
/usr	55 Mbytes	Only SUNWowbcp and SUNWowrqd of the OpenWindows packages should be loaded to the client system.
/opt	9 Mbytes	
swap	32 – 64 Mbytes	

Solaris 2.3 Release

Partition	Size	Notes
/	25 Mbytes	This includes /var
/usr	55 Mbytes	Only SUNWowbcp and SUNWowrqd of the OpenWindows packages should be loaded to the client system.
/opt	9 Mbytes	
swap	32 – 64 Mbytes	

Solaris 2.4 Release — *estimate only*

Partition	Size	Notes
/	30 Mbytes	This includes /var
/usr	99 Mbytes	Only SUNWowbcp and SUNWowrqd of the OpenWindows packages should be loaded to the client system.
/opt	10 Mbytes	
swap	32 – 64 Mbytes	

End User #2 Configuration

An End User Configuration with OpenWindows local to the system has the partitions shown in the tables below. For End User #2 configuration:

- Select the End User cluster

    This selection does not install the OpenWindows demo packages.

Solaris 2.2 Release

Partition	Size	Notes
/	20 Mbytes	This includes /var
/usr	55 Mbytes	
/opt	9 Mbytes	
/usr/openwin	65 Mbytes	
swap	32 – 64 Mbytes	

Solaris 2.3 Release

Partition	Size	Notes
/	25 Mbytes	This includes /var
/usr	55 Mbytes	
/opt	9 Mbytes	
/usr/openwin	70 Mbytes	
swap	32 – 64 Mbytes	

Solaris 2.4 Release — *estimate only*

Partition	Size	Notes
/	20 Mbytes	This includes /var
/usr	58 Mbytes	
/opt	10 Mbytes	
/usr/openwin	75 Mbytes	
swap	32 – 64 Mbytes	

Developer Configuration

A Developer Configuration with OpenWindows local to the system has the partitions shown in the tables below. Compilers can be loaded to the /opt partition or they can be mounted. The following assumes that compliers will be mounted.

Solaris 2.2 Release

Partition	Size	Notes
/	21 Mbytes	This includes /var
/usr	90 Mbytes	
/opt	85 Mbytes	Add ~60 Mbytes if compilers are to be loaded locally.
/usr/openwin	95 Mbytes	
swap	32 – 64 Mbytes	

Solaris 2.3 Release

Partition	Size	Notes
/	25 Mbytes	This includes /var
/usr	90 Mbytes	
/opt	100 Mbytes	Add ~60 Mbytes if compilers are to be loaded locally.
/usr/openwin	115 Mbytes	
swap	32 – 64 Mbytes	

Solaris 2.4 Release — *estimate only*

Partition	Size	Notes
/	30 Mbytes	This includes /var
/usr	95 Mbytes	
/opt	111 Mbytes	Add ~60 Mbytes if compilers are to be loaded locally.
/usr/openwin	120 Mbytes	
swap	32 – 64 Mbytes	

Server Configuration

A Server Configuration with diskless clients should look like the tables below. For systems without diskless clients, ignore the /export partition. For systems that do not use or serve OpenWindows (diskless clients included), ignore the /usr/openwin partition.

For server configuration:

- Select the End User cluster and add the following:
  - 4.1 Heterogeneous install software
  - Automated Security Enhancement Tools
  - Basic networking
  - On-line manual pages
  - On-line Diagnostics Tool
  - OpenWindows Version 3 (all)
  - System accounting

Solaris 2.2 Release

Partition	Size	Notes
/	15 Mbytes	
/var	20 Mbytes + space	Space refers to space for print spooling and mail.
/usr	70 Mbytes	
/opt	25 Mbytes	
/usr/openwin	90 Mbytes	
/export/root	32 Mbytes per client	
/export/swap	estimate swap	Estimate the swap size and multiply it by the number of clients.
/export/exec	5 Mbytes	If other architectures are selected.
swap	48 – 128 Mbytes	

Solaris 2.3 Release

Partition	Size	Notes
/	17 Mbytes	
/var	20 Mbytes + space	Space refers to space for print spooling and mail.
/usr	75 Mbytes	
/opt	30 Mbytes	
/usr/openwin	95 Mbytes	
/export/root	34 Mbytes per client	
/export/swap	estimate swap	Estimate the swap size and multiply it by the number of clients.
/export/exec	5 Mbytes	If other architectures are selected.
swap	48 – 128 Mbytes	

Solaris 2.4 Release — *estimate only*

Partition	Size	Notes
/	17 Mbytes	
/var	20 Mbytes + space	Space refers to space for print spooling and mail.
/usr	75 Mbytes	
/opt	30 Mbytes	
/usr/openwin	75 Mbytes	
/export/root	34 Mbytes per client	
/export/swap	estimate swap	Estimate the swap size and multiply it by the number of clients.
/export/exec	5 Mbytes	If other architectures are selected.
swap	48 – 128 Mbytes	

Sources of Information C ≡

This appendix contains pieces of a list of Frequently Asked Questions (and answers) about Sun Microsystem's Solaris 2.x system in general. The full FAQ can be found by reading the comp.unix.solaris newsgroup. Other FAQs are archived as Solaris2/Porting and Solaris2/x86. This is not a Sun-supported document, but it has a lot of good information.

1. GENERAL

1.3) Should I move to Solaris 2.x now, or later, or never?

That depends—on you, your situation, your application mix, etc. Some year SunOS 4.1.x will go the way of the 3/50—it'll still be around, but Sun will no longer support it. You don't have to upgrade immediately, but you should be planning your upgrade path by now.

1.4) What is Solaris 2? Is it really SVR4 based?

Solaris 2 is an "operating environment" that includes the SunOS 5.x operating system and the OpenWindows 3.x window environment. SunOS 5.x are based on USL's SVR4.0. SVR4.0, in turn, was developed jointly by AT&T and Sun while Sun was developing 4.1.0, which is why things like RFS, STREAMS, shared memory, etc., are in SunOS 4.1.x, and why things like vnodes, NFS and XView are in SVR4.0. (RFS, by the way, is being dropped effective with Solaris 2.3).

1.5) What machines does Solaris 2.x run on?

Solaris 2.0 only ran on desktop SPARCstations and a few other Sun machines. Solaris 2.1 and later comes in two flavors, SPARC and "x86." Solaris 2.1 (and 2.2, ...) for SPARC run on all SPARCstations and clones, as well as all models of the Sun-4 family. The old FPU on the 4/110 and 260/280 is not supported, so floating point will be SLOW, but it does work.

Solaris 2.1 for x86 has been released to end users. It runs on a wide range of high-end PC-architecture machines. "High-end" means: 16MB of RAM and an 80486 (or 33MHz or faster 80386DX). It will not run on your 4 MB 16MHz 386SX, so don't bother trying! Also, floating point hardware (80387-style) is absolutely required. All three buses are supported: ISA, EISA, MCA.

To summarize all this, Jim Prescott gave this chart, which I've updated:

Table C-1

Solaris	SunOS	OpenWin	Comments
1.0	4.1.1B	2.0	4.1.1_U1 2.0 sun3 EOL release (not named Solaris)
1.0.1	4.1.2	2.0	(6[379]0-1[24]0 MP)
1.1	4.1.3	3.0	SP Viking Support
1.1C	4.1.3C	3.0	Downgrade Classic or LX from Solaris 2.x to Solaris 1.x
1.1.1	4.1.3_U1	3.0	4.1.3 + fixes + Classic/LX support
2.0	5.0	3.0.1	sun4c only
2.1	5.1	3.1	SPARC and x86
2.2	5.2	3.2	SPARC only
2.3	5.3	3.3	SPARC only -PostScript instead of NeWS. It is still primarily OPEN LOOK. OpenWin 3.3 is X11R5 based: Display
2.3 MS1	5.3	3.3	Bugfix release for 2.3 (SPARC only)
2.4	5.4	3.4	From this moment on, the SPARC and x86 releases will be in sync. OpenWin will be Motif and COSE-based.

1.8) Where has the XXX command gone now?

There are too many of these changes to include in this FAQ, but here are some key ones:

a. locations are often different hostid /usr/ucb/hostid

   whoami /usr/ucb/whoami

   hostname /usr/ucb/hostname (or use uname -n)

b. some old commands don't exist or have replacements

   4.1.X Solaris 2.X

   pstat -s swap -s (how much swap space?)

   dkinfo /usr/sbin/prtvtoc raw_dev_name

   trace truss

   mount -a mountall

   exportfs share

   bar cpio -H bar (read only)

   mount -a mountall

   exportfs share

   bar cpio -H bar (read only)

This information can be found in the Solaris 2.x Transition Guide—Appendix A (commands), Appendix B (system calls), Appendix C (files).

The guide has undergone some changes from 2.0 -> 2.1 and beyond. Several manuals were combined into this single manual. This manual discusses adminstrative transition and developer transition issues.

The command "whatnow" (for Solaris 2.x) is included in the "Admigration Toolkit" package (see below). The Admigration toolkit can be obtained from:

opcom.sun.ca:/pub/AMToolkit-2.2a.*

Sample output:

```
% whatnow hostname
hostname 4.x command only
hostname /usr/ucb/hostname part of SCP package
hostname /usr/bin/uname -n alternate command
```

The whatnow command is limited in that it may point to one command which may only implement a subset of the old command (e.g., pstat points to sar, while pstat -s is identical to swap -s).

1.9) When I upgrade, should I use SunInstall "upgrade," or start over?

You can't do a SunInstall "upgrade" from 4.1.x to Solaris2. You can use the Admigration toolkit (q.v.) to help you move from SunOS 4.1.x (Solaris 1, actually) to Solaris 2.

If you're moving from Solaris 2.1 to 2.2, or 2.2 to 2.3, then you can use "upgrade" to preserve your existing partitions and local changes (including pkgadd!!), though it runs very slowly (about 1.5-2x the time for a reinstall) and does require that you have enough free space in / and /usr—make these big when you first install! If you run out of space in one of your partitions, you can always remove some components. Those will not be upgraded and can be installed else where after initial upgrade (e.g., you can remove OW, Xil, Dxlib, manual pages, etc.).

There is no need to backout patches before upgrading. In 2.2, the system would back them out for you, in 2.3 it won't back out the patches but removes them without a trace.

The upgrade doesn't work as well as a full install. E.g., the upgrade from 2.x (x<3) to 2.3 will leave aliases for all your ptys in /devices/pseudo.

1.11) Why do some people dislike Solaris 2?

There is a number of reasons why people dislike Solaris.

1) Change. In general people dislike change. Change requires relearning and retraining. Old system administration practices no longer work. Commands have been replaced by other commands, some commands behave differently. And they ask why the change was necessary. SunOS 4.x worked for them.

2) Lack of migration support. Sun did not provide a lot of tools to ease migration. Many applications wouldn't run in the binary compatibility mode. The source compatibility mode was probably compatible with some OS, but it certainly wasn't SunOS. Lot of public domain and third party stuff needed wasn't immediately available for Solaris.

3) Missing functionality. When people migrate, they at first don't tend to notice new functionality. Instead, they stumble upon missing functionality such as screenblank, clear_colormap and the like.

4) Slow and buggy. The initial Solaris releases didn't perform at all well and were extremely instable. This is improving rapidly, but SuperSPARC MP machines need a heavily patches 2.3 to work reliably.

1.12) Do some people *like* Solaris 2?

Yes! There are improvements in Solaris 2.x.

1) OpenWindows 3.3 (in Solaris 2.3). Includes X11R5 and Display PostScript.

2) ANSI-C and POSIX development environment.

3) Multithreaded kernel and real threads.

4) True multi-processing.

5) Goodies: vold, admintool and Wabi.

2. MORE INFO

2.1) How can I RTFM when I don't have it anymore?

"RTFM" is an old saying: Read The Manual. Sun still sells printed manuals, but doesn't automatically distribute them. As with all real UNIX systems, you do get a full set of online "man" pages. As well, a smaller, lighter, bookshelf-friendly :-) CD-ROM called "The AnswerBook"™ contains all the printed documents in machine-readable (PostScript) form, and a keyword search engine. 90% of your introductory questions are answered therein!

In Solaris 2.x the Answerbook set gets increasingly more divided into pieces. It is currently (2.3) split over 4 CDs.

Solaris 2.x CD:
> Solaris 2.x User AnswerBook
> Solaris 2.x administrator answerbook
> Solaris 2.x System Administrator AnswerBook
> Solaris 2.x on Sun Hardware AnswerBook
> Solaris 2.x Reference Manual AnswerBook

Solaris 2.x Software Developer Kit
> All programming manuals

Solaris 2.x Driver Developer Kit
> Device driver developer manuals.

There is some overlap between CDs.

C

As distributed with 2.1 and 2.2, the Answerbook search engine runs only with the OpenWindows ("xnews") server, not with MIT X11. This changed in 2.3. If you are using the MIT server instead of what Sun provides, you'll have to use one of several "answerbook workaround" scripts that are in circulation. The AnswerBook distributed with 2.3 and later runs with the OW3.3 X11R5+DPS server, so it should display on any X11+DPS server, such as on DEC, IBM and SGI workstations. The workaround

You should buy (or print from within Answerbook) at least the reference manual and the System and Network Administration books, because if your system becomes disabled you won't be able to run the Answerbook to find out how to fix it...

2.2) Why is "man -k" so confused?

Solaris man uses a manual page index file called "windex" in place of the old "whatis" file. You can build this index with cd <man-page-directory>; catman -w -M .

But, in 2.1, this will result in numerous "line too long" messages and a bogus windex file in /usr/share/man, and a core dump in /usr/openwin/man. (In 2.2, catman works in /usr/share/man, but says "line too long" in /usr/openwin/man). To add injury to insult, "man" normally won't show you a man page if it can't find the windex entry, even though the man page exists.

There's a "makewhatis" script in /usr/openwin/man that works better than catman. But watch it—by default it searches files in /usr/man, not in openwin, and it only looks in some predefined man subdirectories. Try changing its "for ..." command to "for i in man*", then use it like this: cd /usr/share/man; /usr/openwin/man/makewhatis . cd /usr/openwin/man; /usr/openwin/man/makewhatis .

Still (!), the openwin windex file is somewhat hosed (try "man answerbook" :-(. You can always delete the bogus lines manually... or, you can alias man to "man -F", forcing it to look for the bloody file like you asked.

But wait, there's more! To see the read(2) man page, you can't just type "man 2 read" anymore—it has to be "man -s 2 read". Or, alias man to this little script:

```
#!/bin/sh
if [ $# -gt 1 -a "$1" -gt "0" ]; then
/bin/man -F -s $*
else
/bin/man -F $*
fi
```

2.3) What Software is available for Solaris 2.x?

Most commercial software that ran on 4.x either will run in BCP mode, or is available for Solaris 2.x, or is being ported now. Solaris 2.3 BCP mode finally supports statically-linked executables.

You can obtain a list of official 3rd party porting commitments, maintained by Sun's "Solaris Demand Center" (whatever that is), by sending electronic mail to "solaris2apps@sun.com"—this is an automatic reply server. The list shows what third party applications are currently available for Solaris, and lists expected dates for many more.

A list of freeware (some "public domain", but mostly copyright-but-freely-distributable) [as well as commercial software??] that has been ported to Solaris 2.x is posted monthly to the newsgroup comp.unix.solaris by ric@updike.sri.com (Richard Steinberger). Look for this:

Subject: Solaris SW list. Monthly Post.

If you can't wait, the list is also available via anonymous FTP from updike.sri.com.

2.4) What FTP sites do I need to know about?

SunSite (sunsite.unc.edu) - Sun sponsors an FTP site at the University of North Carolina. Lots of good stuff here.

ftp.x.org (or export.lcs.mit.edu) - the master X11 site

ftp.uu.net - UuNet communication archives

OpCom. (opcom.sun.ca) - run by Sun Microsystems' OpCom group - lots of stuff. Here is some of the stuff that's online:

pub/AMToolkit.* - the Administration Migration (4.1.x to Solaris 2) Toolkit

pub/binaries - binaries/man pages for Solaris 2.0 native binaries.

pub/newsletter - issues of the monthly OpCom newsletter.

pub/docs - assorted documentation, papers, and other information. - all of the RFCs

pub/drivers - information related to device driver writing under under Solaris 2.0 as well as a skeleton SCSI driver.

ls-lR.Z - compressed recursive listing of files available on the server.

pub/tars - compressed tars.

pub/tmp - place for uploading things to the server.

pub/R5 - the unadultered MIT x11r5 distribution.

pub/x11r5 - port of X11r5 to Solaris 2.0, binaries, libraries and headers. A compressed tar of this tree can be found in tars.

prep.ai.mit.edu and the GNU mirrors

pub/gnu/sparc-sun-solaris2 - recent gcc binaries for SPARC

pub/gnu/i486-sun-solaris2 - recent gcc binaries for i486

2.5) What other FAQ's do I need to know about?

All of them :-). But in particular you should see these FAQ's:

1) Newsgroups: comp.sys.sun.admin, comp.sys.sun.misc, comp.unix.solaris, comp.answers, news.answers Subject: FAQ: Sun Computer Administration Frequently Asked Questions

2) The "Solaris 2 Porting FAQ" from David Meyer in this newsgroup. For those developing or compiling software. Archive-name: Solaris2/Porting

3) The "Solaris 2 x86 FAQ" from J. S. Caywood in this newsgroup. Deals with Intel-("x86")-specific issues on Solaris 2. Archive-name: Solaris2/x86 (proposed)

4) comp.windows.open-look - Anything related to OpenWindows or the OPEN LOOK Graphical User Interface

5) The Sun-Managers mailing list (see below) has its own FAQ, maintained by John DiMarco <jdd@cdf.toronto.edu>. FTP from ra.mcs.anl.gov in the sun-managers directory.

6) See also the "Solaris SW list Monthly Post" above and the "whatlist" file.

2.6) What mailing lists should I get?

First, read all the USENET newsgroups with "sun" in their name :-)

1) The Florida SunFlash is a "closed" mailing list for Sun owners. It contains mostly press releases from Sun and third-party vendors. This list contains information on conferences such as the Solaris Developer's Conference as well. It is normally distributed regionally - to find out about a mail point in your area, or for other information send mail to info-sunflash@Sun.COM.

Subscription requests should be sent to sunflash-request@Sun.COM. Archives are on solar.nova.edu, ftp.uu.net, sunsite.unc.edu, src.doc.ic.ac.uk and ftp.adelaide.edu.au.

2) The Sun Managers list is an unmoderated mailing list for *emergency-only* requests. Subscribe and listen for a while, and read the regularly-posted Policy statement BEFORE sending mail to it, and to get a feel for what kinds of traffic it carries. Write to sun-managers-request@eecs.nwu.edu.

2.7) What books should I read?

O'Reilly & Associates specializes in UNIX books. Their "UNIX In A Nutshell" has been updated for SVR4 and Solaris 2.0. Get their catalog by calling 800-998-9938 (1-707-829-0515) 7AM to 5PM PST.

SunSoft Press carries books specific to Solaris 2. Look for the inset with your End User Media Kit that lists the most relevant ones.

Prentice-Hall has reprints of much of the AT&T documentation.

I'm not sure how much of this you need—a lot of the same material is in the Answerbook (see above).

3. SYSTEM ADMINISTRATION

3.2) How can I convert all my local changes that I've made over the years into their corresponding forms on Solaris 2?

1) Do it by hand. You did document every single change and check it into RCS, didn't you?

2) Automate it, using the AMToolkit (Administration Migration Toolkit) from the OpCom FTP server (q.v.)!

3.4) Why can't I write in /home?

This is a common one! SunOS is delivered with the "automounter" enabled. The automounter is designed for NFS sites, to simplify maintenance of the list of filesystems that need mounting. However it is a burden for standalone sites.

The automounter takes over /home and in effect becomes the NFS server for it, so it no longer behaves like a normal directory. This is normally a Good Thing as it simplifies administration if everybody's home directory is /home/<username>.

To kill it off for standalone or small networks, you can comment out the three lines in /etc/init.d/nfs.client that start "if" (from the if to the fi!!), and reboot (Solaris 2.2) or remove the file /etc/rc2.d/S73autofs (Solaris 2.3). You can allways relink that file with /etc/init.d/autofs if you change your mind.

To learn about it, read the O'Reilly book "Managing NFS and NIS," or ftp the white paper "The Art of Automounting" from sunsite.unc.edu in the directory /pub/sun-info/white-papers.

3.5) Why can't I access CDs or floppies?

Solaris 2.2 introduces a new scheme for automatically mounting removable media. It consists of a program "vold" (volume daemon) which sits around watching for insertions of floppies and CD's, handles ejects, talks to the file manager, and invokes a second program called "rmmount" (removable media mounter) to mount the disk.

Note that on most SPARCstations, you must run "volcheck" whenever you insert a floppy, as the floppy hardware doesn't tell SunOS that a floppy was inserted.

Advantages of this scheme:

- no longer need root; users can mount and unmount at will.

- can do neat tricks like automagically start "workman" or other Audio CD player when audio CD inserted.

- extensible - developers can write their own actions

Drawbacks:

- can no longer access /dev/rfd0 to get at floppy; must use longer name like /vol/dev/rdsk/floppy0

- similarly, CD's get mounted on /cdrom/VOLNAME/SLICE, e.g., /cdrom/solaris_2_2/s0 is slice 0 of the Solaris 2 CD (nice that it does mount all the partitions, though!).

To read or write a non-filesystem floppy (tar, cpio, etc), put in the diskette and run "volcheck" to get it noticed; then access /vol/dev/rfd0/unlabeled (e.g. "tar tvf /vol/dev/rfd0/unlabeled").

[Solaris 2.3: /vol/dev/rdiskette0/unlabeled, or /vol/dev/aliases/floppy0.]

If you want the old behaviour, it's been suggested that you can comment out the vold startup in /etc/init.d/volmgt and then reboot; an easier way is # /etc/init.d/volmgt stop.

3.6) What is this junk mail about an error in the crontab entry?

Solaris 2.1 (FCS on SPARC and OEM on Intel) shipped with a blank line at the end of root's crontab file. The result is that root gets mail at boot time and nightly thereafter, complaining about an error in the crontab file and that it has "ignored the entry."

Pretty hard work ignoring that blank line, eh? If the messages bug you (they should), su to root and use "crontab -e" to edit root's crontab and delete the blank line at the end of the file. Fixed in FCS on Intel and 2.2 on SPARC.

3.7) Why are there no passwords in /etc/passwd?

System V Release 4 includes a feature called "shadow passwords". The encrypted passwords are moved out into a shadow password file (called /etc/shadow in this release) that is NOT publicly readable. The passwd file has always been readable so that, for example, ls -l could figure out who owns what. But having the passwd encryptions readable is a security risk (they can't be decrypted but the bad guy can encrypt common words and names &c and compare them with the encryptions).

The Shadow Password feature is mostly transparent, but if you do any passwd hacking you have to know about it! And DO make sure that /etc/shadow is not publicly readable!

3.8) Why can't I rlogin/telnet in as root?

... when I try to rlogin as root ...

it gives me the message "Not on system console - Connection closed.". What have I left out?

Solaris 2 comes out of the box a heck of a lot more secure than Solaris 1. There is no '+' in the hosts.equiv. root logins are not allowed anywhere except the console. All accounts require passwords. In order to allow root logins over the net, you need to edit the /etc/default/login file and comment out or otherwise change the CONSOLE= line.

This file's CONSOLE entry can actually be used in a variety of ways:

1) CONSOLE=/dev/console (default) - direct root logins only on console

2) CONSOLE= - direct root logins disallowed everywhere

3) #CONSOLE (or delete the line) - root logins allowed everywhere

3.9) How can I set up anonymous FTP?

If you need help, ftp the file "solaris2-ftp" from ftp.cs.toronto.edu:/pub/darwin/solaris2.

ftpd(1M) is nearly complete when it comes to setting up anonymous ftp. It only leaves out /etc/nsswitch.conf. [S2.3]

3.10) How can I print from a Solaris 2 (or any System V Release 4) system to a SunOS4.x (or any other BSD) system?

Hmmm, the lp system is totally different than what you're used to. The System V Line Printer System is a lot more, well, flexible. A cynic might say "complicated." Here's a very quick guide—see the man pages for each of these commands for the details.

Let's say your Solaris2 workstation is called "sol" and the 4.1.x server is called "bertha" and you want the printer name to be "printer" (imaginative, eh?).

```
sol# lpsystem -t bsd bertha # says bertha is a bsd system
sol# lpadmin -p printer -s bertha # creates "printer" on "sol"
# to be printed on "bertha"
sol# accept printer # allow queueing
sol# enable printer # allow printing
sol# lpstat -t # check the status
```

Finally, if that's your only printer, make it the default:

```
sol# lpadmin -d printer
```

On some systems you may have to turn on the port monitor.

Q:I did that. Why does it now complain about invalid content types?

I said it was complicated!

For better or for worse, you need to know about printer content types.

See the man page for "lpadmin".

To get transparent mode, try this:

lpadmin -I any -p printer

Q: Isn't there any easier way?

The GUI-based Admintool has a Printer Manager that is supposed to be able to do all this and more. Try it; Sun hopes you'll like it.

Now my jobs print but they stay in the queue after!?

It's a known bug, and probably get fixed in 2.3. There's also a number of lpsched patches out for Solaris: 101025-xx (2.2) and 101317-xx (2.3). Make sure you install those.

[Now you want to set up Solaris 2 as a print server? You're on your own.]

3.11) What if I'd rather use the old familiar BSD-style line printer system?

The 4.3BSD-reno lpr system for Solaris 2, file lpr-sol2.tar.gz or lpr-sol2.tar.Z is available from the following FTP sites:

sunok-wks.acs.ohio-state.edu:/pub/solaris2/src/lpr-sol2.tar.gz

atlas.ce.washington.edu:/pub/lpr-sol2.tar.Z

solomon.technet.sg:/pub/uploads/unix/lpr-sol2.tar.gz

And don't despair. Someday the System V print spooler will be replaced by something new. (See the Solaris 2.3 Open Issues & Late Breaking News For System dministrators)

3.13) What happened to /etc/rc and /etc/rc.local?

They're now fragmented into 12 million tiny little pieces. Look in the following files to get oriented:

/etc/inittab - starting point for init

/sbin/rcS, /etc/rcS.d/* - booting stuff

/sbin/rc2, /etc/rc2.d/*,

/sbin/rc3, /etc/rc3.d/* - stuff for multi-user startup.

 Note that all files in /etc/rc*.d/* are hardlinked from /etc/init.d (with better names), so you should grep in there.

There are many "run levels" to the System V init; the run level 3 is normally used for "multi user with networking."

I can't understand that stuff; can't I have /etc/rc.local back? I just want to keep all my local changes in one place.

No. You can never have rc.local back the way it was. But then, it never really *was* purely a "local" rc file. To have a real "local" rc file with just your changes in it, copy this file into /etc/init.d/rc.local, and ln it to /etc/rc3.d/S99rc.local. Put your startup stuff in the "start" section.

```
----- Cut here -----
# /etc/init.d/rc.local - to be linked into /etc/rc3.d as
# S99rc.local -- a place to hang local startup stuff.
# started after everything else when going multi-user.

# Ian Darwin, Toronto, November, 1992
# As with all system changes, use at own risk!
```

```
case "$1" in
'start')
echo "Starting local services...\c"

if [ -f /usr/sbin/mydaemon ]; then
/usr/sbin/mydaemon 1>/dev/console 2>&1
fi
echo ""
;;
'stop')
echo "$0: Not stopping any service - use ucb shutdown for that."
;;
*)
echo "Usage: $0 { start | stop }"
;;
esac
------ End of Cut Here -----
```

3.14) Speaking of that, why are there two versions of shutdown?

SVR4 (hence SunOS 5.x) tries to make everybody happy. The traditional (slow) System V "shutdown" runs all the rc?.d/* shell scripts with "stop" as the argument; many of them run ps(!) to look for processes to kill. The UCB "shutdown" tells init to kill all non-single-user processes, which is about two orders of magnitude faster. Unfortunately, the UCB version does everything it should *except* actually halt or reboot in SunOS5.1 (and some other SVR4 implementations). This is fixed in Solaris 2.3.

If you run a database (like oracle) or INN, you should install a special /etc/rc?.d/K* script and make sure you always shutdown the long way.

3.15) When will somebody publish a package of the BSD (4.3BSD Net2) "init", "getty", and "rc/rc.local", so we can go back to life in the good old days?

Getty should be easy and was reportedly done at a number of sites. The portmonitor isn't everyones favourite. But given that you can do much more with the SVR4 init, why would you want to change back? It would be much more trouble than it's worth.

3.16) What has happened to getty? What is pmadm and how do you use it?

I was hoping you wouldn't ask. PMadm stands for Port Monitor Admin, and it's part of a ridiculously complicated bit of software over-engineering that is destined to make everybody an expert.

Best advice for workstations: don't touch it! It works out of the box. For servers, you'll have to read the manual. This should be in admintool in Solaris2.3. For now, here are some basic instructions from Davy Curry.

"Not guaranteed, but they worked for me."

To add a terminal to a Solaris system:

1. Do a "pmadm -l" to see what's running.

The serial ports on the CPU board are probably already being monitored by "zsmon".

```
PMTAG PMTYPE SVCTAG FLGS ID <PMSPECIFIC>
zsmon ttymon ttya u root \
/dev/term/a I - /usr/bin/login - 9600 ldterm,ttcompat ttya \
login: - tvi925 y #
```

2. If the port you want is not being monitored, you need to create a new port monitor with the command

```
sacadm -a -p PMTAG -t ttymon -c /usr/lib/saf/ttymon -v VERSION
```

where PMTAG is the name of the port monitor, e.g. "zsmon" or "alm1mon", and VERSION is the output of "ttyadm -V".

3. If the port you want is already being monitored, and you want to change something, you need to delete the current instance of the port monitor.

To do this, use the command

```
pmadm -r -p PMTAG -s SVCTAG
```

where PMTAG and SVCTAG are as given in the output from "pmadm -l". Note that if the "I" is present in the <PMSPECIFIC> field (as it is above), you need to get rid of it.

4. Now, to create a specific instance of ttymon for a port, issue the command:

```
pmadm -a -p PMTAG -s SVCTAG -i root -fu -v 1 -m \
"'ttyadm -m ldterm,ttcompat -p 'PROMPT' -S YORN -T TERMTYPE \
-d DEVICE -l TTYID -s /usr/bin/login'"
```

Note the assorted quotes; Bourne shell (sh) and Korn (ksh) users leave off the second backslash!

In the above:

PMTAG is the port monitor name you made with "sacadm", e.g. "zsmon".

SVCTAG is the service tag, which can be the name of the port, e.g., "ttya" or "tty21".

PROMPT is the prompt you want to print, e.g. "login: ".

YORN is "y" to turn software carrier on (you want this for directly connected terminals" and "n" to leave it off (you want this for modems).

TERMTYPE is the value you want in $TERM.

DEVICE is the name of the device, e.g. "/dev/term/a" or "/dev/term/21".

TTYID is the line you want from /etc/ttydefs that sets the baud rate and stuff. I suggest you use one of the "contty" ones for directly connected terminals.

5. To disable ("turn off") a terminal, run

```
pmadm -d -p PMTAG -s SVCTAG
```

To enable ("turn on") a terminal, run

```
pmadm -e -p PMTAG -s SVCTAG
```

Ports are enabled by default when you "create" them as above.

For more details, see the article:

SUMMARY: Solaris modem/terminal how-to: Rev xx.xx.xx posted periodically to comp.unix.solaris by celeste@xs.com (Celeste Stokely).

3.17) How do I get the screen to blank when nobody's using it?

Under 4.1.x you invoke screenblank in /etc/rc.local, but there's no screenblank in Solaris 2.1. Sun recommends that you have everybody put 'xset s on' in their .xinitrc, but this may be hard to police, and in any event it won't work when nobody is logged in. The simplest workaround is to copy /usr/bin/screenblank from 4.1.x and run it in binary compatibility mode. See "What happened to /etc/rc and /etc/rc.local?" for how to invoke it.

Another possibility is to use xdm, but you'll have to use your own, since the xdm shipped with Solaris 2.1 doesn't work.

The 4.1.x screenblank didn't work for me; I use Jef Poskanzer's freeware screenblank (FTP it from various archive sites, two of them listed in the next item).

Because of a bug in Solaris 2.3, you'll need to change to use latest version of screenblank.

3.18) And what about screendump, screenload and clear_colormap?

You can FTP Jef's screenload, screendump, etc., if you need that functionality, and for free you get a pixrect (clone) library. Get one of these:

netcom.com:pub/jef/raster-pixrect_30dec93.tar.Z

ee.lbl.gov:raster-pixrect_30dec93.tar.Z

The 4.1.x versions of these programs will not run under Solaris 2.2 or later. The pixrect BCP library is no longer supported.

3.19) Where did etherfind go?

There is a replacement for etherfind, but it has changed name; in fact it's a whole new program. It IS better. To find it, though, you would have to realize that network snooping is not really ethernet-specific. To end the suspense :-), here it is:

```
% man -k snoop
snoop snoop (1m) - capture network packets and inspect them
%
```

It works differently - it has an immediate mode, a capture-to-disk mode, and a playback-from-disk mode. Read the man page for details.

3.20) Can I run SunOS4.1.x on my SPARC Classic or LX?

Yes, because users wanted it (and because Clone makers were providing it), Sun has now released a version of Solaris 1 (SunOS 4.1.3) specifically for these machines. That version is called 4.1.3C or Solaris 1.1C. Recently, Sun released a new end-of-life release of SunOS 4.1.x, 4.1.3_U1 (Solaris 1.1.1). This release supports the LX and Classic as well. Suns newest models based on the MicroSPARC II will be supported in a SunOS 4.1.x release as well.

3.21) The "find" program complains that my root directory doesn't exist?

Yes! Actually, messages like

```
find : cannot open /: No such file or directory.
```

are due to a bug in the tree walking function (nftw(3)). If it runs into problems traversing the tree, it gives up and incorrectly complains about the top level directory of the tree. The submitter seems] to recall that the most common case which caused trouble was a directory somewhere in the directory hierarchy which was readable but not executable. With the fix it will just complain about the directory to which it couldn't chdir and skip descending that subtree.

3.22) I'm having troubles with high-speed input on the Sparc serial ports. What should I do?

Try using UUCP. The Solaris 2.x sparc serial driver has trouble receiving data at or above 9600 bps. Symptoms include sluggish response, 'NOTICE: zs0: silo overflow' console messages, sending spurious control-Gs to the serial port, and applications that cannot be killed even with 'kill -9'. This problem surfaces in many applications, including Kermit and tip. UUCP seems immune, though, because its protocol throttles input sufficiently.

3.23) How do I make ksh or csh be the login shell for root?

Root's shell is /sbin/sh, which is statically linked. Don't just insert a 'c' before "sh" as previously, as that would look for /sbin/csh, which doesn't exist. Don't just change it to /bin/csh, since that's really /usr/bin/csh, which is dynamically linked, because:

a) /usr may not be mounted initially, and then you're in deep (the shared libraries are in /usr!), and

b) There is code in the startup scripts that assumes that everything critical is in /etc/lib, not /usr/lib. Approach with caution!

Safer bet - have an alternate root account, like "rootcsh", with uid 0, and /bin/csh as its shell. Put it after root's entry in the passwd file. Only drawback: you now have to remember to change all of root's passwds at the same time.

Third bet - in root's .profile, check if /usr is mounted and, if so, exec /bin/ksh or whatever.

3.24) What is this message: "automount: No network locking on thathost, contact administrator to install server change."?

The other machine (an NFS server) is running 4.1.x and needs a patch from Sun to update its network lock daemon (lockd). If you don't install the patch on the server, file locking will not work on files mounted from "thathost". The 100075-xx patch fixes a bunch of other lock manager problems, so it may be a Good Thing To Get; however, it may also cause the machine on which the patch is installed to have trouble talking to servers with no patch or older patches, so Be Warned.

3.25) How do I make Solaris2 use my Toshiba MK538FB drives?

Append this line to /etc/system and reboot:

```
set scsi_options=0x78
```

This turns off Command Queueing, which upsets the Toshiba something rotten. If you have fast SCSI, you must use:

```
set scsi_options=0x178
```

or you end up disabling fast SCSI as well.

3.26) How do I make Solaris2 use my old ADAPTEC ACB-4000 and Emulex MD-21 disks?

As with any hardware addition, first try the obvious (boot -r after installing and power-cycling everything).

The adaptec is no longer supported; man -s7 sd no longer even lists it! So I guess they go over the cliff. Either that, or take the drives out and put them on a PC, where ST506 MFM drives are still supported.

The MD21 should work.

3.27) Why are there so many patches for Solaris 2.3? It's only been out a month!

Solaris 2.x releases are essentially frozen TWO months before their general release date. During the early access/beta test period bugs are found both in the beta and in the previous release. That's why at the moment a new release comes out a number of patches is ready. Some of those are on the Solaris 2.3 CD. Others were released almost at the same time as 2.3.

Solaris 2.3 is not a bug fix release. Although tons of bugs were fixed, a number of changes have been made and a number of new features were introduced:

• OpenWin moved from NeWS based to X11R5+DPS based.

• PPP (is said not to work with non Solaris 2.3 PPP)

• AutoFS

• CacheFS

• Easier NIS+ conversion

• BCP for statically linked executables.

And another user writes:

Be thankful you don't have to use IBM's AIX. For that you get a new release and then about 100 patches per WEEK!

3.28) Where do I get patches from?

thor.ece.uc.edu:/pub/sun-faq/Solaris2.[123]-patches.

(SunOS 4.1.x patches in: /pub/sun-faq/SunOS4.1.x.Patches)

ugle.unit.no:/pub/unix/sun-fixes

Starting with SunSolve CD 2.1.2 ALL Sun patches are shipped on the SunSolve CD. Contract customers can get patches by ftp from Sun sites or via e-mail and query one of the online sunsolve-databases on the internet.

4. NETWORKING

4.1) Can I use DNS with Solaris 2.x?

It seems that the in.named included in the Solaris 2.1 distribution is terribly unstable. The easiest solution for now I have discovered is to use the OLD (SunOS 4.1.2 in my case) in binary compatibility mode. This works just fine. If it's slower I can't tell. There's also a patch (100902-01) available now for 2.1. [Better now in 2.2 and 2.3 ? - reports please]

4.2) How do I use DNS w/o using NIS or NIS+?

Under SunOS 4.1 it was next to impossible to run DNS name resolution without either a kludge fix or the NIS (V2 I guess). Under Solaris 2.1 it is incredibly simple, but you must ignore what the manual (SunOS 5.1 Administering NIS+ and DNS) says (the manual is fixed in Solaris 2.2). All that is required to make a non-NIS host use the DNS for name resolution is to change the host: line in the /etc/nsswitch.conf file to the following:

```
hosts: files dns
```

(i.e., when looking for hosts, look in /etc/hosts first, if not found there, try DNS, if still not found then give up) and set up a correct version of /etc/resolv.conf to tell the resolver routines (like gethostbyname) how to contact the DNS nameserver. You must have the names of machines which are somehow contacted during boot in the files in /etc and files must appear first in the hosts: line, otherwise the machine will hang during boot (at least ours did). Make sure that /etc/netconfig is using switch.so. (It does from the factory.)

4.3) Speaking of nsswitch.conf, what is it?

An idea whose time has come (it came to Ultrix a few years ago). You can control which of the "resolver" services are read from NIS (formerly YP), which from NIS+, which from the files in /etc, and which are from DNS (but only "hosts" can come from DNS).A common example would be:

```
hosts: nis files
```

which means ask NIS for host info and, if it's not found, try the local machine's host table as a fallback.

Advice: if you're not using NIS or DNS, suninstall probably put the right version in. If you are, ensure that hosts and passwd come from the network. However, many of the other services seldom if ever change. When was that last time *you* added a line in /etc/protocols? If your workstation has a local disk, it may be better to have programs on your machine look up these services locally, so use "files".

Terminology: Sun worried over the term "resolver", which technically means any "get info" routine (getpwent(3), gethostbyname(3), etc.), but is also specifically attached to the DNS resolver. Therefore they used the term "source" to mean the things after the colon (files/DNS/NIS/NIS+) and "database" to mean the thing before the colon (passwd/group/hosts/services/netgroup etc.).

4.4) So what does [NOTFOUND=return] in nsswitch.conf mean, and where does it go?

Type man nsswitch.conf for more info. There is too much detail to summarize here. Briefly, [NOTFOUND=return] means that the name service whose entry it *follows* should be considered authoritative (so that if it's up and it says such a name doesn't exist, believe it and return instead of continuing to hunt for an answer).

5. TROUBLE SHOOTING

5.1) Why can't I run Answerbook on a standalone machine?

This is a bug in openwindows. Using xhost + or starting openwin -noauth works around this problem. This is only recommended for stand-alone machines with no dial-in users.

5.2) Why can't I run filemgr, I get "mknod: permission denied"?

This is a symptom of a bug in filemgr. Either apply patch #101514 or run the following commands at system start-up:

```
mkdir /tmp/.removable
chmod a+rwxt /tmp/.removable
```

6. SOFTWARE DEVELOPMENT

6.1) Where is the C compiler or where can I get one?

Where have you been? :-) Sun has dropped their old K&R C compiler, supposedly to create a market for multiple compiler suppliers to provide better performance and features. Here are some of the contenders:

1) SunPro C:

SunPro, SMCC, and various distributors sell a new ANSI-standard C compiler on the unbundled (extra cost) SPARCcompiler/SPARCworks CD-ROM. There are some other nice tools there too, like a "make tool" and a visual idiff (interactive diff).

(The "no support" price actually includes three months of support under warrantee. One catch with Sun support is that to get *any* support, you have to pay for support for *all* the users at your site. The quantity prices are only available in fixed size chunks. You don't actually buy multiple years up front, but renew each year if desired.)

One misfeature is that these tools use a floating license manager, so your whole staff can't use them without paying large sums of money. Not only that, but as shipped, the tools enforce a 15-minute minimum usage time, to "encourage" you to buy a "floating" license for each and every actual user. This caused so much screaming and tearing of hair that Sun was forced to fix it. New compiler releases after May 1993 have a default 5 minute setting, changeable all the way to zero by having the sysadmin edit the "options file". However, if you set it to zero, the compiler slows down, since it has to talk to the license daemon for every file you compile. Old compilers have a patch available from SunPro to eliminate the 15 minute limit; patch numbers: C: 100966-0x; C++: 100967-0x; Fortran: 100968-0x; Pascal: 100969-0x. These patches are bulky and are not available at many anonymous ftp sites. If you have support, you can get them from Sun.

2) Cygnus GCC:

Cygnus Support and the Free Software Foundation make the GNU C compiler for Solaris, a free software product. Source code and ready-to-run binaries are available by FTP from

ftp.uu.net:/vendor/cygnus, or can be installed from the CDware CD (Volume 4 or 5).

Like all GNU software, there are no restrictions on who can use it, how many people can use it at a time, what machines it can be run on, or how many copies you can install, run, give away, or sell.

Cygnus sells technical support for these tools, under annual support contracts. (If you get the compiler from one of the free distribution sites, there is no cost but no warrantee. Cygnus lets you buy support for any number of users, at $500/user after the first two users at $1400. You don't actually buy multiple years up front, but renew each year if desired.)

The Cygnus distribution includes:

gcc (ansi C compiler), gdb (good debugger), byacc (yacc repl), flex (lex repl), gprof, makeinfo, texindex, info, patch, cc (a link to gcc)

The Cygnus compiler on uunet is starting to show its age a bit. If you want to compile X11R5, you can get the latest version of GCC in source code, from the usual places (prep.ai.mit.edu or one of the many mirrored copies of it). Build and install that compiler using the Cygnus gcc binaries. Or get tech support from Cygnus; they produce a new version for their customers every three months, and will fix any bug you find.

3) Gcc:

Gcc is available from the GNU archives in source and binary form. Look in a directory called sparc-sun-solaris2 for binaries. You need gcc 2.3.3 or later. You should not use GNU as or GNU ld. Make sure you run just-fixinc if you use a binary distribution. Better is to get a binary version and use that to bootstrap gcc from source.

4) Info on Apogee, Lucid C, etc will be added if you send us some.

6.2) What about the linker, the assembler and make?

Solaris ships with everything you need, except for the compiler. All this stuff lives in /usr/ccs/bin and /usr/ccs/lib. If you still can't find it, make sure you have the following packages installed on your system:

- for tools (sccs, lex, yacc, make, nm, truss, ld, as):

  SUNWbtool, SUNWsprot, SUNWtoo

- for libraries & headers:

  SUNWhea, SUNWarc, SUNWlibm, SUNWlibms

- for ucb compat:

  SUNWsra, SUNWsrh

6.3) What do I need to compile X11R5?

There are several "patch kits" for X11R5 under Solaris 2.1. Most of them require gcc 2.3.3 and you must have run "fixincludes" when you install the gcc software.

The recommended patchkit is R5.SunOS5.patch.tar.Z available from ftp.x.org:/contrib. It works with gcc (2.3.3 or later) and SunPRO C.

6.4) Why do I get isinf undefined when linking with libdps?

That's a bug in libdps. Sun compiles and links its software with its own compilers. The isinf() function is shipped with the SunPRO compilers, but not defined in any Solaris 2.x library.

A workaround exists, and consists of adding the following to your program:

```
int isinf(double x) { return !finite(x); }
```

6.5) What happened to NIT? What new mechanisms exist for low-level network access?

See man page DLPI(7). Try NFSWATCH 4.0 for sample code using DLPI. FTP from

harbor.ecn.purdue.edu (128.46.128.76,
128.46.154.76):/pub/davy/nfswatch4.0.tar.Z

gatekeeper.dec.com (16.1.0.2):/pub/net/ip/nfs/nfswatch4.0.tar.Z

Better yet, FTP the paper "How to Use DLPI in Solaris 2.x" by Neal Nuckolls of Sun Internet Engineering. Look in these FTP sites:

opcom.sun.ca:/pub/drivers/dlpi/dlpi-spec.ps.gz

opcom.sun.ca:/pub/drivers/dlpi/dltest.tar.gz

opcom.sun.ca:/pub/drivers/dlpi/howtouseDLPI.ps.gz

ftp.ui.org:/pub/osi/dlpi.ps

ftp.ui.org:/pub/osi/npi.ps

ftp.ui.org:/pub/osi/tpi.ps

6.6) Where are all the functions gone that used to be in libc?

The C library has exploded. The manual page may give an indication where to find a specific function.

Those libraries are essentially split over two directories: /usr/lib and /usr/ccs/lib. Important libraries:

/usr/lib:

libsocket - socket functions

libnsl - network services library

/usr/ccs/lib:

libgen - regular expression functions

libcurses - the SysVR4 curses/terminfo library.

See Intro(3) for more details.

6.7) I'm still missing some functions: bcopy, bzero and friends.

They are in /usr/ucblib/libucb.so. The b* functions are replaced with the ANSI-C equivalents. Look in the Solaris porting FAQ for more details.

6.8) Can I use the source compatibility package to postpone porting?

Not really. The Source code comaptibility package is compatible with BSD 4.2, not SunOS 4.1.x. The consensus is that the library is broken beyond usibility.

6.9) Why doesn't readdir work?

You're probably linking with libucb and didn't read the previous question. (The readdir in libucb.so wants you to include `sys/dir.h`, many SunOS 4.1.x programs included

Glossary

≡

address mask

A bit mask used to select bits from an Internet address for subnet addressing. The mask is 32 bits long and selects the network portion of the Internet address and one or more bits of the local portion. Synonymous with *subnet mask*.

address resolution protocol (ARP)

The Internet protocol used to dynamically map Internet addresses to physical (hardware) addresses on local area networks. Limited to networks that support hardware broadcast.

alias

(1) In electronic mail, an easy-to-remember name used in place of a full name and address. Also, a name used to identify a distribution list— several user names grouped under a single name. (2) An alternate label. For example, a label and one or more aliases may be used to refer to the same data element or point in a computer program. (3) A distortion or artifact in the digital reproduction of an audio waveform that results when the signal frequency is too high compared to the sampling frequency.

architecture

The specific components of a computer system and the way they interact with one another.

ARP

See *address resolution protocol (ARP)*.

auto answer

The feature of a modem that answers incoming telephone calls automatically.

autoconfiguration

The process by which the host fetches SBus IDs and FCodes, beginning at location 0 of each slave used to identify the device.

backbone

The primary connectivity mechanism of a hierarchical distributed system. All systems that have connectivity to an intermediate system on the backbone are assured of connectivity to each other. This does not prevent systems from setting up private arrangements with each other to bypass the backbone for reasons of cost, performance, or security.

background

(1) In the OPEN LOOK GUI, an underlying area on which objects, such as controls and windows, are displayed. (2) To run a system so that the terminal is left free for other uses. See *background process.*

background process

A command that a user has directed the system to work on while the user continues to type commands to the command interpreter.

backup

A copy on a diskette, tape, or disk of some or all of the files from a hard disk. There are two types of backups: a full backup and an incremental backup. Synonymous with "dump." See *full dump* and *incremental dump.*

backup device

The device that receives a backup copy of files—a floppy drive, tape drive, or disk.

banner

The title page added to printouts by most print spoolers. The banner typically includes user information. Also called a "burst page," because it indicates where to burst (tear apart) fanfold paper to separate one user's printout from the next.

block

(1) A unit of data that can be transferred by a device, usually 512 bytes long. (2) A group of audio samples.

block device

A device where block I/O transfers are possible, usually a magnetic or optical disk. Contrast with *character device*.

blocking factor

The size of the chunk of data transferred to or from a *block device*. Common blocking factors are 128, 256, and 512 bytes. See also *block*.

block-special device

See *block device*.

boot

To load the system software into memory and start it running.

boot block

An 8-Kbyte disk block that contains information used during booting; block numbers pointing to the location of the /boot program on the disk. The boot block directly follows the disk label.

boot PROM

In Sun workstations, contains the *PROM monitor* program, a command interpreter used for booting, resetting, low-level configuration, and simple test procedures. See also *ID PROM*, *EEPROM*, and *NVRAM*.

boot server

A server system that provides client systems on the network with the programs and information that they need to start up. The *master server* and *slave servers* can be boot servers.

Bourne shell

The *shell* used by the standard Bell Labs UNIX.

bridge

A device that connects two or more physical networks and forwards packets between them. Bridges can usually be made to filter packets, that is, to forward only certain traffic. Related devices are: *repeaters*, which simply forward electrical signals from one cable to another, and full-fledged *routers*, which make routing decisions based on several criteria. In International Organization for Standardization's open systems interconnection (OSI) terminology, a bridge is a *data link layer* intermediate system.

broadcast

A *packet* delivery system where a copy of a given packet is given to all hosts attached to the network. See also *multicast*.

buffer

(1) A storage device that holds data to be transmitted to another device. (2) A temporary work area or storage area set up within the system memory. Buffers are often used by programs, such as editors, that access and alter text or data frequently.

bundled

(1) A hardware or software product that is sold with a computer as part of a combined hardware and software package. (2) Smaller software programs sold with larger programs. Contrast with *unbundled*.

bus

A circuit over which data or power is transmitted, one that often acts as a common connection among a number of locations.

bus error

A notification that a process has attempted to access an area of memory that is restricted or does not exist. See also *segmentation fault*.

cache

A buffer of high-speed memory filled at medium speed from main memory, often with instructions and programs. A cache increases effective memory transfer rates and processor speed.

CD-ROM

Compact disc, read-only memory. A form of storage characterized by high capacity (roughly 600 megabytes) and the use of laser optics rather than magnetic means for reading data. See also *High Sierra specification*.

central processing unit (CPU)

The part of the computer in which calculations and manipulations take place.

Centronics parallel interface

A *de facto* standard for parallel data exchange paths between computers and peripherals, originally developed by the printer manufacturer Centronics, Inc. The Centronics parallel interface provides eight parallel data lines plus additional lines for control and status information.

character device

A computer device, such as a keyboard or printer, that receives or transmits information as a stream of characters, one character at a time. The characters can be transferred either bit-by-bit (serial transmission) or byte-by-byte (parallel transmission) but are not moved from place to place in blocks. Contrast with *block device.*

character-special device

See *character device.*

client

(1) In the *client-server model* for file systems, the client is a machine that remotely accesses resources of a compute server, such as compute power and large memory capacity. (2) In the client-server model for window systems, the client is an *application* that accesses windowing services from a "server process." In this model, the client and the server can run on the same machine or on separate machines. See also *dataless client, diskless client,* and *diskfull client.*

client-server model

A common way to describe network services and the model user processes (programs) of those services. Examples include the name-server/name-resolver paradigm of the *domain name system (DNS)* and file-server/file-client relationships such as *NFS* and diskless hosts. See also *client.*

client system

A system on a network that relies on another system, called a *server system,* for resources such as disk space.

compute server

See *server.*

console

A terminal, or a dedicated window on the screen, where system messages are displayed.

cron

The UNIX clock *daemon* that executes commands at specified dates and times. See also *crontab file.*

crontab file

A file that lists commands to be executed at specified times on specified dates. See also *cron.*

daemon

A process that runs in the background, handling commands delivered for remote command execution. Typical daemons are the mailer daemon and the printer daemon.

data encrypting key

A key used to encipher and decipher data intended for programs that perform encryption. Contrast with *key encrypting key*.

data encryption standard (DES)

A commonly used, highly sophisticated algorithm developed by the U.S. National Bureau of Standards for encrypting and decrypting data. See also *SUN-DES-1*.

dataless client

A *client system* that relies on a *server system* for its home directory, and on a local disk for its root directory and swap space. See also *diskless client* and *diskfull client*.

data link layer

The second of the seven layers in the International Organization for Standardization's open systems interconnection model for standardizing computer-to-computer communications. The data-link layer is one level above the *physical layer*; it is involved both in packaging and addressing information and in controlling the flow of separate transmissions over communications lines. It is the lowest of three layers (data-link, network, and transport) concerned with actually moving information from one device to another.

device

A hardware component, such as a printer or disk drive, acting as a unit to perform a specific function.

device name

The name that the system uses to identify a device. For example, /dev/rst0 (or just rst0) is the device name for a 1/4-inch tape.

disc

An optical device for storing data such as files. Note the spelling (as opposed to "disk"). This particular spelling is reserved for optical discs, as opposed to magnetic disks, in keeping with the common spelling used in the CD (compact disc) market. See *CD-ROM*.

disk

A round platter, or set of platters, of a magnetized medium organized into concentric tracks and sectors for storing data such as files.

diskette

A 3.5-inch removable storage medium supported by some Sun systems.

diskfull client

A *client* on a network that relies on a *server* for resources, such as files, but has its own local disk storage. Some of its files are local and others are remote. The remote files can be obtained from any machine running as a network file server. Contrast with *diskless client* and *standalone*.

diskless client

A *client* on a network that relies on a *server* for all of its disk storage. Contrast with *diskfull client* and *standalone*.

disk partition

A portion of the *disk* reserved for a specific file system and function.

display device

The hardware device that displays windows, text, icons, and graphical pictures. Typically, a display device is a *frame buffer* and monitor.

distributed file system

A file system that exists on more than one machine, enabling each user to access files on other machines.

domain

(1) In the Internet, a part of a naming hierarchy. Syntactically, an Internet domain name consists of a sequence of names (labels) separated by periods (dots). For example, "tundra.mpk.ca.us." (2) In International Organization for Standardization's open systems interconnection (OSI), "domain" is generally used as an administrative partition of a complex distributed system, as in MHS private management domain (PRMD), and directory management domain (DMD).

domain name

The name assigned to a group of systems on a local network that share administrative files. The domain name is required for the network information service database to work properly. See also *domain*.

domain name system (DNS)

The distributed name/address mechanism used in the Internet.

dump

See *full dump* and *incremental dump*.

EEPROM

Electrically erasable PROM (programmable read-only memory). A nonvolatile PROM that may be written to as well as read from. In Sun workstations, an EEPROM holds information about the current system configuration, alternate boot paths, and so on. See also *boot PROM*, *NVRAM*, and *ID PROM*.

EPROM

(Pronounced "ee-prom.") Acronym for erasable programmable read-only memory. A nonvolatile memory chip that is programmed after it is manufactured. EPROMs are a good way for hardware vendors to put variable or constantly changing code into a prototype system when the cost of producing many PROM chips would be prohibitive. EPROMs differ from PROMs in that they can be erased (generally by removing a protective cover from the top of the chip package and exposing the semiconductor material to the ultraviolet light) and can be reprogrammed after having been erased. See also *EEPROM*, *PROM*, and *ROM*.

Ethernet

A type of local area network that enables real-time communication between machines connected directly together through cables. Ethernet was developed by Xerox in 1976, originally for linking minicomputers at the Palo Alto Research Center. A widely implemented network from which the IEEE 802.3 standard for contention networks was developed, Ethernet uses a bus topology (configuration) and relies on the form of access known as CSMA/CD to regulate traffic on the main communication line. Network nodes connected by coaxial cable (in either of two varieties known as thin and thick) or by twisted-pair wiring. Thin Ethernet cabling is 5 millimeters (about 0.2 inch) in diameter and can connect network stations over a distance of 300 meters (about 1000 feet). Thick Ethernet cabling is 1 centimeter (about 0.4 inch) in diameter and can connect stations up to 1000 meters (about 3300 feet) apart.

export

The process by which a server advertises the file systems that it allows hosts on a network to access.

fiber distributed data interface (FDDI)

An emerging high-speed networking standard. The underlying medium is fiber optics, and the topology is a dual-attached, counter-rotating token ring. FDDI networks can often be spotted by the orange fiber "cable."

file handle

In *NFS*, a data structure that allows systems to uniquely identify files over the network. A *stale NFS file handle* is one that has data in it that is out of date with respect to the file it refers to.

filesystem

In the SunOS operating system, a tree-structured network of files and directories through which the user can move to access the files and directories contained there.

filesystem hierarchy

The structure of the *filesystem*, consisting of a tree of files and directories, with a root directory at the top and directories that act as parent directories and child directories throughout.

floppy drive

An electromechanical device that reads data from and writes data to floppy disks. This drive is standard on most desktop *SPARC* workstations. The floppy disk is a 3.5-inch disk encased in rigid plastic.

formatting

(1) Arranging text or data into a suitable visual form. (2) Preparing a disk for use.

frame buffer

Display memory that temporarily stores (buffers) a full frame of picture data at one time. Frame buffers are composed of arrays of bit values that correspond to the display's pixels. The number of bits per pixel in the frame buffer determines the complexity of images that can be displayed.

full dump

A copy of the contents of a *filesystem* backed up for archival purposes. Contrast with *incremental dump*.

gateway

The original Internet term for what is now called a *router* or more precisely, IP router. In modern usage, the terms "gateway" and "application gateway" refer to systems that do translation from some native format to another. Examples include X.400 to/from RFC 822 electronic mail gateways.

group

A collection of users who are referred to by a common name. Determines a user's access to files. There are two types of groups: default user group and standard user group.

group attribute

An attribute attached to a file or directory that determines a user's access. See also *permissions*.

halt

To intentionally stop the system from running, for example, in preparation for turning off the power.

hard link

A directory entry that references a file on disk. More than one such directory entry may reference the same physical file.

heterogenous network

A network composed of systems of more than one *architecture*. Contrast with *homogeneous network*.

High Sierra specification

An industry-wide format specification for *CD-ROM* data. The High Sierra specification defines the logical structure, file structure, and record structures of a CD-ROM disc; it served as the basis for the *ISO 9660*, an international format standard for CD-ROM. High Sierra was named for the location of a seminal meeting on CD-ROM held near Lake Tahoe in November 1985.

home directory

The directory assigned to the user by the system administrator; usually the same as the *login directory*. Additional directories the user creates stem from the home directory.

homogeneous network

A network composed of systems of only one architecture. Contrast with *heterogenous network*.

host computer

(1) In a network, a computer that primarily provides services such as computation, data base access, or special programs. (2) The primary or controlling computer in a multiple computer installation.

hostid

See *system ID*.

ID PROM

In the Sun workstation, a PROM (programmable read-only memory) that contains workstation-specification information, such as workstation serial number, Ethernet address, and system configuration information. See also *boot PROM*, *NVRAM*, and *EEPROM*.

incremental dump

A duplicate copy of the files that have changed since a certain date. An incremental dump is used for archival purposes. Contrast with *full dump*.

inode

An entry in a predesignated area of a disk that describes where a file is located on that disk, the file's size, when it was last used, and other identification information.

Integrated Services Digital Network (ISDN)

An emerging technology that is beginning to be offered by the telephone carriers of the world. ISDN combines voice and digital network services in a single medium making it possible to offer customers digital data services as well as voice connections through a single "wire." The standards that define ISDN are specified by CCIT.

internet

A collection of networks interconnected by a set of routers that enable them to function as a single, large virtual network.

Internet

(Note the capital "I") The largest internet in the world consisting of large national backbone nets (such as MILNET, NSFNET, and CREN) and a myriad of regional and local campus networks all over the world. The Internet uses the Internet protocol suite. To be on the Internet the user must have IP connectivity, that is, be able to connect via *Telnet* to—or *ping*—other systems. Networks with only email connectivity are not actually classified as being on the Internet.

Internet control message protocol (ICMP)

The protocol used to handle errors and control messages at the Internet protocol layer. ICMP is actually part of the Internet protocol.

ISDN

See *Integrated Services Digital Network*.

ISO 9660

An international format standard for CD-ROM, adopted by the International Organization for Standardization (ISO). See also *High Sierra specification* and *CD-ROM*.

kernel

The core of the operating system software. The kernel manages the hardware (for example, processor cycles and memory) and supplies fundamental services, such as filing, that the hardware does not provide.

kernel architecture

The type of kernel on a system, such as sun4c for the SPARCstation system.

key encrypting key

A key used to encipher and decipher other keys, as part of a key management and distribution system. Contrast with *data encrypting key*.

loadable kernel module

Software used to enhance the system *kernel*.

local area network (LAN)

A group of computer systems in close proximity that can communicate with one another via some connecting hardware and software.

logical disk

A section of a formatted disk allocated by the software. Synonymous with *partition*.

logical unit number

See *major/minor device numbers*.

login directory

The directory the user is placed in after logging in. Usually, the *home directory*.

login name

The name by which the computer system knows the user.

mailer daemon

> See *daemon*.

mail gateway

> A machine that connects two or more electronic mail systems (especially dissimilar mail systems on two different networks) and transfers messages between them. Sometimes the mapping and translation can be quite complex, and generally it requires a store-and-forward scheme whereby the message is received from one system completely before it is transmitted to the next system after suitable translations.

major/minor device numbers

> A numbering sequence for devices connected to the computer. Sometimes called *logical unit number*.

master server

> The server that maintains the master copy of the network information service database. It has a disk and a complete copy of the operating system.

modem

> Short for modulator/demodulator. A device that enables a machine or terminal to establish a connection and transfer data through telephone lines. Because a computer is digital and a telephone line is analog, modems are needed to convert digital into analog and vice versa. When transmitting, modems impose (modulate) a computer's digital signals onto a continuous carrier frequency on the telephone line. When receiving, modems sift out (demodulate) the information from the carrier and transfer it in digital form to the computer. Modems operating over telephone lines typically transmit at speeds ranging from 300 to 9600 baud. Higher rates of operation are also possible but are generally constrained by the limitations of the telephone lines themselves.

multicast

> A special form of broadcast where copies of the packet are delivered to only a subset of all possible destinations. See *broadcast*.

multihomed host

> A computer connected to more than one physical data link. The data links may or may not be attached to the same network.

netgroup

> A network-wide group of machines granted identical access to certain network resources for security and organizational reasons.

net number

See *network number*.

network

Technically, the hardware connecting various systems enabling them to communicate. Informally, the systems so connected.

network address

The address, consisting of up to 20 octets, used to locate an OSI transport entity. The address is formatted into an initial domain part that is standardized for each of several addressing domains, and a domain specific part that is the responsibility of the addressing authority for that domain.

network information center (NIC)

Originally, there was only one NIC, located at SRI International and tasked to serve the ARPANET (and later the defense data network (DDN)) community. Today, there are many NICs, operated by local, regional, and national networks all over the world. Such centers provide user assistance, document service, training, and much more. See *network operations center.*

network information service (NIS)

A distributed network database containing key information about the systems and the users on the network. The NIS database is stored on the *master server* and all the *slave servers.*

network mask

A number used by software to separate the local subnet address from the rest of a given Internet protocol address.

network number

A number that the *network information center (NIC)* assigns to your network. The network number forms the first part of a host's Internet protocol address.

network operations center (NOC)

Any center tasked with the operational aspects of a production network. These tasks include monitoring and control, troubleshooting, user assistance, and so on.

NFS

A distributed file system developed by Sun that enables a set of computers to cooperatively access each other's files in a transparent manner.

NIS

See *network information service (NIS)*.

NIS+

A new version of Sun's *network information service (NIS)* that allows for decentralized administration and incremental updates to the data.

NIS domain

A master set of *network information service (NIS)* maps maintained on the NIS master server and distributed to that server's NIS slaves.

NIS maps

Database-like entities that maintain information about machines on a local area network. Programs that are part of the NIS service query these maps. See also *network information service (NIS)*.

node

An addressable point on a network. Each node in a Sun network has a different name. A node can connect a computing system, a terminal, or various other peripheral devices to the network.

nonvolatile memory

A storage system that does not lose data when power is removed from it. Usually used in reference to memory devices, such as *ROM, PROM, EEPROM,* and *NVRAM*.

NVRAM

Nonvolatile random-access memory. A type of *RAM* that retains information when power is removed from the system. See also *EEPROM, boot PROM, ID PROM,* and *nonvolatile memory*.

open boot

With regard to SBus profiles, the facility by which the FCodes program interrogates the host and determines the state of various parameters it addresses.

operating system

A collection of programs that monitor the use of the system and supervise the other programs executed by it.

package

> (1) A collection of software grouped for modular installation. (2) A computer application consisting of one or more programs created to perform a particular type of work—for example, an accounting package or a spreadsheet package.

panic message

> The message printed on a system's console when it crashes.

partition

> The unit into which the disk space is divided by the software.

password

> A security measure used to restrict access to computer systems and sensitive files. A password is a unique string of characters that a user types in as an identification code. The system compares the code against a stored list of authorized passwords and users. If the code is legitimate, the system allows the user access, at whatever security level has been approved for the owner of the password.

patch

> (1) In programming, to repair a deficiency in the functionality of an existing routine or program, generally in response to an unforeseen need or set of operating circumstances. Patching is also a common means of adding a feature or a function to an existing version of a program until the next version of the software, which presumably will have that feature or function included in its design, is released. (2) In computer graphics, a portion of an *object* surface defined by some number of points. Patches are separately defined and then pieced together to form the skin of an object, like a patchwork quilt. Surface patches can either be planar (flat) or curved.

PC file system (PCFS)

> A file system specification that provides the capability to read and write files in DOS format on the *SPARC* workstation internal *floppy drive*. The PC file system is mounted to the workstation's file system as /pcfs.

permissions

> The attribute of a file or directory that specifies who has read, write, or execution access.

physical layer

The first, or lowest, of the seven layers in the International Organization for Standardization's open systems interconnection model for standardizing computer-to-computer communications. The physical layer is totally hardware-oriented and deals with all aspects of establishing and maintaining a physical link between communicating computers. Among specifications covered on the physical layer are cabling, electrical signals, and mechanical connections.

physical memory

Main memory. The memory connected to the processor that stores instructions, which the processor directly fetches and executes, and any other data the processors must manipulate.

pid

See *process ID*. Also called process number.

ping

Packet Internet groper. A program used to test reachability of destinations by sending them an *Internet control message protocol (ICMP)* echo request and waiting for a reply. The term is used as a verb: "Ping host X to see if it is up!"

platform

The foundation technology of a computer system. Because computers are layered devices composed of a chip-level hardware layer, a firmware and operating-system layer, and an applications program layer, the bottom layer of a machine is often called a platform, as in "a *SPARC* platform." However, designers of applications software view both the hardware and systems software as the platform because both provide support for an application.

POSIX

An acronym created from the phrase "portable operating system interface," an IEEE standard that defines a set of operating-system services. Programs that adhere to the POSIX standard can be easily ported from one system to another. POSIX was based on UNIX system services, but it can be implemented by other operating systems.

power-on self test (POST)

A set of routines stored in a computer's read-only memory (ROM) that tests various system components such as RAM, the disk drives, and the keyboard to see if they are properly connected and operating. If problems are found, the POST routines alert the user by displaying a message, often accompanied by a diagnostic numeric value, to the standard output device. If the POST is successful, it passes control to the system's bootstrap loader.

print queue

A temporary lineup of print jobs waiting to be printed on a printer.

print spooler

Computer software that intercepts a print job on its way to the printer and sends it to disk or memory instead, where the print job is held until the printer is ready for it. The term "spool" is an acronym for "simultaneous peripheral operations on-line."

process

A particular computer activity or job.

process ID

A unique, system-wide, identification number assigned to a *process*.

PROM

(Pronounced "prom.") An acronym for programmable read-only memory. A type of read-only memory (ROM) that allows data to be written into the device with hardware called a PROM programmer. After the PROM has been programmed, it is dedicated to that data and cannot be reprogrammed. See also *EEPROM*, *EPROM*, and *ROM*.

PROM monitor

A command interpreter, stored in the workstation *boot PROM*, used for booting, resetting, low-level configuration, and simple test procedures.

QIC

Working Group for Quarter-Inch Cartridge Drive Compatibility. A number of standard interfaces to 1/4-inch tape drives.

query

(1) The process by which a master station asks a slave station to identify itself and give its status. (2) The process of extracting data from a database and presenting it for use. (3) A specific set of instructions for extracting particular data repetitively. For example, a query might be created to present sales figures for a particular region of the country. This query could be run periodically to obtain current reports.

queue

(1) A line or list formed by items in a system waiting for service. (2) To arrange in, or form, a queue. (3) A multielement data structure from which (by strict definition) elements can be removed only in the same order in which they were inserted; that is, it follows a first-in-first-out (FIFO) constraint.

RAM

Semiconductor-based memory that can be read or written by the CPU or other hardware devices. The storage locations can be accessed in any order. Note that the various types of ROM memory are capable of random access. The term RAM, however, is generally understood to refer to volatile memory, which can be written as well as read. Compare with *ROM*.

RARP

See *reverse address resolution protocol*.

readme file

A file containing information that the user either needs or will find informative and that might not have been included in the documentation. Readme files are placed on disk in plain-text form (such as ASCII) so that they can be read easily by word-processing programs.

reduced instruction set computer (RISC)

A type of microprocessor design that focuses on rapid and efficient processing of a relatively small set of instructions.

release

(1) To stop pressing a mouse button. (2) As a noun, a particular version of a piece of software, most commonly associated with the most recent version (as in "the latest release"). Some companies use the term release as an integral part of the product name. (3) As a verb, for an application to relinquish control of a block of memory, a device, or other system resource, thereby returning control to the operating system.

remote file system (RFS)

A distributed file system, similar to *NFS*, developed by AT&T and distributed with their UNIX *System V* operating system.

remote network

A *network* that does not physically connect to your system but with which your system can still communicate.

remote procedure call (RPC)
> An easy and popular paradigm for implementing the client-server model of distributed computing. A request is sent to a remote system to execute a designated procedure, using arguments supplied, and the result is returned to the caller. There are many variations and subtleties, resulting in a variety of different RPC protocols.

remote shell
> A command interpreter that you initiate on one machine, but that executes on another machine specified on the command line.

repeater
> A device that propagates electrical signals from one cable to another without making routing decisions or providing packet filtering. In International Organization for Standardization's open systems interconnection (OSI) terminology, a repeater is a *physical layer* intermediate system. See *bridge* and *router*.

request for comments (RFC)
> The document series, begun in 1969, which describes the *Internet* suite of protocols and related experiments. Not all (in fact, very few) RFCs describe Internet standards, but all Internet standards are written up as RFCs.

reverse address resolution protocol (RARP)
> The Internet protocol that a diskless host uses to find its Internet address at startup. RARP maps a physical (hardware) address to an Internet address. See *address resolution protocol (ARP)*.

RFC
> See *request for comments (RFC)*.

RFS
> See *remote file system (RFS)*.

RISC
> See *reduced instruction set computer (RISC)*.

ROM
> Read-only memory. See also *PROM, EEPROM, EPROM,* and *boot PROM*.

router

A system responsible for making decisions about which of several paths network (or Internet) traffic will follow. To do this, it uses a routing protocol to gain information about the network, and algorithms to choose the best route based on several criteria known as "routing metrics." In International Organization for Standardization's open systems interconnection (OSI) terminology, a router is a network layer intermediate system. See *gateway, bridge,* and *repeater.*

routing

The process of determining a pathway for data to get from one machine in a network to another machine throurgh a *gateway.*

RPC

See *remote procedure call (RPC).*

RS-232-C standard

An accepted industry standard for serial communications connections. Adopted by the Electronic Industries Association (EIA), this recommendation standard (RS) defines the specific lines and signal characteristics used by serial communications controllers to standardize the transmission of serial data between devices. The letter C denotes that the current version of the standard is the third in a series. See also *RS-422/423/449 standard.*

RS-422/423/449 standard

Standards for serial communications with transmission distances over 50 feet. RS-449 incorporates RS-422 and RS-423. See also *RS-232-C standard.*

SBus controller

The hardware responsible for performing arbitration, addressing translation and decoding, driving slave selects and address strobe, and generating timeouts.

SBus device

A logical device attached to the SBus. This device may be on the motherboard or on an *SBus expansion card.*

SBus expansion card

A physical printed circuit assembly that conforms to the single- or double-width mechanical specifications and that contains one or more *SBus device*s.

SBus expansion slot

An SBus slot into which a *SBus expansion card* can be installed.

SBus ID

A special series of bytes at address 0 of each SBus slave used to identify the *SBus device*.

script

A type of program that consists of a set of instructions to an application or utility program. A script usually consists of instructions expressed using the application's or utility's rules and syntax, combined with simple control structures such as loops and if/then expressions.

seek

Usually refers to a disk seek, that is, positioning the read/write head of the disk so that data can be read or written.

segmentation fault

A process has attempted to access an area of memory that is restricted or does not exist. See also *bus error*.

server

(1) In the *client-server model* for file systems, the server is a machine with compute resources (and is sometimes called the compute server), and large memory capacity. Client machines can remotely access and make use of these resources. In the client-server model for window systems, the server is a process that provides windowing services to an application, or "client process." In this model, the client and the server can run on the same machine or on separate machines. (2) A *daemon* that actually handles the providing of files.

server system

A system that is on a *network* and provides resources, such as disk space and file transfers, to other systems.

single in-line memory module (SIMM)

A small circuit designed to accommodate surface-mount memory chips. SIMMs use less board space and are more compact than more conventional memory-mounting hardware.

single-user mode

A mode that allows a user to log in to a system as superuser and perform administrative tasks without interference from other users.

slave server

A server system that maintains a copy of the *network information service (NIS)* database. It has a disk and a complete copy of the operating system.

slot

(1) An SBus entity for which there is an independent slave select wire.
(2) An abbreviation for *SBus expansion slot*.

small computer systems interface (SCSI)

An industry-standard bus used to connect disk and tape devices to a workstation.

SMD

See *storage module device (SMD)*.

SMTP

Simple mail transfer protocol. The Internet electronic mail protocol. Defined in RFC 821, with associated message format descriptions in RFC 822.

SNMP

Simple network management protocol. The network management protocol of choice for *TCP/IP*-based internets.

socket

A software endpoint for network communication. Two programs on different machines each open a socket in order to communicate over the network. This is the low-level mechanism that supports most networking programs.

SPARC

The 32-bit Scalable Processor ARChitecture from Sun. SPARC is based on a reduced instruction set computer (RISC) concept. The architecture was designed by Sun and its suppliers in an effort to significantly improve price and performance. SPARC is now a registered trademark of SPARC International, Inc.

stale NFS file handle

A *file handle* that contains data that is out of date with respect to the file it refers to.

standalone

(1) A computer that does not require support from any other machine. It must have its own disk; it may or may not be attached to an Ethernet network. It must have some type of medium, such as CD-ROM or tape drive, for software installation. Synonymous with single system. (2) A standalone diagnostic means the program can load from either local disk or Ethernet and runs in a non-UNIX environment.

storage module device (SMD)

An industry-standard interface used for large capacity, high-performance disks.

subnet

A working scheme that divides a single logical network into smaller physical networks to simplify routing.

subnet mask

See *address mask*.

subnet number

The part of an *Internet* address that refers to a specific subnet.

subnetwork

A collection of International Organization for Standardization's open systems interconnection (OSI) end systems and intermediate systems under the control of a single administrative domain and using a single network access protocol. Examples: private X.25 networks, collection of bridged LANs.

SUN-DES-1

One of the authentication protocols that X11/NeWS uses to authenticate client connections. The SUN-DES-1 authorization protocol was developed by Sun Microsystems. It is based on Secure RPC (remote procedure call) and required DES (data encryption software) support. The authorization data is the machine-independent netname, or network name, of a user. This data is encrypted and sent to the server as part of the connection packet. The server decrypts the data and, if the netname is known, the connection is allowed. The SUN-DES-1 protocol provides a higher level of security than does the MIT-MAGIC-COOKIE-1 protocol.

superuser

A special user who has privileges to perform all administrative tasks on the system. Also known as *root*.

swap

To write the active pages of a job to external storage (*swap space*) and to read pages of another job from external page storage into real storage.

swap space

The memory used for the transfer of a currently operating program from system memory to an external storage device. Also known as swapping area.

symbolic link

A special file or directory that points to another file or directory so that both files or directories have the same contents.

sync

(1) The process of synchronizing the scanning of receiving, processing, or display equipment with a video source. (2) A signal comprising just the horizontal and vertical elements necessary to accomplish synchronization. (3) The component of a video signal that conveys synchronizing information.

syntax

The order in which you type the parts of an operating system command.

syntax error

An error in the use of language syntax; a statement that violates one or more of the grammatical rules of a language and is thus "not legal."

system ID

A sequence of numbers, and sometimes letters, that is unique to each system and is used to identify that system.

System V

(Pronounced "system five.") A version of the UNIX operating system produced by AT&T.

TCP/IP

Acronym for transport control protocol/interface program. The protocol suite originally developed for the Internet. It is also called the *Internet* protocol suite. SunOS networks run on TCP/IP by default.

Telnet

The virtual terminal protocol in the Internet suite of protocols. Enables users of one host to log in to a remote host and interact as normal terminal users of that host.

thread

(1) In programming, a process that is part of a larger process or program. (2) In a tree data structure, a pointer that identifies the parent node and is used to facilitate traversal of the tree.

time-out

A situation in which the SBus controller terminates a bus cycle which a slave has failed to acknowledge. In a system that is correctly designed and is operating properly, time-outs should happen only during system configuration.

TP4

International Organization for Standardization's open systems interconnection (OSI) transport protocol class 4 (error detection and recovery class). This is the most powerful OSI transport protocol, useful on top of any type of network. TP4 is the OSI equivalent to TCP.

transceiver

Transmitter-receiver. The physical device that connects a host interface to a local area network, such as *Ethernet*. Ethernet transceivers contain electronics that apply signals to the cable and sense collisions.

transport control protocol (TCP)

The major transport protocol in the Internet suite of protocols providing reliable, connection-oriented, full-duplex streams. Uses IP for delivery. See *TP4* and *TCP/IP*.

TTY

This term originally meant Teletypewriter equipment. It has since become associated with any dumb terminal that can be used to access a computer.

twisted-pair wiring

Wiring that uses two separately insulated strands twisted together. Twisted-pair wiring is used to reduce signal interference introduced by a strong radio source such as a nearby cable.

UART

Universal asynchronous receiver-transmitter. A module, usually composed of a single integrated circuit, that contains both the receiving and transmitting circuits required for asynchronous serial communications.

UDP

See *user datagram protocol (UDP)*.

unbundled

> Not included as part of a complete hardware and software package. This term specifically applies to a product that was previously *bundled*, as opposed to one that has always been sold separately.

user datagram protocol (UDP)

> A transport protocol in the Internet suite of protocols. UDP, like TCP, uses IP for delivery; however, unlike TCP, UDP provides for exchange of datagrams without acknowledgments or guaranteed delivery. See also *TCP/IP*.

UUCP

> UNIX-to-UNIX copy program. A protocol used for communication between consenting UNIX systems.

virtual memory

> A storage hierarchy in which a virtual image of a program is stored in secondary storage while main memory only stores active program segments. When a system has virtual memory, a user program can be larger than physical memory.

VMEbus

> An interfacing system that connects data processing, data storage, and peripheral control devices in a closely coupled configuration. The VMEbus structure can be described in two ways: mechanically and functionally. The mechanical specification includes physical dimensions of subracks, backplanes, and plug-in boards. The functional specification describes how the bus works, what functional modules are involved in each transaction, and the rules that define behavior.

wide-area network (WAN)

> A network consisting of many systems that provide file transfer services. This network may cover a large physical area, sometimes spanning the globe.

window system

> A system that provides the user with a multiuse environment on the display device. Separate windows are like separate displays on the monitor screen. Each window can run its own application. The user brings up some number of windows for various applications, and the window system handles the communications between each of the applications and the hardware.

XGL

Sun graphics library.

zones

Administrative boundaries within a network domain, often made up of one or more subdomains.

Index

new home directory designation, 25
root partition, 23-24
sample script, 276
swap space, 24
/usr partition, 24-25
Disk software, 221-34
format utility, 223-31
mt (magnetic tape handling program),
  239-40
newfs command, 231-32
Online DiskSuite tools, 241
probe-scsi, 221-23
reconfiguring, 223
Disk utilities, 219-41
disk hardware, 219-20
disk software, 221-34
Domain Naming Service (DNS), 170-71

E

EEPROM check, ASET, 196
EEPROM entries, changing, sample, 276
Encryption, 182-84, 200-201
Engineering network, 147-48
gateways to, 147
server systems on, 148
workstations on, 148
/etc/bootparams, 17
/etc directory, 12-13
/etc/ethers, 37
/etc/inittab, 129-32
actions in, 129-30
generic file, 130
/etc/nodename, 139
/etc/nsswitch.conf, 16, 140-41, 156
values for, 140
/etc/system, 136-37
/etc/vistab, 137-38
Ethernet address, updating NIS domain with,
  41

F

File descriptors, 10
Filesystem mounting, 137-38
/etc/vistab, 137-38
Filesystems, and newfs command, 231-32
Finish scripts (samples), 273-74

format utility, 223-31
disk defects, extracting, 225
formatting the disk, 225-26
new format types for disks, adding, 225
partitioning, 226-31
calculating partition size, 228-30
partition menu, 226-28, 230-31
Frame buffer changes, name changes, 10

H

Hardware requirements, installation, 19-20
Home directories, 23, 25
permissions on, 200
sharing, 177-78
Home directory server, 176-78
Host Manager, 112, 121-22
launching, 121
NIS+, 122
NIS, 122
Host maps, updating, 40-41
-hosts map, 156

I

Included maps, 156
Indirect maps, 157
Installation, 19-54
AutoInstall, 44-54
automatic, 28
automounter files, 99
base operating system, 21-22
booting, 25-27
from local CD, 55-57
diskless or dataless client support, 99
disk partitioning, 23-25
hardware requirements, 19-20
home directories, 23
manual, 28
network requirements, 30-31
optional software, 22-23
preparing for, 28
and root password, 98
server installation, 84-97
software requirements, 20-23
special files to save, 29
windowing system, 22
See also AutoInstall

T

Tape devices, name changes, 9-10
Tape handling, 239-40
`tar` command, 236-38
Terminal port, configuring, 117-19
Timezone map, updating, 42-43
`/tmp` directory, 12
`tunefs` command, 233

U

`ufsdump` command, 238-39
UNIX operating system, 21
User Account Manager, 112, 122-25
    launching, 123
    Modify User Window, 124-25
User accounts, and login security, 185
User logins, 184-85
`/usr` directory, 21-22
`/usr` partition, 24-25

V

Volume manager, 138-39

W

Wabi, 251-59
    configuration, 254-59
        disk devices, 258
        floppy drives, 258-59
        printers, 256-57
        serial ports, 255-56
    installation, 251-54
        application, 251-52
        Microsoft Windows, 253-54
    licensing, 259
    server management issues, 259
Windowing system, 22